"John Walton has been writing insightfully about the book of Genesis for over twenty-five years. His important reminder that the books of the Bible were not written 'to us' but rather 'for us' underscores the importance of reading the books of the Old Testament in their ancient Near Eastern context. John has helped us do just that for years, and in this new book, he revisits the topics that he has treated earlier on the book of Genesis to give us his most recent and best thinking on that foundational book. I recommend *New Explorations in the Lost World of Genesis* for all readers of the Bible."

Tremper Longman III, distinguished scholar and professor emeritus of biblical studies at Westmont College and author of *How to Read the Psalms*

"John Walton, who has significantly shaped discussions on the early chapters of Genesis, continues to advance and enrich these conversations with his latest book. Drawing from a wealth of knowledge acquired over decades of research, John again provides insightful analysis of some of the Old Testament's most debated chapters with the clarity and expertise of a master teacher. His characteristic erudition and creativity are on display throughout, making this book an essential and engaging resource for students of Scripture interested in exploring the theology of the early chapters of Genesis."

Adam E. Miglio, professor of Old Testament and archaeology at Wheaton College and author of *The Gilgamesh Epic in Genesis 1–11: Peering into the Deep*

"As one who is a church leader and also involved in academics, I can say that reading *New Explorations in the Lost World of Genesis* is, without exaggeration, a mind-blowing, heart-expanding, Scripture-focused adventure. This book causes you to grow incredibly more excited about studying the early chapters of Genesis, with so many insights into what was happening in that ancient world to bring fuller color and more clarity to understanding what is there. I highly, highly, highly suggest anyone studying the early chapters of Genesis to include this in your studies."

Dan Kimball, author of *How (Not) to Read the Bible*, vice president of Western Seminary, and founder of Vintage Faith Church in Santa Cruz, California

"John Walton is a master teacher. Here he makes his approach to Genesis 1–3 crystal clear, explaining advances in his thinking about both method and substance since his previous Lost World books. Careful attention to this book will make scholars better communicators and lay Christians much better readers of the Bible."

J. Richard Middleton, professor emeritus of biblical worldview and exegesis at Northeastern Seminary, Roberts Wesleyan University

"Fifteen years ago, John Walton taught us that the Bible was written *for* us but not *to* us. His Lost World books open our eyes to the ancient cultures of the Old Testament, with a wealth of new insights that deepen our understanding of God's Word while upholding scriptural authority. For those who know Walton, this book compiles his latest thinking and shows a humble scholar at work. Much of the book is responses to common questions, a friendly dialogue format accessible for first-time readers."

Deborah Haarsma, BioLogos

"In this thought-provoking book, the author critically examines his understandings of the Genesis texts published over the past decades, greatly assisted by contributions from his son and coauthor. As a result, some perspectives are further nuanced, whereas in one case there is a radical re-interpretation. Whatever conclusions the reader comes to themselves, they will be challenged to grapple with the texts afresh in their ancient Near East contexts, a valuable exercise for anyone interested in Biblical hermeneutics."

Denis Alexander, emeritus director for the Faraday Institute for Science and Religion in Cambridge, United Kingdom

"Mention Genesis and biologists flee. This book should bring them to a screeching halt. John Walton reveals how God determines the foundations of order, and in doing so, he radically reshapes the many topics—not least Adam and Eve, the fall, and the seven days—that will provoke any Christian to fresh insights. But scientists need this book as well, both to reset their often simplistic assumptions and to ponder that as God's agents, even as products of evolution, we have a unique role."

Simon Conway Morris, professor of evolutionary paleobiology at the University of Cambridge and author of *From Extraterrestrials to Animal Minds*

"We still need Walton's Lost World Series. This is true for several reasons, but most of all because we still have readers in the church who continue to misappropriate Genesis simplistically by assuming that our cultural context today is sufficient as background for interpreting the book. And yet, if one considers the distance between Shakespeare (for example) and our own post-industrial and post-modernist context, it seems obvious that reading the Bard demands quite a lot of us if we are to understand him properly. How much more so the distance between us and the world of Genesis? Walton's agenda in the series has been to illumine the cultural river of the ancient world (to borrow his metaphor), among whose currents swirl Israel's ideas and ways of thinking. In this latest volume of the series, Walton (with the help of son J. Harvey Walton) has once again shown himself to be a dependable guide to exploring the currents of thought that informed Israel's Scriptures. As with other volumes in the series, the reader will benefit greatly by learning the currents flowing through ancient culture, which are so very different from the currents in which we swim in today's cultural river. All readers today will benefit from this latest contribution from the Waltons."

Bill T. Arnold, Paul S. Amos Professor of Old Testament Interpretation at Asbury Theological Seminary

NEW EXPLORATIONS IN THE LOST WORLD OF GENESIS

ADVANCES IN THE ORIGINS DEBATE

JOHN H. WALTON

WITH CONTRIBUTIONS BY J. HARVEY WALTON

InterVarsity Press
P.O. Box 1400 | Downers Grove, IL 60515-1426
ivpress.com | email@ivpress.com

©2025 by John H. Walton

All rights reserved. No part of this book may be reproduced in any form without written permission from InterVarsity Press.

InterVarsity Press® is the publishing division of InterVarsity Christian Fellowship/USA®. For more information, visit intervarsity.org.

All Scripture quotations, unless otherwise indicated, are taken from The Holy Bible, New International Version®, NIV®. Copyright © 1973, 1978, 1984, 2011 by Biblica, Inc.™ Used by permission of Zondervan. All rights reserved worldwide. www.zondervan.com. The "NIV" and "New International Version" are trademarks registered in the United States Patent and Trademark Office by Biblica, Inc.™

The publisher cannot verify the accuracy or functionality of website URLs used in this book beyond the date of publication.

Cover design: Faceout Studio, Jeff Miller
Interior design: Jeanna Wiggins

Image credit: © Kristian Bell / Moment / Getty Images

ISBN 978-1-5140-0491-3 (print) | ISBN 978-1-5140-0492-0 (digital)

Printed in the United States of America ∞

Library of Congress Cataloging-in-Publication Data
Names: Walton, John H., 1952- author. | Walton, J. Harvey (Jonathan Harvey) contributor.
Title: New explorations in the Lost World of Genesis : advances in the origins debate / John H. Walton ; with contributions by J. Harvey Walton.
Description: Downers Grove, IL : IVP Academic, [2025] | Series: The Lost World series | Includes bibliographical references and index.
Identifiers: LCCN 2024038230 (print) | LCCN 2024038231 (ebook) | ISBN 9781514004913 (paperback) | ISBN 9781514004920 (ebook)
Subjects: LCSH: Bible. Genesis–Criticism, interpretation, etc. | Bible. Genesis–Historiography. | Creation. | Biblical cosmology.
Classification: LCC BS1235.52 .W353 2025 (print) | LCC BS1235.52 (ebook) | DDC 231.7/65–dc23/eng/20241122
LC record available at https://lccn.loc.gov/2024038230
LC ebook record available at https://lccn.loc.gov/2024038231

32 31 30 29 28 27 26 25 | 13 12 11 10 9 8 7 6 5 4 3 2 1

Contents

Acknowledgments xiii

Abbreviations xv

1 INTRODUCTION: HOW WE GOT HERE 1

Excursus 1: Rhetorical Strategy of Genesis 2–4 12

2 METHODOLOGY 17

Summary of Previous Material 17

New Explorations. 18

Answers to Frequently Asked Questions 28

   1. Is understanding ancient Near Eastern culture really that
important to reading the Old Testament?   28

   2. Do we have enough ancient Near Eastern literature to
give us any level of confidence about how people thought
back then? How much can we trust what we find in it?   30

   3. Why should we assume that the Israelites thought like
their ancient Near Eastern neighbors?   31

   4. If Scripture is constrained by ancient cultural understandings,
then was God in effect misleading the rest of us?   33

   5. Does the Old Testament borrow from other ancient
Near Eastern texts and cultural understandings?   33

   6. Since ancient Near Eastern culture is based in mythology
but the Old Testament is not, doesn't it devalue the
Old Testament when you refer to pagan mythology?   34

   7. Is it possible that scholars are underestimating the
understanding of the Israelites and the ancient world
when they suggest that people back then believed in
a solid sky or that people actually thought with their hearts?   36

   8. Are we overestimating the impact of cultural differences?
After all, people are people, and humanity has not changed
significantly over time.   44

   9. Shouldn't we be content that, since the Bible is what God
has given us, it is all we need?   44

10. How can anyone read Scripture with confidence if so much information that we don't have access to is needed? 45

11. Why should we believe that we would need to use tools that most people have not had and do not have to interpret the Bible? 47

12. By using ancient Near Eastern mythology to understand Genesis 1–3, aren't you treating Genesis 1–3 as myth and thereby undermining its historicity and compromising its truth? 48

13. Since Genesis 12–50 is clearly intended to reflect real people in a real past, why should we think that we need to treat Genesis 1–11 differently? 50

14. Doesn't your interpretation differ from that found in the New Testament? 53

15. How tightly are we constrained by the author's intentions? 55

16. Since your interpretation is different from what has been taught in the church, doesn't it undermine two thousand years of Jewish and Christian interpretation? 56

3 GENESIS 1: CREATION ACCOUNT FOCUSED ON FUNCTION/ORDER INSTEAD OF PHYSICAL/MATERIAL OBJECTS. 70

Summary of Previous Material 70

New Explorations. 72

Answers to Frequently Asked Questions 97

1. Why can't Genesis 1 include both origination of material objects and establishment of order (that is, both a house story and a home story)? 97

2. Does Genesis 1 affirm creation out of nothing? 102

3. If throughout the history of the church people have thought of the creation account in Genesis in material terms, why *should* we think differently now? 105

4. If we were to find a creation account that explained material origins, what would we expect it to look like? 107

5. Isn't there evidence that people in the ancient Near East did think of creation in material terms? 108

6. Aren't there many examples of *bārā'* referring to material objects? 110

4 GENESIS 1: COSMIC TEMPLE AND REST 112

Summary of Previous Material 112

New Explorations. 113

Answers to Frequently Asked Questions 117

1. How can the seventh day be about a temple when
   there is no mention of a temple? — 117

2. Do any ancient Near Eastern creation accounts use
   a seven-day period? — 118

3. Granting that the seven-day structure has a literary rather
   than chronological purpose and that it mirrors the seven-day
   temple inaugurations, what is the significance of the number
   seven that it should be used in these contexts? — 118

4. Divine rest in the ancient Near East is often in temples
   but also often involves sleep. Is the idea of the god resting
   on a throne in the temple found in the ancient Near East? — 120

5. If the seventh day is more interested in God ruling than in
   relaxing, what does Sabbath observance look like for humans? — 122

6. Isn't God's throne in heaven? How can it be on earth? — 124

7. Did God need a home? — 124

8. Would the Israelites in the Old Testament, including those
   who penned Scripture, have considered the seventh day
   to be about God's rule? — 125

9. It appears that Jewish interpretation, as evidenced in the
   New Testament and in the Mishnah, focuses entirely on
   resting from work. Did the Jews outside the Old Testament
   ever understand the seventh day in terms of God's rule? — 126

10. The term *šabbāt* is widely recognized to refer to ceasing,
    and that is the only term for divine resting in the seven-day
    account. What is the support for divine rest in Genesis
    being connected to divine rule? — 127

11. How should we think about Sabbath as we factor in the
    New Testament and think about application today? — 130

5 GENESIS 2: THE GARDEN AND THE TREES 133

Summary of Previous Material 133

New Explorations. 135

Excursus 2: The Relationship Between the Divine Realm
and Human Order 136

Answers to Frequently Asked Questions 147

1. Should we consider the garden to be a pristine paradise? 147

2. Are we heading back to Eden? 148

6 GENESIS 2: ADAM AND EVE 150

Summary of Previous Material 150

New Explorations. 153

Excursus 3: What Are Adam and Eve Archetypes Of?. . . 160

Answers to Frequently Asked Questions 161

1. What is the significance of naming the animals? 161

2. What is the significance of God "closing up the flesh"
(Gen 2:21)? 162

3. What is the significance of their nakedness (Gen 2:25)? 163

4. You have said that Adam and Eve are functioning in the text
as archetypes. Does that mean that they are allegorical? 164

5. How important is it that Adam and Eve are real people
in a real past? 166

6. What is meant by Eve being the "mother of all living"? 170

7. Was humanity created immortal? 171

8. Was Adam perfect? 174

7 GENESIS 3: THE FALL. 179

Summary of Previous Material 179

New Explorations. 180

Answers to Frequently Asked Questions 185

1. If the serpent is not identified with Satan in the Old Testament,
how should we understand the serpent and its role? 185

2. Was there death before the fall? 188

3. Was there pain and suffering before the fall? 189

4. Is the origin of sin the focus of Genesis 3? 192

Excursus 4: What Is Paul's Interest in Adam in Romans 5? 195

5. Are Adam and Eve being punished for sin? 197

6. Is Genesis 3 a theodicy? 201

8 GENESIS 3: THE PRONOUNCEMENT 203

Summary of Previous Material 203

New Explorations. 205

Excursus 5: What Is Going On in Genesis 3:16? 209

Answers to Frequently Asked Questions 212

1. Should we consider Genesis 3:15 messianic? 212

2. Does Genesis 3 have anything to contribute to questions
concerning the roles of women? 213

3. What is the significance of the guardian with the sword? 213

4. Why does Genesis 3:22 use the plural form ("like one of us")? 215

9 GENESIS AND SCIENCE 217

Summary of Previous Material 217

New Explorations. 218

Answers to Frequently Asked Questions 221

1. How can you claim that the Bible is compatible
with evolutionary models, given that those models
are by nature godless? 221

2. If one believes that the Bible is inerrant and should be
read literally, can one also accept an evolutionary model? 222

3. Where can I learn more about committed Christian scientists
who also adopt an evolutionary model of creation? 223

4. Why would God use an instrument of creation that entailed
endless millions of years of animal suffering through predation? 224

5. Don't the biblical genealogies make an old earth,
and therefore evolution, impossible? 225

6. What about all the arguments that people use to refute or
at least undermine evolutionary models? 225

7. How is your view the same or different from
Stephen Jay Gould's proposal that science and religion
are nonoverlapping magisteria? 227

8. Some have claimed that all of your conclusions in
   Genesis are proposed only to accommodate an
   evolutionary model. Is this true?   229

9. Is there a war between science and the Bible?   230

10 Conclusion **233**

For Further Reading   242

Scripture Index   245

Acknowledgments

I am very grateful for the careful reading of the manuscript and the many helpful suggestions by my wife, Kim, and my son, J. Harvey Walton. I acknowledge also his kind permission to publish some of his core ideas before he has had the chance to do so.

Abbreviations

AMD	Ancient Magic and Divination
AMP	Amplified Bible
ANE	Ancient Near East
AOAT	Alter Orient und Altes Testament
CEB	Common English Bible
CEV	Contemporary English Version
col.	column
ERV	Easy-to-Read Version
ESV	English Standard Version
G1AC	Walton, John H. *Genesis 1 as Ancient Cosmology*. Winona Lake, IN: Eisenbrauns, 2011.
GNT	Good News Translation
GW	God's Word Translation
HCSB	Holman Christian Standard Bible
LWAE	Walton, John H. *The Lost World of Adam and Eve: Genesis 2–3 and the Human Origins Debate*. Downers Grove, IL: InterVarsity Press, 2014.
LWF	Longman, Tremper, III, and John H. Walton. *The Lost World of the Flood: Mythology, Theology, and the Deluge Debate*. Downers Grove, IL: InterVarsity Press, 2018.
LWG1	Walton, John H. *The Lost World of Genesis One: Ancient Cosmology and the Origins Debate*. Downers Grove, IL: InterVarsity Press, 2009.

LWIC	Walton, John H., and J. Harvey Walton. *The Lost World of the Israelite Conquest: Covenant, Retribution, and the Fate of the Canaanites.* Downers Grove, IL: InterVarsity Press, 2017.
NCV	New Century Version
NET	New English Translation
NIrV	New International Readers Version
NIV	New International Version
NLT	New Living Translation

1

Introduction

How We Got Here

The *Lost World of Genesis One* appeared in 2009. Many of the ideas there had already been introduced earlier in my commentary on Genesis.[1] Two years later, a full academic monograph, *Genesis 1 as Ancient Cosmology*, was published to fill in the details for a scholarly audience. Two other Lost World books pertaining to Genesis then followed, *The Lost World of Adam and Eve* (2014) and *The Lost World of the Flood* (2018).

For the story of how the ideas took shape, however, we have to begin a couple of decades earlier. I was raised in a family where the Bible mattered. My four siblings and I learned biblical content early and well. Our context was nondenominational, traditional, and evangelical, and therefore passively young-earth creationists (though others in that same context would have been more militant on that count). No other options besides a young earth were considered, but it was not a big issue. That continued to be my default position even through much of my time teaching at Moody Bible Institute (1981–2001). Nevertheless, alternative ideas were subtly taking shape in my mind.

As early as my master's work (Wheaton College, 1975), I had taken an interest in Genesis as I began to learn Hebrew and study the Old Testament academically. When I got into my doctoral program (Hebrew Union College, 1976–1981), I began to understand the

---

[1]John H. Walton, *Genesis*, NIV Application Commentary (Grand Rapids, MI: Zondervan, 2001).

untapped significance provided by interacting with the cultures and literature of the ancient world. I studied Akkadian, Ugaritic, and Aramaic, and translated texts as well as studying the history and culture. As I did so, the cognitive environment of the ancient world unfolded. I was particularly interested in comparative studies that brought an understanding of the ancient world alongside the Old Testament to unpack cultural ideas inherent in the text. This led to my decision to do my dissertation on the Tower of Babel. In that work, I first began to combine a close, fresh reading of the Hebrew text with an exploration into the world of the ancient Near East. I investigated what type of tower this was, how such towers functioned, and what they stood for. I also researched what it meant to "make a name" in the Bible particularly and in the ancient Near East in general.[2]

It was never my intention nor inclination to suggest that the biblical authors borrowed and adapted literature from Babylon or Egypt (though many working in comparative studies have those preconceptions). I was more intrigued by the light that the literature shed on how people in the ancient world thought differently from us in so many ways. Besides issues of general comparison, I also wanted to interact with ancient Near Eastern background information as I performed exegetical analysis on particular passages such as the Tower of Babel to see what additional insight our knowledge of the ancient world could provide.

When I began teaching at Moody Bible Institute, I regularly taught a book-study course in Genesis. When asked, I used to tell my classes that I held an "uncomfortable young-earth position." Young earth had been my default position since childhood, and I had read widely about other alternatives. I found proposals such as the gap theory or the day-age theory to be inconsistent with the grammar and syntax of the Hebrew text.[3] So I remained in the young-earth camp because I could

---

[2]Some of the results of my dissertation research, along with how those ideas have developed over the years, can be found in *LWF*.

[3]Details and analysis can be found in Walton, *Genesis.*

Introduction: How We Got Here   3

not see another option that would preserve what I considered essential to the demands of biblical authority. If I were to stretch the language in the ways required by those views, I would no longer be tracking with the authors of Scripture. Even so, I described myself as uncomfortable with the position because all the research and reading that I had done in Genesis and in the ancient Near East increasingly gave me an unsettled feeling. I became convinced that I was missing something important, but I could not put my finger on it. I struggled to put all the pieces together—careful reading of Hebrew, ancient Near Eastern perspective, and commitment to biblical authority—and I just could not work it out. Were questions about the age of the earth tracking with the authors of Scripture? That seemed dubious to me, but I could not identify an alternative path.

During those years at Moody, I also used to take my fourth-semester Hebrew students through Genesis 1, and that is the context in which all the pieces finally fell into place for me. It actually happened during a class session. I was putting them through their paces in the Hebrew text and had posed my typical set of questions. I pointed out to them that the seven days of creation began with elements such as earth and water already there (Gen 1:2). We talked about the fact that as the days began, the activities focused on issues such as time (day and night) and fecundity (sprouting of plants)—not on things such as terraforming mountains and lakes. I finally asked aloud the very simple, yet complexly significant question, "What kind of creation account is this, anyway?" And the shoe dropped. All the pieces that I had been working with over decades of study fell into place. I had finally framed the right question, and we cannot get good answers if we are not asking the right questions.

In a lecture in 1856, Louis Pasteur was talking about how discovery works, in light of the fact that so often it looks like it happened suddenly, by accident—by chance. He proposed, "In the fields of observation, chance favors the mind that is prepared." Decades of preparation had led up to that moment in Genesis class, and very suddenly, a new approach became not only possible but almost obvious and inevitable. My modern context and my presuppositions had prevented me from recognizing that there were other ways to think about creation and that those needed to be explored. The rest of the class period (not to mention the rest of my life) was spent unpacking the new approach opened up by new questions.[4]

As the publications began appearing, I was increasingly asked to speak on these topics. By now I have given presentations hundreds of times, from classes at Wheaton to lectures on both Christian and secular campuses across the country, from churches and pastors' conferences to academic conventions, from lectures in dozens of countries around the world to over a hundred podcasts and radio interviews. The books have additionally been translated into a number of other languages.

It has been a great privilege to have these opportunities, but perhaps one of the most important benefits is that as I have strived to communicate new ideas clearly and have interacted with audiences (whether friendly, nervous, confused, or even passively hostile), I have *learned*. I have found that some terminology was not as clear as it needed to be, so I have chosen alternatives. I have figured out what aspects of the presentation needed to be addressed at the beginning and how to approach some of the more controversial issues, anticipating the struggles my audiences will be experiencing. I have gotten better at packaging challenging ideas in ways that people can receive them. I have heard just about every question imaginable and have found that there is some consistency to them.

I also continue to learn how important tone is. I have never been a confrontational person; I am not an in-your-face debater who is going

---

[4]Only three or four students were enrolled in that course, and two of them are now valued colleagues, Ryan Peterson (Talbot) and Adam Miglio (Wheaton—his office is right next to mine). We often think back to that day.

Introduction: How We Got Here

to take down the other position. I want to understand where people are coming from that may lead them to disagree with me. I understand the young-earth position (since I was raised that way) and respect that those who hold it feel they are defending the integrity of Scripture. I do not want to dampen that passion. Occasionally those passions turn into anger, and I have learned that the angrier an antagonist gets, the more gentle and conciliatory I need to be. Hostility is best met with graciousness, which is not always easy. I have tried to find ways to express that I am still learning and growing and that there is still much that continuing scholarship can contribute to broaden and widen our understanding of the Genesis account. A refrain that I often repeat is that it is not my intention to present the "right" answer and to expect everyone to adopt my conclusions. Instead, my job is to be a faithful interpreter and to put information on the table that others may not have so that they can make more informed decisions. I have learned that even when I have heard a question dozens of times, I need to listen carefully to the way it is posed to try to understand what concerns the questioner has.

People sometimes get concerned that if interpretation requires a technical level of information, that it makes the Bible inaccessible to them. I have heard the complaint that the need for linguistic, literary, and especially cultural information effectually takes the Bible out of their hands and makes them dependent on specialists.[5] The fact is, however, that we depend on specialists all the time for information that is important to us. Andrew Brown makes the point convincingly:

> Now I defend the right of the thinking person to be a self-starter in any area of knowledge and not wait humbly at the gate to be invited in and shown around. We cannot remain at the mercy of the academic elite. But when I suspect something is wrong with

---

[5]I intend to address this issue in more detail in my forthcoming book *The Crisis of Biblical Authority* (InterVarsity Press).

my car, I could prop up the hood and, with my limited insight into automotive engineering, begin to unplug anything that looks plugged in, clean anything that looks dirty, and pour some liquid into any convenient-looking opening. It would be better to open a service manual for the car before attempting any remedies beyond checking the oil level. Even better, I could consult my local mechanic, tap into his years of experience, and learn some of the "theory" of car repair and maintenance.[6]

Why should we not make the same sort of efforts to read the Bible well? Some have accused me of relying on hidden, secret information. But the information I use is not secret or mystical; it is actually recoverable from ancient literature that I seek to make accessible. Some have accused me of elitism, promulgating the idea that only the scholars can interpret the text. My response is that we all have gifts to contribute to the church, and scholarship is the one that I have to give. The idea of the church is that we are all dependent on one another for what we each have to contribute. That is what spiritual gifts are all about. I am not hoarding what I know; I am sharing it. I have tried to incorporate all of these experiences into the writing of this book.

Beyond taking advantage of opportunities to communicate ideas, I have also been trying to develop deeper understanding and new ideas through ongoing research and thinking. This has led to the continual development of new insights and perspectives. These have come not only through my own research and thinking but in interaction with conversation partners of all sorts. Probably no one has had more influence on my thinking than my son Jon (publishing under J. Harvey Walton). His influence began when he was in his midteens and I was writing my Genesis commentary. We would often walk the dog together in the evenings, and he would ask what passage or issue I had

---

[6]Andrew Brown, *Recruiting the Ancients for the Creation Debate* (Grand Rapids, MI: Eerdmans, 2023), 11.

Introduction: How We Got Here 7

been working on that day. In the resulting conversations, he asked important questions and offered amazingly insightful observations. Such exchanges continued over the years as he read my work, interacted with it, and eventually collaborated with me on several books. As he did his doctoral dissertation at St Andrews on Genesis 2–4, he constantly challenged me to think in new directions, and many of his ideas are incorporated in this book. That is not to say that we always agree; it only means that what each one of us brings to the conversation strengthens the whole. Furthermore, when our ideas or conclusions clash, we then seek ways to qualify and adjust—an extremely beneficial process of give and take.

Such is the story of how we have arrived at this point, now twenty-five years after the first emergence of an idea and fifteen years after the publication of the first of the Lost World books. People frequently ask how the "Lost World" label came about, and I am quick to admit that not only was it not my idea but that I was somewhat skeptical about it when the publisher suggested it. As I understand it, the initial suggestion was made by Dan Reid, then academic editor at InterVarsity Press. The marketing people liked it, and I eventually agreed, despite continuing reservations. It turned out to be a great decision, as it has communicated how in these books I have been trying to uncover an understanding of the Old Testament that has been lost to us through time as culture has shifted slowly but surely, inevitably and dramatically. Culture has evolved from those ancient ways of thinking to produce the ways we think today, and memory of those cultures has faded. That is the lost world that needs to be recovered for us to gain the full benefit of Scripture that, as I maintain, has been written for us but was not written to us.

What Is This Book About?

The idea of this book is to update the discussions pertaining to the lost world of Genesis (primarily Gen 1–3, since the *Lost World of the Flood* just came out in 2018). In most cases this does not revise the previously published material but supplements it, though on occasion readers might find a shift in emphasis or terminology that represents some rethinking. Unavoidably, yes, there are topics about which I have changed my mind (summarized in the conclusions chapter).

We will proceed in eight parts:

Chapter 2: Methodology: How should we approach the text?

Chapter 3: Genesis 1: What kind of creation account is it? (functional ontology)

Chapter 4: Genesis 1: The seventh day and its significance (temple and rest)

Chapter 5: Genesis 2: The garden and the trees (sacred space and priestly roles)

Chapter 6: Genesis 2: Adam and Eve (archetypes, dust and rib)

Chapter 7: Genesis 3: The serpent and the fall

Chapter 8: Genesis 3: The pronouncement and aftermath

Chapter 9: Genesis and Science

In each part we will approach the material in several sections:

1. Summary of the position presented in the previously published material

2. Presentation of new insights, clarifications, illustrations, and so on—these are the new explorations to which the title of this book refers

3. Answering frequently asked questions and addressing common critiques, particularly regarding traditional Christian interpretation and theological ideas. This list of sixty FAQs has been developed from question-and-answer sessions after lectures, from course presentations as I engage with students, from emails that I receive most days, and from published academic reviews.

Introduction: How We Got Here   9

That third section is an important aspect of due diligence. As anyone would expect, there are those who disagree with the Lost World proposals, whether in the realm of methodology or exegesis. One cannot talk about these seminal passages and expect that no one will have objections. I do not mind that people disagree with me. We can each present our evidence as best we can and let people decide what they think is most convincing. I find that I struggle more when reviewers misrepresent me, speculate on my motivations, draw conclusions about my thinking that are inaccurate, or simply fail to grasp the nuances that I am presenting. Sadly, some have persisted in repeating their points publicly even after I have confronted them with how inaccurately they understand my view. In this book I will address their concerns but not them personally. The issues that they raise will be dealt with topically as they come up in the book.

My hope for this book is that it will (1) help those who have adopted the Lost World perspective to understand it more fully, (2) help those who have been confused and uncertain to gain more clarity, and (3) help those who have been resistant and critical to perhaps correct what they believe about me or about the position so that the conversation can move forward in more healthy ways, even if they continue to disagree. In the end, I hope that as I offer more depth of understanding and more alternatives, Christians will come to understand that faithful interpretation can still result in a variety of opinions on interpretation of specific passages. Our common ground in the authority of Scripture unites us, and the gospel message is clear for any reader, young or old.

Synopsis of the Message of Genesis 1–3

Before moving into the individual chapters, it will be helpful for me to offer a summary of how I view the message of these early chapters of Genesis. From an academic perspective, this could be referred to as the rhetorical strategy of the discourse. Here I would like to summarize what I believe the author (= final compiler) of Genesis was trying to communicate to his audience. For me, this text-in-context analysis represents the authoritative message to be found in the affirmations of this section of Scripture. This is a summary I will unpack in the rest of the book.

Genesis 1:1 offers a descriptive phrase explaining the topic that the chapter is going to address, and Genesis 1:2 describes the opening situation. As the story begins, no order has yet been established on the earth. I call this condition nonorder; others call it chaos. It is not an evil situation but describes the undesirable default condition that order bringing will rectify. The scene is set for creation to take place.

In the ancient world, people did not primarily think of God's acts of creation of the cosmos in terms of making objects; they thought of it as bringing order. Order is understood as a stable and secure situation where everything is working the way it is supposed to work. It is an ideal but not perfection and can be relative. I believe the seven-day creation account describes that ordering activity. The main message of this account is that God brings order with a purpose in mind. Two aspects of this purpose can be inferred. The first pertains to God and humanity and is the highlight of day six. As image bearers, humanity's designated role is to work alongside God as partners in bringing order. This implies a working relationship between God and humanity. The second purpose pertains to God and the cosmos and is the highlight of day seven. It eventually takes shape in the temple. In the ancient world, divine rest took place in temples and reflected divine presence and rule. This implied God's intention to be present among humanity.

Though neither relationship nor presence is fully explained in the seven-day account and therefore cannot be identified as the author's main message, the foundation for them is laid here. It is worth noting that both elements, relationship and presence, are of interest in the wider ancient Near East, but the Old Testament develops both in very different directions. For Israel, God's presence is not a mechanism by which his needs can be met—he has no needs. The idea of relationship

Introduction: How We Got Here 11

with God is also qualitatively different from what was found in the ancient Near East. Nothing compares to the idea that Israel is Yahweh's treasured possession or to the metaphor of marriage that defines the relationship.[7] Again, I admit that these are not developed in these early chapters of Genesis, but they would have been in the mind of the Israelite audience, as is demonstrated by the rest of the Old Testament.[8] Both relationship and presence are going to find their focus in the covenant patronage relationship that leads to the divine presence specifically locating itself in the temple in Jerusalem. Genesis 1–11 is leading to the covenant (Gen 12), where relationship and, eventually (in Ex 40), presence, will become the centerpiece of God's work to bring order to the world, but here those ideas are only nascent. These ideas will eventually take shape as the unfolding of his plans and purposes to bring about his kingdom.

I am suggesting neither that Israel was given the mission to promote these ideas nor that it is the mission of the church to do so. Rather, I suggest that relationship and presence represent God's sovereign purposes, and he calls on his people of all ages to participate in them with him. For preexilic Israel, this took the form of a stable and secure political structure. For postexilic Israel, it projected restoration to a stable and secure situation. For us, it calls us to bring honor to the

---

[7]The relationship proceeds from humanity as coworkers, to Israel as vassal and client, to Israel as a patron in the covenant. The ANE also has variants on these relationships. Eventually, however, the OT will see that covenant relationship as taking on a level of *ḥesed* that transcends what we find in the ANE. *Ḥesed* is present when someone is acting to fulfill an obligation, formal or informal, stated and agreed on or inherent in the normal expectations of human interaction or protocol. It involves conforming to an understood expectation and therefore addressing propriety. The closest English rendering is *commitment*. As a patronage agreement, the covenant relationship of Yahweh with Israel is the foundation for such mutual behavior and does not exist in the same way elsewhere in the ANE—that is, between gods and people groups. Likewise, though the presence of deity in a temple is a foundation for worship in the ANE, in Israel it transcended those ideas in that Yahweh's presence was not just a mechanism for meeting his needs.

[8]We should not try to view Genesis through the eyes of the characters (Adam, Noah, Abraham, Jacob) but through the eyes of the narrator and his audience. Regardless of its date of composition, Genesis reflects Israelites writing to Israelites.

reputation of God in our world as his Spirit indwells us, facilitated by the relationship made available in Christ. My current view of the rhetorical strategy of Genesis 2–4 has aligned with that developed by J. Harvey Walton, here summarized by him.

EXCURSUS 1: RHETORICAL STRATEGY OF GENESIS 2–4

J. HARVEY WALTON

The subject of the discussion in the Primordial History (Gen 1–11) is human order and where the highest state of desirable human existence can or cannot be found. The search for order in Genesis is conceptually very similar to the search for meaning in Ecclesiastes. In Ecclesiastes, Qoheleth searches for meaning in all the places that his culture expected to be able to find it—hard work, wisdom, righteousness (the "fear of the Lord"), pleasure, wealth, legacy—and comes up empty every time. He nonetheless affirms that all these things are better to have than not, even if none of them ultimately provide the remedy to meaninglessness. The analysis of Ecclesiastes includes several anecdotes about (presumably) real people (i.e., Eccles 2:4-9; 4:7-8; 9:13-16), some of whom would have been persons of historical significance (the king in Eccles 1:1, 12), but the book is not interested in any of these people in and of themselves. The story of their achievements or lack thereof is instead a commentary on the value and ultimate futility of whatever they are trying to do. The goal is not to describe what people did but to describe the inability of their efforts to create meaning.

In the same way, Genesis includes anecdotes about (presumably) real people whose lives and actions may have had some kind of historical significance, but the purpose of the text is not to record those lives and actions but rather to comment on the search for order. The people depicted in Genesis 1–11 are trying to achieve order in all the ways that ancient Near Eastern conventional wisdom thought it could be done, just like Ecclesiastes is trying to achieve meaning in the way conventional wisdom said it could be done. The text of Genesis depicts humans failing as a commentary on where order cannot be found.

Genesis 2–4 identifies several attempts to establish order, which include living like the gods as immortals in the divine realm, being given the gift of agriculture, being given a community and the ability to propagate that community through future generations, being given divine enlightenment (becoming "like the gods, knowing good and evil"), wearing clothes (a distinctive sign of becoming human), building cities, establishing the arts of civilization, and recounting noteworthy achievements. None of these things turn out to be capable of achieving order, even though most of them are better to have than not, just as things such as wisdom, wealth, and the fear of the Lord do not achieve meaning in Ecclesiastes but are better to have than not. The Genesis narrative emphasizes failure by depicting a nonordered, undesirable condition that persists even after the attempt to achieve order has been put into place. Genesis 2–4 is therefore not a documentary about how a specific attempt to achieve order failed; it is an *evaluation* of where order can or cannot be found and of what kinds of attempts will be futile for those attempting to achieve it.

As the text proceeds to the subsequent *toledoth*s,[9] other potential sources of order that are considered and rejected are annihilation of humanity (the flood), establishment of national-political entities (Gen 10), and bringing God's presence down by their own initiative (Tower of Babel) to fuel a system of mutual codependence (people meeting God's needs so that he will meet their needs).[10]

In this view, these accounts are not about sins and are not describing institutions or behaviors that are sinful (though some of them might incidentally be so); they are in conversation with the ancient world from which they derive as they consider what it is that can achieve order in the world. These values are subverted as they are evaluated as insufficient. These are also the pathways to order that continue to be attractive to us today, which makes the cautionary message of Genesis vital in modern discourse. The message in Genesis 2–11 is not to tell readers (ancient or modern) where to find order; this section of Genesis helps them (and us) to see where we will not find it.

As I will discuss in the pages below, the text-in-context intention of Genesis 3 is not to document the first sin or to provide an explanation for evil in the world. Instead, it shows how humanity is characterized by a desire for godlike autonomy, taking the fruit of the knowledge on their own initiative in the face of divine warning to the contrary, as they seek order on their own terms. I understand their act as an appropriation of a divine capacity now driven by self-will. Their order-bringing attempts going forward are not only inadequate but marred, tainted by self-will. This is evident in Cain, Lamech, the "sons of God," the flood generation, and the tower builders.

---

[9] *Toledoth* is the Hebrew term that is used to introduce the sections of Genesis. Traditionally translated "generations" ("These are the generations of . . .") now often "This is the account of . . ."

[10] These ideas are developed in J. Harvey Walton, "Knowing Good and Evil: Values and Presentation in Genesis 2–4" (PhD diss., University of St Andrews, 2023), http://hdl .handle.net/10023/27738, though he has a different interpretation of the Tower of Babel.

When created in God's image, the plan was that humanity was delegated to partner with God to continue the process of bringing order in the world—God's order according to God's plans and purposes, eventuating in his kingdom.[11] In the Old Testament the focus is primarily on the kingdom of God based in Jerusalem. Eventually, however, particularly in the prophets and specifically in Daniel, the kingdom takes on a more universal shape, though without losing the central role of Israel. When humans choose to be like God, it reflects a desire and determination to be order bringers out on their own, with their own benefits in view. This can be inferred since it is then what humanity does in Genesis 2–11, what Israel does throughout the Old Testament, and what we all do in every place and every time. People are always happy for God's help and want to recruit him to their efforts, but the focus was and is on their own perspectives. Genesis 3 is not so much about how that all started; it is about how that always has characterized all of humanity. We have all strayed as we go our own way. It is not so much about human failure as about our misguided efforts to seek our own benefit. As the text devalues ancient Near Eastern options for achieving order (such as being godlike), it also deconstructs humanity's universal inner drive toward self-will.[12] As such, these texts do not offer prescriptions or commands; they offer wisdom.

Humanity has universally chosen this path to forge order on its own. This does not mean that our institutions of order (civilization, cities, family, community) are bad or contrary to the will of God. The problem is that we place too much confidence in them and too easily exploit them to our own ends. Yet, God is at work carrying out his plans and purposes despite our waywardness. He does so through the covenant—his plan for establishing relationship and his presence

---

[11]In the ANE this was the role of the king, and it was generally assumed that the king's decisions would be endorsed by the god. In Israel, however, there was little such optimism about God and humanity being in sync.

[12]To be clear, J. Harvey Walton's view proposes the idea of deconstructing ANE values, but he would strongly disagree with the idea that it also deconstructs the exercise of self-will.

Introduction: How We Got Here   15

among the people he created as he works toward the establishment of his kingdom.[13] God's plans and purposes eventuate in his kingdom; our plans and purposes eventuate in our kingdom. This contrast is picked up much later in the Lord's Prayer—"Your kingdom come" (implied: not ours), "your will be done" (implied: not ours). The covenant strategy is what Genesis 1–11 is laying the foundation for, and it gets there by devaluing the usual ways and places that ancient (and often modern) people seek order.

As is evident from the above synopsis, I do not see Genesis as feeding a metanarrative of sin and salvation, a view that has long been common in Christian thinking. The long-standing problem for theologians has been that it is difficult to demonstrate that the Israelite authors and audiences were aware of such a metanarrative. Instead, I maintain that these opening chapters of Genesis, while not articulating a metanarrative, use the rejection of ancient ideals of order to launch a different metanarrative, one that centers on relationship and presence, particularly as it is reflected in the covenant.[14] Interest in these issues is pervasive in the Old Testament, evident, for example, in the covenant expression that Yahweh will walk among them and be with them, that he will be their God and they will be his people (Lev 26:11-12; 1 Kings 8:57; Ezek 34:30; 37:26-28). Even prior to the covenant, these factors are evident in Genesis 5:24, where Enoch walks with God (relationship and presence). This focus extends into the metanarrative of the New Testament as well (Jn 1:14; Mt 28:20;

---

[13]It should be noted that Israel is not a replacement image of God. Humanity, as the image of God, was delegated to be order bringers. Israel, as the people of God though the covenant, were incorporated into the divine identity as God identified himself with Israel, and they were with him. In this they are not new order bringers; rather, they have God's order imposed on them (Torah).

[14]I call this "Immanuel theology." For my sermon explaining it, see "Immanuel Theology: What God Has Always Wanted- Dr. John Walton," YouTube, March 14, 2019, 40:49, www.youtube.com/watch?v=knyUtOf_O6s. For a published summary, see John H. Walton, *Old Testament Theology for Christians* (Downers Grove, IL: InterVarsity Press, 2017), 27-28, or John Walton and Kim Walton, *Bible Story Handbook* (Wheaton, IL: Crossway, 2010), 28-30.

2 Cor 6:16; Rev 21:3). The incarnation extends the presence of God, and the death and resurrection of Jesus provide for relationship in a full way. Pentecost features the presence of God in his people as a seal of the relationship forged with them through Christ. New heaven and earth are characterized by God's presence and relationship with him. This can therefore be identified as a canonical metanarrative, though the New Testament did not launch it; it just gave it new expressions as God's plans and purposes unfolded in Jesus. Genesis 1–3 launched the core ideas, which were then developed in the context of Yahweh's covenant with Israel.

2

Methodology

SUMMARY OF PREVIOUS MATERIAL

The methodology used for interpretation in the Lost World books is founded on the premise of biblical authority. Those who take the Bible seriously often boldly affirm biblical authority in theory, but many have not worked out all the implications of that for the methods that they use in their interpretation.[1] The operating methodology in the Lost World books is that God's authority is vested in the human instruments he used to produce Scripture. It is God's authority but their agency—that is, working through their language, their communication style, their genres, and their cultural understandings. This process that God has chosen means that for us to receive the authoritative message of God, we have to get it through the human instruments he used. That requires us to engage with their language, their communication style (rhetoric), their genres, and their cultural understandings, because God accommodated his communication in those areas.[2] I point out that all effective communication requires

---

[1] I have addressed the methodology for interpretation in *Wisdom for Faithful Reading: Principles and Practices for Old Testament Interpretation* (Downers Grove, IL: InterVarsity Press, 2023).

[2] When I speak of *accommodation*, I am simply referring to the unspoken social contract of communication whereby ethical authors use words in a way that they have confidence will be intuitively understood by their audience. This stands in contrast to an alternate understanding of accommodation that imagines an unethical author pandering to the audience by presenting false ideas as true. For more on authority and accommodation, see Iain Provan, *The Reformation and the Right Reading of Scripture* (Waco, TX: Baylor University Press,

accommodation to the audience. God's communication accommodated Israel's language and culture, not ours. That is why I insist throughout the Lost World Series that the Bible was written for us but not to us.

The approach used in the Lost World Series therefore seeks to penetrate those various levels of communication in order to recover to the best of our ability the literary intentions built into the text. This means that at times we will not be able to interpret well if we are lacking understanding of the meanings of words, the conventions of rhetoric, the uses of genre, or the inherent aspects of culture that are intuitive to insiders (Israelites) but opaque to outsiders (us). In the introductions of the various Lost World books, readers can find many examples of this phenomenon from our own culture.

NEW EXPLORATIONS

Cultural river. Though the basic ideas of cultural differences are addressed in all the books, it was not until 2017 that I developed the metaphor of the "cultural river," so that was not used in *The Lost World of Genesis One* or *The Lost World of Adam and Eve*.[3] In those earlier works I use examples such as big-city traffic reports to demonstrate how very extensive and specific cultural knowledge was necessary to understand certain technical types of communication. I refer to it as high-context communication. I also use examples of cosmic geography (such as the ancient belief in a solid sky) and physiology (what the ancients believed about the functions of the internal organs and their relationship to cognition) to demonstrate some of the ways that ancient Israelites thought very differently than we do. The metaphor of the cultural river not only helps us to recognize the cultural distance

---

2017), 313-31; John W. Hilber, *Old Testament Cosmology and Divine Accommodation: A Relevance Theory Approach* (Eugene, OR: Cascade, 2020).

[3]I use it first in *Old Testament Theology for Christians* (Downers Grove, IL: InterVarsity Press, 2017) and, in the Lost World Series, in *LWIC*.

Methodology   19

between them and us; it provides two very important methodological insights: (1) the necessity of trying to set aside elements we can identify as characteristic of our cultural river (e.g., consumerism, social media, democracy, expanding universe) when interpreting, and (2) the distinction between reference and affirmation.

First, then, let me explain the metaphor. The idea is that we can describe the way we think about the culture in which we live with all its elements of values, assumptions, politics, economics, history, religion, science, communication, traditions, conventions, and much more as a river with currents. We exist in that river, and everything we do or think is in the context of that river. We do not necessarily agree with everything in the river, nor do we necessarily like it. Nevertheless, it is what it is—we cannot escape it. All of our conversations and disputes take place within it. Broadly speaking, it is our context. We may reject its legitimacy and try to resist its perspectives, but the currents are strong. Even when we personally adopt an opposing position, our position is taken relative to the cultural river as we oppose *it*. The more academic way to express this concept is that the cultural river represents our cognitive environment. Specific aspects of our modern Western (especially the US) cultural river include freedom/liberty, personal rights, individualism, capitalism, globalism, consumerism, democracy, social media, Big Bang cosmology, tolerance, diversity, market economy, technological progress, a nonsupernatural view of disease, empiricism, statutory law, educational advancement, and many others that could be named. These are not necessarily unique to modern Western culture, but they are characteristic of it.

The first observation derived from this metaphor concerns how we interact with people or literature from another culture. Even today, when we engage with those of other cultures, it would be presumptuous and inappropriate for us to think that they have the same set of assumptions we do. We are aware of the challenges we face in bridging the cultural gaps (not just the obvious language gaps). We need to recognize that this is also the case, and more extremely so, when we want to interact with the ancient Israelite literature that we call the Old Testament. Just as we could not assume that someone of another culture today would share our assumptions or would understand the intricacies of our cultural river, we must give the same respect to the Old Testament. For communication to be successfully received from another culture, we must achieve a level of cultural literacy.

Furthermore, we cannot assume that the Israelite biblical authors knew, anticipated, or would even understand our cultural river. They would not have any meaning to associate with the terms we use to describe it, even if somehow we could translate it into their words. Though we may well acknowledge that God knows all cultural rivers, we cannot seek hidden messages about our cultural river in the biblical text. God spoke in ways that accommodated the Israelite culture and in ways that had meaning to the people then. The authority of the text could not be found in any purported hidden meanings because the authority of the text is linked to the literary intentions of the authors.

Beyond the reality that this metaphor expresses, the significance I want to highlight here is that, once we recognize the cultural-river principle, it is incumbent on us to attempt to mentally set our cultural river aside when we seek to interpret Old Testament texts. If our cultural river provides no cognitive scaffolding to understand their literature, we must try to immerse ourselves in their cultural river. That is a challenging undertaking and to some degree is unachievable. That does not mean that we should not make the attempt. Despite all the limitations that constrain our ability to make the transition, even if we only succeeded in recognizing the way that our own cultural assumptions were influencing our interpretation, we can make great progress. We recognize this principle even when we discuss how to have conversations about our faith with unchurched neighbors. We know that we must strip out Christian jargon if we hope to have a meaningful

Methodology 21

conversation. In a similar way, we must strip out our cultural river to have meaningful conversation with the Old Testament authors as we seek to understand the messages God has given through them. They thought more like Babylonians or Egyptians than they thought like us. To get on their wavelength, we need to minimize the distorting static with which our own wavelength distracts us.

Kurt L. Noll offers an example of this with something as basic as our understanding of our god-concept, which inevitably is contingent on social, economic, and political conceptions. He points out that in our modern Western culture, "Many people believe their god guarantees human equality and freedom of conscience" and also "take for granted that their god knows about the natural universe, such as how galaxies were formed, what atomic energy is, and how planet Earth orbits the sun." Furthermore, "many people presume as self-evident that their god approves of a capitalist economic system and a political democracy."[4] Perhaps to the surprise of some readers, he points out that only a few centuries ago there was no one who held those beliefs.

> People in Medieval Europe believed that their god ordained rigidly defined social stations, including aristocracy, commoners and slaves. Also, their god knew that planet Earth rested at the centre of the universe and the sun orbited Earth. This god guaranteed the right of kings, not the right of people to vote for a leader, and outlawed the lending of money at interest, the backbone of capitalism.[5]

The problem I have described above finds confirmation as he identifies the undesirable state of affairs that should not be as shocking as it is. "Today, professional theologians interpret the Bible so that the Bible

---

[4]Kurt L. Noll, "The Patron God in the Ancient Near East," in *Patronage in Ancient Palestine and in the Hebrew Bible: A Reader*, ed. Emanuel Pfoh (Sheffield: Sheffield Phoenix, 2022), 41-66, here 41.

[5]Noll, "Patron God," 41.

affirms their modern values, just as medieval theologians interpreted the Bible so that the Bible affirmed their medieval values."[6] What I have proposed above finds confirmation in his conclusion:

> With these observations as a foundation, it is easy to see why it is necessary to erase from our minds any assumptions that we might have about a god today and any modern religious community's theological interpretation of the Bible, for otherwise it is impossible to understand what a god was in the ancient Near East. Even familiar biblical passages are, in reality, unfamiliar territory, for the ancient who wrote, read or heard those passages presupposed a network of beliefs that our culture does not share.[7]

The second implication of the metaphor pertains to how we read what we find in their cultural river, what I referred to above as reference and affirmation. In *The Lost World of Scripture* I discuss the nature of inerrancy and the conventional qualification that it is associated with "all that Scripture *affirms*." That qualification is generally used sparingly to recognize that, for example, words of Satan are not inerrant and not something that the text affirms (the advice of Job's friends is another example). I go beyond those traditional confines to suggest that when ancient perspectives about cosmic geography or physiology and so on are evident, those should likewise not be considered affirmations.

We can now bring greater clarity to our understanding of the affirmations of Scripture. What was lacking was a way to describe the category of texts that were not to be considered affirmations. The term proposed to classify those texts that are not affirmations is *reference*, because the authors are *referring* to their cultural river.[8] This is

---

[6]Noll, "Patron God," 41.

[7]Noll, "Patron God," 41.

[8]Reference and affirmation are discussed at greater length in John H. Walton and J. Harvey Walton, *Demons and Spirits in Biblical Theology* (Eugene, OR: Cascade, 2019), introduced on 16-18, then applied throughout the book.

Methodology 23

unavoidable because communication takes place in the context of a cultural perspective. The text may refer to a solid sky or a physiological assumption widely held in the ancient world, but no scriptural affirmation is thereby being made. That is, the Bible is not making authoritative statements about physiology or cosmic geography that God's people need to adopt as truth.

Once we make this distinction, we can recognize a much broader use for the category of reference than we might think. A few examples can help.

- In Acts 7, Stephen makes a long speech recounting Israelite history just prior to his execution. Luke's account of that speech is reference—it records how Luke presents what Stephen said in a way that serves the rhetorical purposes of Luke. *Acts* is inspired (not Stephen). Stephen's speech itself is not thereby confirmed to be a totally accurate record of history. It represents his recollection and view of history filtered through Luke's rhetorical strategy as he presents the affirmations of his book.

- In the Old Testament, when God conveys wisdom to Israel concerning what constitutes order for their living in his presence (whether ritual or law), that would be characterized as reference. That is, the text accurately refers to the content of those covenant stipulations. These texts are included to convey how God worked with Israel. That is what is affirmed, and its relevance to us follows that same line. It is not affirming that the same behavior is demanded of everyone.

- Cultural assumptions also can be classified as reference. Cases include Jacob's understanding of herd management (Gen 30:37-42) and dietary perspectives (Lev 11).[9]

---

[9]Note that most Christian interpreters have considered aspects of the Mosaic law as irrelevant to Christians. In that way they are references to what God told Israel, not affirmations of what all must do. See Michael Graves, *The Inspiration and Interpretation of Scripture: What the Early Church Can Teach Us* (Grand Rapids, MI: Eerdmans, 2014), 7.

24 New Explorations in the Lost World of Genesis

- Beliefs that Israelites held by default and in common with others in the ancient Near East are in the category of reference. They believed, for example, that there was a nondescript netherworld where everyone went after death and from which spirits could be summoned (1 Sam 28). Israelites held even very basic beliefs in common with their neighbors. For example, everyone believed that the divine world was real and that the inhabitants of that world cared how people lived. That would not be new information for Israel. Yet Yahweh had affirmations to offer that transcended those basic shared beliefs.

Though this reference category has long been recognized, at least tacitly, as we confront it we can now see that it poses some potential problems to interpretation. How does one tell? For example, is the idea of a divine council (1 Kings 22) reference or affirmation? Are fruit trees with incredible properties and a talking snake reference or affirmation? Are cherubim and seraphim reference or affirmation? What about Leviathan? Once we are aware that there are two categories, determination of which category is appropriate in a passage becomes a significant interpretive decision.

Yet, even these examples somewhat miss the point. The affirmations that the text makes need to be made at the discourse level. That is, since authority is resident with the author, we want to know what the author is doing with these elements. His affirmations may not be tied to facts (about snakes or trees); alternatively, he may be using these elements from his world and cultural context to communicate ideas.[10]

I propose, first, that we must recognize that since communication takes place in a cultural context, not in a vacuum, everything can be identified at some level as reference. Yet, the author also has affirmations to make in his larger discourse. References thereby serve as the

---

[10]Note that I am using the masculine singular forms here for the implied authors, not in defiance of inclusive language but in recognition that the consensus assessment is that all the writers in the Bible happened to be male.

Methodology   25

building blocks of discourse that in turn carry the affirmations. That is, this is not an either-or question but reflects the need to determine when something is both/and. Second, I propose that the most important determining factor as to whether something is affirmation is whether what it says is a *departure from* the default thinking in the ancient world (most likely affirmation) or a *reflection of* the default thinking in the ancient world (most likely reference only). More importantly, however, we need to pay attention to how the discourse wants to change how the audience thinks about the subject matter. One of the ways to answer the question "Why is this here?" is to ask "What did this change in their thinking?"—though this is not the only guide.[11]

For example, as noted above, everyone in the ancient world believed there was a netherworld where people went when they died, even though there were vastly different concepts about that netherworld (for instance, between Egyptian and Babylonian views). A thorough study of the Old Testament reveals that the Israelites did not have any distinctive views about the netherworld. Instead, they reflect a very similar understanding to what one would find in Babylon. No distinctive hallmarks characterize what we find in the Bible concerning the netherworld. That would suggest that, in the absence of new revelation to Israel, everything we find in the Old Testament about the nature of the netherworld is reference, not affirmation. The Old Testament has nothing to teach about the nature of the netherworld, and therefore nothing we find there can be used to construct doctrine founded on the authority of Scripture.[12]

Other cases are more complicated. For example, we find nothing in ancient Near Eastern literature that quite compares with a single

---

[11]Criteria developed in conversation with J. Harvey Walton.

[12]I would say that the same is true of the divine council. Texts that feature it do not even make an effort to clarify whether the council members are gods. It is difficult to find any aspect of the Israelite concept of a divine council that would distinguish it from the view of Israel's neighbors.

man and woman being placed in a garden with the fruit of a particular tree being forbidden (Gen 2–3). If it is truly unique, does that mean that it is automatically an affirmation? Before that question can be answered, we again must consider the distinction between details and discourse. The narrative clearly has an affirmation to make. But affirmations occur on the discourse level. If the narrator's discourse concerns whether being like God can produce order (see excursus 1), the details of the narrative (human couple, snake, trees) may not be the point of the affirmation, possibly then leading to the conclusion that they are reference.

Another option for the discourse is that the Israelites are giving a new series of answers to common questions about what brings ultimate order in their world. We do have stories in the ancient world about how wisdom was gained and the chance at immortality was lost (Gilgamesh). We have stories about the encroachment of forces of chaos and the disruption of order (Anzu; Erra). The stories take a very different shape in the Babylonian telling, but they deal with the same questions. This is no surprise because they represent the most fundamental and persistent questions that haunt humanity.

How much, then, of what we find in Genesis 2–3 is affirmation, and how much of it is reference? What is being affirmed by the parts that are affirmation? Interpreters will differ, but this leads to another guideline. One of the assumptions in the proposed methodology is that every discourse has something it intends to affirm. Again, trying to determine what that is becomes the task of the interpreter.

All of this in turn raises other worries. Would this not mean that some of the Bible is not true? To respond to that very legitimate question, I begin with the reminder: inerrancy claims that the Bible is true *in all that it affirms*. What it affirms is true. References may truly reflect the culture or the speech, but that does not mean that they stand as something that the Bible affirms in its authority. Am I

Methodology 27

saying that not all of the Bible is God's Word? No, not at all. The Bible is God's Word by virtue of its inspiration. The doctrine of inspiration makes the claim that its source is God. Since God is communicating through human instruments and into a particular human culture, he uses both reference and affirmation together. The source is still God. Both reference and affirmation come from God because communication cannot take place without reference.

Theologians often describe inspiration as being both verbal and plenary, and the differentiation of reference and affirmation does not change that. Each word (verbal) comes from God (inspired), whether reference or affirmation. At the same time, the whole message throughout (plenary) comes from God (inspired) in its combined use of reference and affirmation, producing discourses. Though we may be most interested in the affirmations, references are not without their role and significance, and affirmations cannot be made without the use of reference. These important distinctions can help us to ask better questions when we interpret text. They help us to be more informed readers and bring more nuance to our reading.

To be more specific, what are these better questions?[13]

- Who is the (implied) audience? What do they care about?
- What does the audience believe by default, and what did the author/redactor/editor/compiler change?
- How do those changes modify the default beliefs of the audience (why is this in here?)
- What are we supposed to learn/do as a result of watching the audience have their beliefs altered in this specific way?
- Is the author contributing something to our understanding of God or his plans and purposes?

---

[13]Provided by J. Harvey Walton in personal communication.

28 NEW EXPLORATIONS IN THE LOST WORLD OF GENESIS

ANSWERS TO FREQUENTLY ASKED QUESTIONS

The common questions and critiques in the area of methodology involve three general categories: (1) the proper use of the ancient Near East, (2) the genre and historicity of the early chapters of Genesis, and (3) reconciling this new approach with how these chapters of Genesis have been interpreted in the past. Each category can be addressed through several questions, which I will try to answer individually.

Questions about the significance and use of perspectives and material from the ancient Near East

1. Is understanding ancient Near Eastern culture really that important to reading the Old Testament? It depends how deeply you would like to go into the Old Testament and how many of its nuances you want to understand. If you care only about seeing the grand scheme of how God worked with and through his people in the centuries leading up to Jesus, the basic ideas will probably come through. If you want only to meditate on God's greatness, you will find some easy, low-hanging fruit. Nevertheless, important nuances even on major topics await those who seek to be informed about the cultural context. If, therefore, you are interested in interpreting individual Old Testament passages, the ancient Near East can often supply enlightening perspectives and on some occasions can provide the key to revolutionize interpretation with information that you would otherwise have no way of knowing. If knowledge of the cultural context is not informing your understanding, it is likely that your theological and traditional presuppositions are.

Examples of revolutionary thinking in the Lost World books include the nature of God's rest (Gen 2:1-3; Ex 20:8-11), understanding the sons of God and the Nephilim (Gen 6:1-4), the Tower of Babel (Gen 11:1-9), and what was going on in Joshua's prayer for the sun and moon to wait and stand (Josh 10:12-15).[14] Examples of

---

[14]For discussion of rest, see *LWG1*, 71-76; on the Tower of Babel, see *LWF*, 129-42; on sons of God, see *LWF*, 122-28; on the sun and moon, see appendix C to *LWIC*, "Joshua 10:12-15 and

Methodology   29

enlightening are much more widespread and reflect the need for cultural literacy:

- We need to appreciate how marriage was practiced in the ancient world to understand the narratives in Genesis 12–37. Arranged marriages with clan identity in mind and featuring exchange of wealth, specifically for the purpose of producing the next generation, made for a very different institution from the institution of marriage today in the Western world.

- We need to recognize that genealogies played a different role in the ancient Near East than they do today. For people then, the claims of descent had rhetorical value for one's identity beyond the biological and historical details.

- We need to understand the nature of bovine images in the ancient world to interpret the golden calf incident in Exodus 32, including an understanding of the varying ways that images functioned.

- To understand the sacrificial system in Israel, we need to have information about the ritual institutions of the ancient world for both similarities and differences.[15]

- Many of the legal provisions of the Old Testament are opaque to us at best. This is true even of basic materials such as the Ten Commandments.[16]

- People in the ancient world thought about history, law, and prophecy differently from how we do. Learning how they thought can help us to avoid imposing our own ideas on the Old Testament.

The fact is, we all know that when we read the Old Testament, we encounter many things we do not intuitively understand. Knowledge of

---

Mesopotamian Celestial Omen Texts," available at www.ivpress.com/Media/Default/Downloads/Misc/5184-appendix.pdf.

[15]T. M. Bolin, "Exchange, Justice, and Mercy in Genesis 18–19," in Pfoh, *Patronage in Ancient Palestine*, 282-97.

[16]See John H. Walton and J. Harvey Walton, *The Lost World of the Torah: Law as Covenant and Wisdom in Ancient Context* (Downers Grove, IL: InterVarsity Press, 2019), 231-57.

30 NEW EXPLORATIONS IN THE LOST WORLD OF GENESIS

the cultures and literature of the ancient world can help fill that gap in many important ways. If you would like to go beyond a superficial summary of the Old Testament and understand it in all its fullness, the material from the ancient Near East is essential. Furthermore, since we consider the Old Testament to be God's revelation to us, I contend that we ought to desire to understand the text as deeply as we can.[17]

2. Do we have enough ancient Near Eastern literature to give us any level of confidence about how people thought back then? How much can we trust what we find in it? No matter how much of the ancient Near Eastern cultures and literature we recover, we will always be aware of the gaps in both our knowledge and our understanding. Nevertheless, in the century and a half that has passed since the discoveries began in earnest, we have become remarkably well informed. Besides Egyptian tombs, temples, and wall reliefs, over one million cuneiform tablets in Sumerian, Akkadian, Hittite, and Ugaritic have come to light and have now been translated and analyzed. Archaeological excavation has produced countless artifacts, from the ubiquitous pottery to inscriptions and figurines, as well as providing information about houses, palaces, temples, fortifications, and city planning, often supported by literary texts. The literature that has become available begins early in the third millennium at the dawn of writing. Though a large percentage of the texts are administrative business documents, thousands of literary texts (myths, proverbs,

---

[17]For tools that will provide the material from the ANE, see Craig S. Keener and John H. Walton, eds., *NIV, Cultural Backgrounds Study Bible* (Grand Rapids, MI: Zondervan, 2016), also available in NRSV and NKJV; John Walton, Victor Matthews, and Mark Chavalas, *The IVP Bible Background Commentary: Old Testament* (Downers Grove, IL: InterVarsity Press, 2000); John Walton, ed., *The Zondervan Illustrated Bible Backgrounds Commentary: Old Testament* (Grand Rapids, MI: Zondervan, 2009). For more about the methods and further detailed examples, see John H. Walton, *Wisdom for Faithful Reading: Principles and Practices for Old Testament Interpretation* (Downers Grove, IL: InterVarsity Press, 2023). For a description of many of the ways that people thought in the ANE, see John H. Walton, *Ancient Near Eastern Thought and the Old Testament: Introducing the Conceptual World of the Hebrew Bible*, 2nd ed. (Grand Rapids, MI: Baker, 2018). For a more technical but extremely informative elaboration, see Beate Pongratz-Leisten, *Religion and Ideology in Assyria*, Studies in Ancient Near Eastern Records (Berlin: de Gruyter, 2017).

Methodology 31

royal inscriptions, letters, divination texts, prayers, incantations, apocalypses, legal texts, and more) provide ample insight into the ancient world.

We can trust that the literature and iconography give us reliable snapshots of the ancient world, though, as with any attempts to understand another culture, not everything is clear. Nevertheless, these resources can help us recognize the ways in which our cultural river is very different from that of the ancient world. All of this material improves the level of cultural literacy we bring to our interpretation of the text, and the more we can understand about ancient culture, the better our position to be faithful readers.

3. Why should we assume that the Israelites thought like their ancient Near Eastern neighbors? The short answer is, why should we conclude they thought differently if the Bible does not indicate that they did and when the evidence is so abundant that they were full participants in that ancient cognitive environment? The most important observation to make in this regard is that no culture ever exists in a vacuum. Archaeology in Israel and the ancient Near East has conclusively demonstrated countless ways in which Israel was embedded in the world around it. One example is the similarity of the architectural design of Solomon's temple to those found in the same period in the ancient world. Our knowledge of the literature from the ancient world has only confirmed how extensive the cultural commonalities are. Bruce Waltke puts it well: "The Bible originates not only in an ancient Near Eastern language, but also in the garb of ancient Near Eastern literature."[18] Still, there were always differences. As is true today, as each culture has its own individuality, so Israelite culture was distinguishable from the other cultures that populated the region even as Egyptian and Mesopotamian cultures were different from each other.

Nevertheless, what we can say with confidence is that Israelites thought more like their neighbors than they did like us. It is therefore

---

[18]Bruce Waltke, *An Old Testament Theology* (Grand Rapids, MI: Zondervan, 2007), 195. Waltke's entire discussion is insightful and worthwhile reading (188-203).

to our benefit to use the ancient Near Eastern literature to help us to identify thinking that is characteristically modern or Western so that we can eliminate those elements from our interpretation. Yet, it would be foolhardy to believe that the Israelites thought exactly the same as Babylonians or Egyptians. In some respects, Israelite thinking would have more resembled Babylonian thinking; in others, more similarity might be observable in comparison to the Egyptians. Regardless of the nature of the similarities and which cultures were more similar or less so, the important fact is that there *were* similarities, which means that we can find help there.

Consequently, we are deeply interested in recognizing both similarities and differences. Egyptians were different from Babylonians, and second-millennium Babylonians were different in some degree from first-millennium Babylonians.[19] Israelites were characterized by important differences from all of them. These differences must not be taken lightly or neglected. A principle I use is that if I can find anywhere in the ancient Near East a parallel to concepts or phrases I find in the Old Testament, that is sufficient to suggest that Israel was not being innovative on that point (or, if one prefers, that God was not leading Israel to an entirely unique way of thinking). Yet, as previously discussed, the innovations that make Scripture what it is are generally going to be found on the discourse level—that is where the authors' affirmations are going to reveal what significance the information has.

Our interpretation will be strongest when we take advantage of everything we know of both similarities and differences. Even places where there are differences will become clearer when we read the Old Testament in light of what common ancient Near Eastern thinking was. My default is to assume that the Israelite thinking would be similar to what can be determined about their neighbors unless I find

---

[19]Angelika Berlejung, "From One Theology to Many Theologies in Babylonia," in *Divine Secrets and Human Imaginations* (Tübingen: Mohr Siebeck, 2016), 183, indicates that plurality of concepts could occur even within a single piece of literature.

Methodology 33

evidence in the biblical text that would differentiate them from their contemporary cultural river.

4. If Scripture is constrained by ancient cultural understandings, then was God in effect misleading the rest of us? Not at all. Just as communication calls for a mutually understood medium (common language, symbols with agreed meaning, even body language), so it calls for a mutually understood cultural context. Therefore, if God intended to communicate, he would understandably have chosen a language and culture by which to do so. By choosing one, he does not mislead the others. Instead, every reader, no matter what era or culture they are a part of, is expected to recognize that the communication was, as it must be, culturally conditioned. It is our job to become informed readers, always recognizing that we are outsiders trying to penetrate an insider-to-insider communication.

5. Does the Old Testament borrow from other ancient Near Eastern texts and cultural understandings? Though many scholars who compare the Old Testament and the ancient Near East have been and continue to be interested in literary dependence, that is not the direction that my research takes. Perhaps scholars may find Old Testament texts that they believe are in some ways more or less dependent on pieces of known literature from the ancient Near East. The biblical authors were undoubtedly aware of the classic literature of their day. Some of these pieces would likely have been in the curriculum of the scribal schools and the tales that were widespread in the ancient world and would have circulated, at least as oral traditions, in Israel as well. Israelite traditions could plausibly have contained echoes of such literature or even argued against it. God's inspiration of Israelite texts could have interacted with discourse structures, genres, and even content of well-known texts. As interesting (and often speculative) as such inquiries might be, that is not what my studies are doing. I am not working on the premise that Genesis is indebted to other pieces of literature from the ancient world. Moreover, even if the Israelites were specifically

34   NEW EXPLORATIONS IN THE LOST WORLD OF GENESIS

working with a particular piece of ancient literature, what is most important is what they did with it, not where it came from. Nevertheless, I build my research on the idea that Israelite thinking is embedded in the conceptual world of the ancient Near East.

Consequently, I am not interested in discussing whether Genesis borrowed from the Babylonian creation epic (Enuma Elish) or any other piece of Sumerian or Egyptian cosmology. I am interested in the cultural discourse, that is, how the biblical authors may be in conversation with the literature and traditions of the day. God communicated into that ancient world to Israelites who had their own particular interests and conceptions. An investigation of embeddedness will ask questions such as:

- What did people in the ancient world consider to be the most important aspects of creation?
- How did they tend to frame creation accounts?
- Since creation is bringing something into existence, how did they think about existence?
- Were they more interested in terraforming or formation of identity?

This is just a sampling but illustrates the difference between literary indebtedness and cultural embeddedness. Literary borrowing is not an element in my use of the ancient Near East.[20]

6. Since ancient Near Eastern culture is based in mythology but the Old Testament is not, doesn't it devalue the Old Testament when you refer to pagan mythology? The word *mythology* is a slippery one. Today we often use it to refer to literature of another culture or an earlier time that reflects what we consider to be made-up stories containing traditions, superstitions, and fanciful activities of gods we do not believe in. In popular discourse, it is treated as a category of fiction and closely associated with fairy tales. People who take the Bible seriously

---

[20]A helpful discussion of comparative method can be found in Nathan Chambers, *Reconsidering Creation Ex Nihilo* in Genesis 1 (University Park, PA: Eisenbrauns, 2020), 7-44.

Methodology 35

understandably desire to avoid devaluing the Bible by so categorizing it. They believe that the Bible is true and embrace it as reflecting the deepest and most important realities of their faith. How could Babylonian or Egyptian mythology play any significant role, then, in our understanding of the Old Testament?

The first item to address is this understanding of mythology. Instead of comparing it to fairy tales, we should realize that this literature is a reflection of cultural identity. Even when we do not believe in the gods that are portrayed in the literature, we should recognize that the people of those cultures did. As a result, they believed that this literature reflected reality—not necessarily the reality of events but a reality about the relationships between the gods themselves, and between the gods and the world and the people who lived there. This was a transcendent reality and conveyed their deepest sense of what was real. It is deeply reductionistic for us to label it fairy tale or even fiction. To take this literature seriously is not to adopt or affirm the beliefs of the culture but to recognize that we can learn a lot about the culture by studying what the people in it believed.

Over the centuries, a common question about Genesis is whether we should consider it an example of Israelite mythology.[21] One can see that if we were to adopt the popular definition of mythology described above (fairy tale), we would reject such a label. For others who are more inclined to adopt the more nuanced viewpoint described in the last paragraph (cultural identity), it would be easy to acknowledge that Genesis corresponds to ancient mythology in the sense that it is a reflection of cultural identity and represents a transcendent reality—that which was most essentially real to them. One of the key remaining differences would be that we continue to believe that the God of Israel exists.[22]

---

[21]For an extensive and helpful treatment of this question, see Paul K.-K. Cho, *Myth, History, and Metaphor in the Hebrew Bible* (Cambridge: Cambridge University Press, 2019).

[22]Though, at the same time, note that what we believe about that existent God is very different from what ancient Israelites believed about that same God (for example, they were not trinitarian).

A recognition of such correspondence does not devalue the Bible. Instead, comparison helps us to consider how Israel viewed identity and reality in ways similar to their neighbors, even though they believed in different gods. Genesis served a similar function for Israelites as Babylonian and Egyptian myths served for those cultures. It is vital for interpretation that we understand their cultural perspectives about and perceptions of reality. The literature from the ancient Near East, and particularly the mythological literature, offers us windows to their conceptual world, and since Israel extensively shared that conceptual world, this literature is valuable to us.

Some have felt that using the material from the ancient Near East is a violation of the battle cry of the Reformation, *sola Scriptura*—that only Scripture carries authority. Two brief observations should dispel the discomfort represented in that concern. First, I am not suggesting in any way that the literature of the ancient Near East carries authority or that it stands next to Scripture. It provides a reliable window to how people thought in the ancient world and therefore provides meaning that is essential to the interpretation process. Second, when we read the Reformers in context, their insistence on *sola Scriptura* can be seen as holding Scripture's authority above and apart from the church's authority, particularly in interpretation.[23] That has little to do with the issues that we are discussing here, though interpreters today who propose meaning in Scripture that the authors could not have had are likewise placing authority in the interpreter (themselves or the traditions), not in the Scripture. They have merely switched that authority from the magisterium of the church to their own personal readings.

7. Is it possible that scholars are underestimating the understanding of the Israelites and the ancient world when they suggest that people back then believed in a solid sky or that people actually thought with their

---

[23]See the excellent discussions in Provan, *Reformation and the Right Reading*, 294-302; Kevin J. Vanhoozer and Daniel J. Treier, *Theology and the Mirror of Scripture: A Mere Evangelical Account* (Downers Grove, IL: InterVarsity Press, 2015), 102-10.

Methodology   37

hearts? This question turns to some of the particulars of ancient belief. Have we got it right, or are we making the mistake of reading language literally when we should be reading it figuratively? It has been widely recognized that even in today's modern discourse, we retain vestiges of language that we use only figuratively. We speak of the sun rising and setting though we know that the sun is not moving. Such language reflects an observational perspective, which for a long time was all people had to go on. Yet, no one suggests that people in the ancient world knew that the sun was stationary and that its appearance of rising and setting was the result of the rotation of the earth. Other aspects of cosmic geography that could be discussed include whether the earth is spherical or flat, whether there is only one continent, whether the sun, moon, and stars are inside a solid sky that holds back waters, and whether sun, moon, and stars are even physical objects at all or are manifestations of the gods. Our questions could extend beyond cosmic geography to, for example, physiology. Did the ancients actually believe that cognitive and emotive processes took place in internal organs such as the heart, liver, and kidneys, or did they have at least a basic understanding that the heart was a blood pump and that people thought with their brains?

These are important questions, and discovering the answers can require complicated investigations for cultural outsiders such as ourselves. We want to avoid the mistake of reductionistic and naive assessment of others as primitive by reading their literature and language without a robust understanding of their nuances. Likewise, we want to avoid adopting the default assumption that they thought like we do.

It is their literature that can help us to sort out what was figurative in their minds and what was a literal understanding. In each of the cases listed above, I believe that sufficient information is available in the literature to suggest that their understanding was not just a figurative way to express ideas that in the end are similar to the modern world. Here I will offer a very brief rundown of each point mentioned above to present my reasoning for understanding their concepts in a nonfigurative way.

On a flat earth. Probably one of the strongest pieces of evidence that the ancients believed the world was flat is the ubiquitous concept that when the sun set in the west, it traveled beneath the earth (through the netherworld) to rise in the east. Another is the idea that the earth was held up by something like pillars. This appears in the Babylonian boundary stone known as the "unfinished kudurru" that portrays the various levels of the cosmos.

On a solid sky with sun, moon, and stars inside. Othmar Keel, in his highly respected work on iconography, contends that we have read the ancient texts naively on this point. "People in the ancient Near East did not conceive of the earth as a disk floating on water with the firmament inverted over it like bell jar, with the stars hanging from it."[24] Instead, Keel and Silvia Schroer contend that these are merely symbolic ways of describing the cosmos. In their view, such textual expressions represent a conceptual perspective rather than a literal one and reflect the conventions of their time.[25] We should take such cautions seriously. Yet, at the same time, we must be willing to recognize that, symbolic though they may be, such conceptions cannot be easily dismissed. This is especially true as we recognize that the ancients did not have at their disposal the ways of knowing that provide our view of the cosmos.

In contrast to the assertions of Keel and Schroer, Assyriologist Francesca Rochberg offers a historical study of the concept of a solid sky holding back the waters:

> Throughout the period from late antiquity to the Middle Ages, none of the natural philosophers or theologians who engaged

---

[24]Othmar Keel and Silvia Schroer, *Creation: Biblical Theologies in the Context of the Ancient Near East* (Winona Lake, IN: Eisenbrauns, 2015), 78.

[25]Chambers, *Reconsidering Creation Ex Nihilo*, 43, chooses a more cautious position that the language is not making literal claims.

Methodology 39

with the cosmological implications of the biblical six days of creation had the luxury of recognizing the ancient Near Eastern background of the "waters above the firmament." Yet this ancient Near Eastern mythological motif entered the stream of Western cosmological thought and remained, albeit reinterpreted, as part of the picture of the ancient world until the final dismantling of the ancient-mediaeval world view.[26]

That ancient peoples believed in a solid sky is evidenced by the texts that speak of various levels of the heavens made up of varying types of stone, an idea that may also be reflected in Exodus 24:10.[27] Egyptian art consistently portrays the sky god being held up by the air god, and the Babylonian Shamash stele portrays the throne of the god resting on the waters.[28] That Yahweh's throne is "founded on the waters" (presumably those held back by the solid sky) suggests a similar cosmic geography. In the ancient world the sky had to be held up by something, and people had various opinions of how that worked: pillars, mountains, chains, and so on. Consequently, when the Old Testament refers to the pillars of heaven, even though in poetry (Job 26:11), we have no reason to believe that for them it was only figurative. A couple of different Hebrew terms have been identified as referring to the solid sky, but that debate continues.[29] Origen and Augustine interpret the waters above allegorically as referring to spiritual waters. "Basil depicted a dome-shaped roofed structure with a flat underside to hold in the waters."[30] Others speculated that the waters above were frozen

---

[26]Francesca Rochberg, "A Short History of the Waters of the Firmament," in *From the Banks of the Euphrates: Studies in Honor of Alice Louise Slotsky*, ed. Micah Ross (Winona Lake, IN: Eisenbrauns, 2008), 227-44, here 228.

[27]Wayne Horowitz, *Mesopotamian Cosmic Geography* (Winona Lake, IN: Eisenbrauns, 1998), 3-15; Rochberg, "Short History," 235; J. Edward Wright, *The Early History of Heaven* (Oxford: Oxford University Press, 2000), especially 32-37.

[28]Christopher E. Woods, "The Sun-God Tablet of Nabû-apla-iddina Revisited," *Journal of Cuneiform Studies* 56 (2004): 23-103.

[29]*GIAC*.

[30]Rochberg, "Short History," 237, 239.

40 NEW EXPLORATIONS IN THE LOST WORLD OF GENESIS

or crystalline. Based on Ptolemaic planetary models, cosmologists of the fourteenth and fifteenth centuries "moved toward viewing the heavens as composed of solid hard orbs, and this trend continued and culminated in the sixteenth century."[31]

We should also recall that even up to the time of the Reformation, theologians were prone to argue about how thick the solid sky was and the material from which it was made. By this time, we can see that even though the concept of the solid sky continued to be maintained, it had taken on a very different understanding from that which constituted the ancient Near Eastern view. Rochberg confirms this as she acknowledges that Christian writers and medieval cosmologists had no awareness of the ancient Near East traditions but based their understanding on the biblical text without realizing how ancient Near East concepts were embedded in them.[32]

Akkadian texts are clearest about the stars being engraved on the underside of the solid sky, though Egyptian art also portrays the stars as being on the underside of the body of Nut, the sky god. Egyptians show Amun-Re, the sun god, sailing across the waters above the solid sky, but the sun itself is below the god Nut, who swallows the sun each evening and gives birth to it each morning.[33] In the Old Testament, we note that the sun and moon are "in" the *rāqîaʾ*. Whether the *rāqîaʾ* is the solid sky (firmament) or the space (expanse) between the solid sky and the earth, the sun and moon are inside not outside.[34] This is logical

---

[31]Rochberg, "Short History," 241.

[32]Rochberg, "Short History," 241.

[33]We should note that Egyptologist James Allen demurs slightly by offering the nuance that in their perception, the sky may have been more of an interface than something solid. See Allen, *Genesis in Egypt* (New Haven, CT: Yale University Press, 1988), 5.

[34]In *LWGI* I took the former position, but in *GIAC* I changed my mind and adopted the latter. For a recent and thoroughgoing article that attempts to refute the idea of a solid sky, see Randall W. Younker and Richard M. Davidson, "The Myth of the Solid Heavenly Dome: Another Look at the Hebrew *rāqîaʾ*," in *The Genesis Creation Account and Its Reverberations in the Old Testament*, ed. Gerald A. Klingbeil (Berrien Springs, MI: Andrews University Press, 2015), 31-56. For the view that *rāqîaʾ* refers to the solid sky of ANE literature, see Rochberg, "Short History," 235. For a carefully nuanced examination of *rāqîaʾ* in relation

Methodology 41

since they can be *seen*, which would not be possible if they were in the realm of the gods, beyond the waters above.

On heavenly bodies as nonmaterial manifestations of the gods. Much discussion still surrounds the relationship between the heavenly bodies and the gods they represent, particularly in Mesopotamian studies.[35] Regardless of how that relationship is defined, nothing in ancient literature suggests that ancient people considered the heavenly bodies to be material objects. Massive amounts of omen literature address the movements in the heavens, but nothing betrays any sense of a material reality. Instead, the ancient diviners were most interested not in their materiality or even their motion but in the periodicity, and, as Rochberg observes, their approach "did not depend on a physical framework."[36] Though the Old Testament rejects the idea that heavenly bodies are gods, the Israelites struggled to adopt that view, as the prophets had to keep reprimanding them about worshiping astral deities (2 Kings 17:16; 21:3-5; 23:5; Jer 8:2; 19:13; Zeph 1:5). Nevertheless, even when the Israelites adopted the view that these were not gods, they still referred to them as "lights" (Gen 1).

The idea that the moon was a material object was rejected by Plato but had been adopted by his older contemporary Anaxagoras, a radical idea for which he was exiled. The Babylonians were highly skilled in astronomical observation and inference, yet it was not until

---

to Hebrew, Greek, Mesopotamian, and Egyptian data, see Oliver A. Hersey, "Genesis 1:6-8 and Ancient Near Eastern Celestial Perspectives," in *"Now These Records Are Ancient": Studies in Ancient Near Eastern and Biblical History, Language and Culture in Honor of K. Lawson Younger, Jr.*, ed. James K. Hoffmeier, Richard E. Averbeck, J. Caleb Howard, and Wolfgang Zwickel (Münster: Zaphon, 2022), 159-75. He provides ample evidence from all quarters for the belief in a solid sky. He nevertheless concludes that the term *rāqîaʾ* is semantically more invested in its role as a boundary between the divine and the mundane realms than in the material of which it consisted. That leaves unanswered the question of why in Gen 1 it is said to separate the waters rather than the realms.

[35] Francesca Rochberg, "'The Stars and Their Likeness': Perspectives on the Relation Between Celestial Bodies and Gods in Ancient Mesopotamia," in *What Is a God? Anthropomorphic and Non-anthropomorphic Aspects of Deity in Ancient Mesopotamia*, ed. Barbara Nevling Porter (Winona Lake, IN: Eisenbrauns, 2009), 41-92.

[36] Francesca Rochberg, *Before Nature* (Chicago: University of Chicago Press, 2016), 276.

about 600 BC that they began to realize that the movements of the heavenly bodies were regular and could be predicted. Even then, they had not reached the conclusion that they were material.[37] The Babylonians adopted a level of cognitive dissonance as they accepted the regularity but also the omenological significance. The Old Testament rejects the divinization of the heavenly bodies, but no evidence suggests that the Israelites also concluded, against everyone else in their world, that the heavenly bodies were . . . bodies! We cannot conclude that the Israelites departed from the ways that everyone else in their world thought if we have no biblical information to suggest it.

On the roles of the heart, liver, and kidney in cognition versus the brain. That the ancient understanding of cognitive physiology focused on the internal organs such as the heart, liver, and kidneys rather than on the brain can be attested from various directions. I will identify two of the most obvious. First, Egyptian mummification was devised as a means of preserving the identity of the person for the afterlife. Therefore, anything that constituted the person or self was given particular attention. Their process involved removing the liver, lungs, intestines, and stomach and preserving them in canopic jars filled with natron so that they could go with the person to the afterlife. The heart usually remained in the body.[38] In general, for example, the heart was considered the center of the will, and the liver was considered the center of emotion. In contrast, the brain was customarily removed by a hook often inserted through the nasal cavity and was not preserved.[39]

---

[37]Marc Van de Mieroop, *Philosophy Before the Greeks* (Princeton, NJ: Princeton University Press, 2016), 138-39.

[38]This general statement has to be qualified by the fact that practices differed over time and differed between the elites and the commoners, and by the evidence of the actual mummies that have been recovered, some of which have their hearts and others of which do not. Most of our information about mummification comes from classical authors rather than Egyptian sources. For more information, see Andrew D. Wade and Andrew J. Nelson, "Heart Treatment in Ancient Egyptian Mummification," *Anthropology Presentations* 3 (2011), https://core.ac.uk/download/pdf/61628586.pdf.

[39]According to one article, about 20 percent of examined mummies still have the brain intact. See Andrew D. Wade, Andrew J. Nelson, and Gregory J. Garvin, "Another Hole in the

Methodology 43

In Mesopotamia, the evidence comes from an entirely different quarter yet points to the same conclusions. Rather than mummification, it is the divinatory practice of extispicy that can inform us. The Babylonians used the examination of the exta (viscera, primarily from sheep and goats) to receive answers from the gods. The liver and kidneys were of most interest. These viscera in people, along with the heart, were typically associated with the emotions, will, intellect, and personhood. In extispicy, the stomach, gallbladder, lungs, and intestines were also significant. The brain plays no role in these aspects of identity and self. There is an Akkadian word that refers to the brain, but none is known in Hebrew (there likely was one, but it is never used in the OT).[40] When translations use the word *mind*, the Hebrew is generally literally either "heart" (Deut 28:28) or "kidneys" (Jer 11:20; 17:10; 20:12). My conclusion is therefore that the Israelites shared the same view as the Egyptians and Babylonians in believing that the physiology of cognition was associated with the viscera and not with the brain.

Even if we accept the evidence from ancient literature that all of this was characteristic of the thinking in the ancient world, is there reason to conclude that the Israelites thought in the same way? Again, my default is that if the Old Testament does not clarify that they thought

---

Head? Brain Treatment in Ancient Egyptian Mummies," *Anthropology Presentations* 5 (2010), https://ir.lib.uwo.ca/anthropres/5. Sofia Aziz indicates that the brain was intact in 36 percent of mummies, compared to the heart being intact in 30 percent. She also notes that there is no evidence of the brain being preserved in any way. She finds evidence that by the New Kingdom, doctors showed awareness that the brain had importance for bodily functions, though there is no indication that they knew of its role in cognitive functions. See Aziz, *The Human Brain in Ancient Egypt*, Archaeopress Egyptology 45 (Oxford: Archaeopress, 2023).

[40] The Akkadian term *muḫḫu* (generally a reference to the top of something) was used to refer to both the skull and the soft tissue inside the skull, that is, the brain, but also referred to the marrow within bones. It is very rarely referred to in omens, but, according to A. R. George, most likely as foodstuff for the king's table (lamb brains being a delicacy). See George, *Babylonian Divination Texts Chiefly in the Schøyen Collection*, Cornell University Studies in Assyriology and Sumerology 18 (Bethesda, MD: CDL, 2013), 283-84. It tells us nothing about a physiology associated with the brain.

differently, I assume they thought similarly. They could not come to different conclusions except by scientific insight or divine revelation. There is no indication of the former, so we look for the latter. In one of the above cases, we do indeed have biblical texts that call the Israelites to a different way of thinking. Many passages insist that the heavenly bodies are not manifestations of the gods (implied by, e.g., 2 Kings 17:16; 21:3-5; 23:5; Jer 8:2; 19:13; Zeph 1:5), but this revelation provides no insight into our current understanding of astronomy.

All of this suggests that when we read the Old Testament, we must read it in light of these ancient ideas rather than our modern ones. This has nothing to do with pagan mythology but demonstrates how the Israelites were embedded in the ancient world. We must read the text against that backdrop. It also helps us to understand the distinction between reference and affirmation.

8. Are we overestimating the impact of cultural differences? After all, people are people, and humanity has not changed significantly over time. The premise that people have not changed is true enough. To understand that cultures are nevertheless different, however, we only have to compare cultures today. People in Asia, Europe, Africa, and North America are all equally selfish and greedy as well as equally generous and kind, yet we are well aware of the cultural differences that separate us. Human nature is different from human culture. I am trying to understand the cultural differences and use that knowledge to understand their texts better.

9. Shouldn't we be content that, since the Bible is what God has given us, it is all we need? Scripture offers little to define itself. In Christian theology it is considered the unique and autonomous revelation from God. It is considered to include revelation of his plans and purposes and of his plan of salvation for the world. At that level, Scripture is sufficient; we need look nowhere else. Having said that, we realize that we have more interest in Scripture than in mapping that general (and most important) trajectory. Anyone who reads the Old Testament

Methodology 45

recognizes that there are many individual passages that are opaque to us. A few examples should suffice:

- We read the ritual laws in Leviticus and are justifiably perplexed. We cannot easily determine how passages we find in that book should contribute to modern discussions if we do not understand what they meant in the Israelite culture.
- The Bible does not clarify for us what the Israelites were actually thinking the golden calf was.
- Readers cannot go somewhere else in the Bible to help them to understand the sons of God and daughters of men (Gen 6:1-4).

Since the Old Testament was written by Israelites to Israelites, that is, insiders to insiders, the authors do not unpack all of the cultural ideas so that outsiders (like us!) could understand what was going on. There is instead a high level of assumption regarding the cultural knowledge of the audience—knowledge we do not intuitively possess. The Bible is not sufficient in and of itself to bring understanding of those cultural issues that can be necessary for sound interpretation. In a similar fashion, the Bible does not teach the reader Hebrew—the authors assume the reader knows Hebrew. To learn Hebrew, one has to go outside the Bible to something like a Hebrew grammar. This is different from the Bible's sufficiency for knowing how to be in relationship with God and to be participants in his plans and purposes.

10. How can anyone read Scripture with confidence if so much information that we don't have access to is needed? The response to this follows naturally from the previous response. We can be confident that we know what God wants from us (faithful commitment and participation in his plans and purposes)—we know what to do and what God has done for us. Our confidence should be more measured when we are dealing with the complexities of individual passages, and the more culturally encoded they are, the less confidence we can have. When we are trying to decipher culture to gain a clearer understanding, we should hold our conclusions lightly in recognition of our necessarily limited knowledge of their ways of thinking.

Another aspect to take into account here is that we can achieve a literary understanding even when our cultural understanding is uncertain or incomplete. For example, we still do not have clear precedent in the ancient Near East by which to understand why Abraham does what he does in Genesis 15—dividing the animals in two and arranging the halves with a path between. We have some guesses but certainly not confident understanding. Moreover, our intuition will not suffice. We likewise do not have clear insight into the nature of the censer and torch symbols by which Yahweh (apparently) passes between the pieces. Someday we may find some literature that helps us understand these elements. Nevertheless, we can feel confident that we understand this passage literarily and theologically. Literarily, the author is using this to present the next step in the progress of the covenant Yahweh is making with Israel. Theologically, it is the ratification of the covenant offered in Genesis 12. There is no serious doubt about these conclusions—but we still do not understand the cultural background with confidence. We have enough to get what we need; we do not have near enough to get all that we would like. But if we had such information, we would welcome it, and it could potentially enhance our interpretation. In the meantime, we ought to avoid imaginative theological or allegorical speculation about the torch and censer.

A second example is found in the three narratives in which the patriarch (Abraham in Gen 12; 20; then Isaac in Gen 26) tries to pass off his wife as his sister. Are Abraham and Isaac simply liars? Does their charade show a lack of faith? Those have been some of the answers offered intuitively. But why would Abraham and Isaac choose this strategy? What would it accomplish and why? We do not yet have sufficient information from the culture to give confident answers, so we should be willing to admit that we do not know and therefore be slow to issue blanket condemnations of their decisions. Nevertheless,

Methodology 47

we can again understand the literary role of these narratives in the discourse. Each of the three cases involves a different level of jeopardy to the covenant (one of the key themes of Gen 12–50), and each one has different features. When we investigate each one for the jeopardy it poses and how that jeopardy is resolved, we can understand what the *narrator* was doing with these episodes even if we do not have clear understanding of all the cultural or personal reasoning behind why the *characters* were doing what they did.

Scripture is sufficient to our need, and the Spirit can work in us through Scripture even if our understanding is limited. Nevertheless, the lack of cultural understanding can at times hinder us from grasping everything that might contribute to our interpretation. Our ignorance may furthermore lead to unwarranted accusations.

11. Why should we believe that we would need to use tools that most people have not had and do not have to interpret the Bible? In the fourth to fifth century AD, Jerome was severely criticized for using the Hebrew text rather than the popular Greek version the church was using (the LXX) when he translated the Old Testament into Latin. Would we claim that he should not have used this tool since others did not have it and previous interpreters had not used it? Even his famous predecessor, Origen, "felt it was his responsibility to use every tool available to him to grasp the literal sense."[41] For Origen, this included textual criticism, geography, and grammar—to which others certainly did not have access. The Reformers insisted on a return to the Hebrew text rather than the Latin, and they were sharply criticized. Erasmus was soundly rebuked for using textual criticism to establish a more accurate understanding of the Greek New Testament. These and other examples demonstrate that the criticism of using new tools is not itself new, but the church, fortunately, has a long history of being willing to adopt new tools as they become available if those tools can enhance

---

[41]Christopher A. Hall, *Reading Scripture with the Church Fathers* (Downers Grove, IL: InterVarsity Press, 1998), 154.

our understanding of God's Word. We can safely conclude, then, that if Origen, Jerome, Desiderius Erasmus, and John Calvin had had information from the ancient Near East available to them, they would have been eager to use it, as should we.

Questions about the historicity of the early chapters of Genesis and their genre

12. *By using ancient Near Eastern mythology to understand Genesis 1–3, aren't you treating Genesis 1–3 as myth and thereby undermining its historicity and compromising its truth?* Not in the least. Using ancient Near Eastern myths to understand the world of the Israelites cannot be construed as treating Genesis as myth on a par with ancient Near Eastern literature. When I use ancient Near Eastern mythology, it is not because I credit the belief systems of ancient Babylon or Egypt. Likewise, it is not because I consider Genesis to be of the same value or quality. I am using the literature that is contemporary with the Israelites to understand the cultural assumptions of the ancient world, because those assumptions are going to be different from our modern cultural assumptions—different from our cultural river. I will use every piece of literature at my disposal to pursue that goal, whether it be hymns and prayers to Marduk, royal inscriptions of Tiglath-pileser, Sumerian wisdom literature, Assyrian incantations against demons, Babylonian celestial divination texts, or, yes, mythology. That does not imply that Genesis is any of those things or that they are of equal value as Scripture. That literature, however, offers insight into how people thought in the ancient world. That sort of information can aid us as we develop increased levels of cultural literacy. Consequently, when I use ancient Near Eastern mythology, I am not implying that Genesis is the same sort of literature or diminishing its value as Scripture. Such research into the ancient world has no effect on the question of the historicity of Genesis (for more discussion on that, see the next question).

Beyond the benefit of providing us a more informed cultural literacy, examining the literature of the ancient world, particularly the

Methodology   49

mythology, helps us to understand Israel's conversation partners. This does not compromise the Bible's truth but helps to understand its truthful affirmations better. Every culture writes in conversation with the world and literature of its day. This is demonstrably true even of the early Christian writers. For example, we understand that Justin Martyr was in conversation with someone named Trypho as he offered defense of Christian theology pertaining to Jesus against the Jewish resistance of his day.[42] When we read Ephrem the Syrian's commentary on Genesis, we must do so realizing that he was interacting with Bardaisan and critiquing the Gnostic perspective that Bardaisan represented. When we study Augustine, we must do so realizing what the conversation of his day was—he was arguing against Pelagius about issues of free will and the concept of original sin, and we should read him in that context. When we read Martin Luther, we respect his writing most when we can identify the people that he was in conversation with—the papal community and Desiderius Erasmus, for example. John Calvin and Jacob Arminius were in conversation, and in each generation today, theologians have their interlocuters. When we acknowledge these conversation partners, we can be better readers of the literature since such context will prevent us from extrapolating sentences to use beyond what the writers would have been addressing. The same is true when we read Genesis in the context of its ancient background. That Genesis is interacting with ancient mythology does not make it mythological any more than Ephrem would be considered a Gnostic.

Whatever the Genesis author is doing in Genesis 1–11, it is in conversation with ancient literature (not with modern science or modern theological discussions). That does not mean that he is simply reframing that ancient literature or that he is doing the same thing that those ancient literatures are doing. Our consultation of mythological

---

[42]Some consider Trypho to be fictional, while others identify him with a Jewish rabbi. In either case, Justin is arguing against the Jewish perspectives of his day.

50   NEW EXPLORATIONS IN THE LOST WORLD OF GENESIS

literature (as well as many other types) is due diligence. We seek to learn everything that we can about the conversation partners in order to increase our understanding of the nuances of the conversation. The biblical authors are not in conversation with us but with the ancient world in which they were situated. That is one more reason we say the Bible is written for us but not to us.

13. *Since Genesis 12–50 is clearly intended to reflect real people in a real past, why should we think that we need to treat Genesis 1–11 differently?* Every reader realizes that Genesis 1–11 has a broader scope than the family histories of Genesis 12–50. In that way, at least, it represents a different sort of literature. It is also universally recognized that a variety of genres occur within Genesis, so if the author chose to mix genres, nothing would have prevented him from doing so. Our job as readers is to be attentive to what the authors are doing so that we can track with them. An author may use historical events in order to affirm and address those events and the actions of the people involved in them (example: the passion and resurrection). Alternatively, an author may use historical events as a springboard for discussing important concepts and ideas, in which case the events and people fade into the background and become decreasingly significant (example: the exile of Jehoiachin; 2 Kings 24:8-17; 25:27-30).[43] As a third option, authors may choose to present events and people in selective or stylized ways that will enhance the ideas they are trying to convey (example: the assassination of Sennacherib; 2 Kings 19:37).[44] As a fourth alternative, an author could devise a character, perhaps with archetypal or stereotypical characteristics, or conflating numerous characters, to draw readers into an important conversation (example: Haman and Mordechai).[45] Each of these four possibilities has been defended, for

---

[43]Jehoiachin's exile is significant as the official beginning of Israel's exile.

[44]This is given as Yahweh's defeat of Sennacherib, even though the described assassination did not happen until twenty years later.

[45]The author is careful to indicate that Mordecai is from the line of Kish (Esther 2:5), who was the father of King Saul, and that Haman is an Agagite (Esther 3:1). Saul had been

Methodology 51

example, in interpretations of the book of Job, which wrestles with how to view the characters and events in a highly literary piece. These options have also been raised as possibilities for interpreting Adam as well as other characters in the early chapters of Genesis.[46] It is not our job as readers to simply select the option that most appeals to us. We have to try to determine what the author is doing.

The characters in Genesis 1–11 certainly are *literary* characters—that is not in dispute, since we encounter them in literature rather in the world. The question is whether they are *also* real people in a real past, and, if so, how much of their historical identity is essential to what the author is doing with them, because he is certainly doing something with them. Our first job is to understand them as the literary characters that the author has made of them in the (inspired) text. We can then determine to what extent his use, portrayal, and development of them carries historical entailments.

As interpreters continue to assess the situation, they increasingly recognize that it is not unusual for ancient texts to intertwine what we, in our modern perspectives, label history and myth. This should warn us against naively thinking that these are two exclusive poles.[47] Consequently, John Van Seters declares, "It can clearly and easily be established that texts reflecting mythical modes of thinking can be found alongside of historical texts in all the ancient civilizations."[48] Nevertheless, what conclusions should we draw concerning the historicity of Genesis 1–11?

One of the main problems concerns the word *historical*. The concept itself, and its application to any particular sort of literature,

---

instructed to wipe out the Amalekites, whose king was Agag. Here the characters are more than the real people; they represent centuries of conflict and enmity.

[46]See the discussion in Dennis R. Venema and Scot McKnight, *Adam and the Genome* (Grand Rapids, MI: Brazos, 2017).

[47]Christopher M. Hays and Stephen Lane Herring, "Adam and the Fall," in *Evangelical Faith and the Challenge of Historical Criticism*, ed. Christopher M. Hays and Christopher B. Ansberry (London: SPCK, 2013), 24-54, here 29.

[48]John Van Seters, *Prologue to History* (Louisville, KY: Westminster John Knox, 1992), 28.

has many cultural entailments. That is to say, the conventions and assumptions we associate with historical reports in our cultural river may be very different from the conventions and assumptions in the ancient world, and in fact the consensus among historians of the ancient world confirm that to be so. Even Samuel, Kings, and Chronicles cannot confidently be read through the filter of our modern conventions and assumptions about history writing, and the same is true for Genesis 12–50. This is why I am reluctant to apply the term *historical* to Genesis 1–11. It is not because I consider these chapters fictional or mythological; it is because our label (historical) is reductionistic and unnuanced, fraught with cultural baggage. My reticence is not based in skepticism but reflects a desire to treat the ancient authors with integrity. This is the due diligence we owe to authors in different cultural rivers, and especially to those whom God used to produce Scripture. It never undermines the Bible to draw careful distinctions between what the authors are and are not doing.

What do I imagine they are doing? I view Genesis 1–11 as offering vignettes to explore the human search for order, not as the story of human history.[49] We must understand how the literature is functioning. I contend that Genesis 1–11 is engaged in the important task of deconstructing ancient views of how to think about the world by examining what constitutes order in the interrelationships between God, humans, and the world. In the literature of the ancient world, what we call their myths and epics are likewise seeking to understand what constitutes order, though in the framework of their polytheistic presuppositions. Nevertheless, such articulation of what constitutes order is not limited to their mythology; it is found in their wisdom literature and their prayers as well.

---

[49]Christoph Levine, "Genesis 2–3: A Case of Inner-Biblical Exegesis," in *Genesis and Christian Theology*, ed. Nathan MacDonald, Mark W. Elliott, and Grant Macaskill (Grand Rapids, MI: Eerdmans, 2012), 85-100, here 91.

Methodology   53

In our modern world, such a quest for understanding order is the task of all of what we call the natural and social sciences. This is not a matter of a specific literary genre but can encompass many genres or be reflected in them. When people look at the past, they may use a variety of ways to understand the big questions about who we are and what the world is all about. Francesca Rochberg suggests that descriptions of events in literary contexts reflect "not empirical but metaphysical value, which is to say, not facts but truths."[50] Some readers would probably not make as stark a distinction as that, but her assessment provocatively prompts us to ask a different set of questions. The distinction she makes would also be made about the parables in the Gospels, though parables are not the only genre that has such a focus. We must inquire about the objectives of the author and what literary styles and techniques he might use to accomplish those objectives successfully in the literary world of his cultural setting. That is why we may be wise to treat Genesis 1–11 as a different sort of literature from Genesis 12–50.

Questions about the relationship between my interpretation and that of the last two thousand years (Christian, Jewish, New Testament)

14. Doesn't your interpretation differ from that found in the New Testament? Most who ask this question are particularly interested in my focus on two issues, materiality and historicity. Those specific aspects will be discussed in other sections in the book, but in this discussion of methodology it is pertinent to address the matter of whether we should expect to find different perspectives when comparing Old Testament and New Testament, and if we find them, whether we should be concerned.

As I read the interaction of the New Testament writers with the Old Testament, I find them to be engaged in offering fresh insights in light of the ministry and teaching of Christ and doctrinal

---

[50]Rochberg, *Before Nature*, 22.

perspectives for the church as it develops. Since these insights are prompted by these transformative events, the authors are devising readings that are intended to contribute to the development of thinking in their contemporary situation. Consequently, I do not view these New Testament authors as engaged in an exegetical process of trying to determine the literary, linguistic, and cultural interpretation of Old Testament texts in context. They are offering redeployment of the Old Testament texts tailored to their particular interests and issues. Validity of interpretation was associated more with the teacher than with a particular methodology.

It is therefore not only a possibility but a probability that the New Testament authors offer a reading that serves their purposes. Their interests, purposes, and intentions are not the same as those of the Old Testament authors, but that does not pit them against one another. Genesis was crafted by ancient Israelites with their own particular literary and theological interests. Those interests are legitimate, and we should pay careful attention to what they are, since they carry the authority of God's Word. If the New Testament authors choose to use those texts to draw our attention to different perspectives, that is their prerogative. Their insights, though different, are not in conflict with the Old Testament, and they also carry the authority of God's Word. We expect such diverse insights to be compatible, but we should not be inclined to merge them or impose one on the other. They should be understood as being in harmony even when they do not speak in unity; they each have unique contributions to make.

As an example, Paul does something different with Abraham than Genesis does. Paul uses Genesis 15:6 to make a point about salvation by faith—a topic with which Israelites would have had no familiarity. He uses Hagar and Sarah allegorically to discuss the Jews and Gentiles, certainly not an issue in the focus of Genesis. We can recognize these different focuses in Old Testament and New Testament without disparaging either one. We are interested in the points that Genesis is

Methodology 55

making when we read Genesis and interested in the points Paul is making when we read Paul. This sort of thinking will be important when we discuss New Testament views, where we will build on this methodological foundation.

15. How tightly are we constrained by the author's intentions? Let me clarify what I mean by the author's intentions. I am not suggesting that we could successfully read his mind or intuit what motivates him to write what he has. We cannot know him as a person, assess his personality type, psychoanalyze him, or determine what issues lead him to say what he says. Instead, I am simply referring to a basic premise that we all share in practice—we assume that communication is possible, that someone who writes something does so with the expectation that someone else can read it and derive a sensible understanding of what the speaker or author wanted to say. Even though we recognize that we hear through our own filters that can distort, we generally have great faith in the possibility of communication.

When I refer to the author's intentions, then, I refer to my commitment to read the text in its linguistic, literary, cultural, and theological context. I am referring to his *communicative* intentions—his *literary* intentions, related to the one who gave the book its final shape (and correspondingly its purpose, which we characterize as inspired). If we did not believe that such a thing was achievable, we would not write books, articles, essays, blogs, and so on. This concept is all the more important for those who attach some concept of authority to the biblical text. When we speak of biblical authority, we declare our assumption that the text has meaning apart from what we bring to the text as readers (not denying that we inevitably *do* bring ourselves into our reading). If we claim that this is God's Word, not our own, we must believe that it could potentially run against the grain of our own sensibilities, intuition, and inclinations.

Therefore, when I express a commitment to the author's intentions, I do so as a reflection of my belief in biblical authority. That is what

56   NEW EXPLORATIONS IN THE LOST WORLD OF GENESIS

leads me to look for what God has communicated through his chosen human instruments—a message that is not simply the cogitations and formulations of my own mind.[51]

We are constrained to read this way because the quality of authority we attach to the Bible depends on it. We cannot feel free to use the Bible to pursue our own questions or agendas. When we do that, the authority is ours, not the text's. The authority of God that is resident in the text was vested in the authors, editors, and compilers whom God used in that process. We are therefore constrained by our convictions about biblical authority.[52]

16. Since your interpretation is different from what has been taught in the church, doesn't it undermine two thousand years of Jewish and Christian interpretation? For some today, concerns about my interpretation arise from the fact that throughout most of church history, interpreters had no access to the ancient Near Eastern world that was the context of ancient Israel. Why would God allow them to be without this information if it is so important? If we need that ancient cultural information to interpret well, does that not suggest that Christian writers for two thousand years have not been interpreting well and indeed were incapable of doing so? Does that not potentially undermine all of two thousand years of doctrine and preaching?

Here I offer some of my perspectives regarding interpretation from the early Christian writers up to the Reformers.[53] The main point I make is that the history of interpretation is not undermined, because

---

[51]For fuller discussion of this idea, its place in methodology for interpretation, and its theological significance and necessity, see Walton, *Wisdom for Faithful Reading*.

[52]Again, this is developed at length in Walton, *Wisdom for Faithful Reading*, as well as in the forthcoming *The Crisis of Biblical Authority* (InterVarsity Press).

[53]Presumably the Reformers also believed that many of the interpreters who preceded them were misguided at least on some points. That means that such decisions are sometimes warranted. For book-length treatments of these issues, see Graves, *Inspiration and Interpretation*; Hall, *Reading Scripture*; Ronald E. Heine, *Reading the Old Testament with the Ancient Church* (Grand Rapids, MI: Baker, 2007); Manlio Simonetti, *Biblical Interpretation in the Early Church: An Historical Introduction to Patristic Exegesis* (Edinburgh: T&T Clark, 1994).

Methodology

earlier interpreters had different objectives and used different methods from those used today. I will address the issues under four points:

- appeal to the Spirit
- objectives and methods
- higher sense and figurative interpretation
- looking for Jesus and validating Christianity

Appeal to the Spirit. Throughout the long history of Christianity, controversies have existed about the nexus of biblical authority. Though a common thread is found in the idea of the role of the Spirit as validating Scripture's authority (albeit unaddressed in the creeds), less consensus has existed about how concerned we ought to be about the author's literary intentions. In the views of early Christian writers, details were intentionally embedded in Scripture by the Holy Spirit with mystical or symbolic meaning that communicated higher truths.[54] They believed that since Scripture was supernaturally inspired, it must have a spiritual nature that only the Spirit could reveal, and consequently the true meaning of Scripture could only be perceived through the Spirit.[55] The important caveat is that such work of the Spirit was available only to the ecclesial authorities.

This is the polar opposite from the view I take (as addressed in the previous question). These observations demonstrate that these interpreters were not doing the same thing that we are doing today when we interpret. For example, Willemien Otten points out that Augustine uses to great extent the idea of the distinction between letter and spirit as a hermeneutical principle and consequently is "prepared to accept a considerable degree of exegetical liberty." Consequently, "As long as the love of God and neighbor is the firm and fixed goal of biblical

---

[54]Graves, *Inspiration and Interpretation*, 26.
[55]Graves, *Inspiration and Interpretation*, 42. Note also Provan's observations that this was a matter of significant dispute in the Reformation period (*Reformation and the Right Reading*, 294-95).

interpretation, all readings are permitted. Biblical exegesis is thus identified with finding creative interpretive readings of selected biblical passages, as long as they fit Augustine's scheme of the centrality of love."[56]

As addressed in question fourteen above, I insist that authority and meaning are found in the author's intentions, that is, in what earlier interpreters would have referred to as the literal sense.[57] In my view, the objective is to determine the authoritative message of the text as supported by evidence rather than the alternative, the objective of offering inspirational and theological insights supported by creative imagination. Verifiable evidence can only be found in reference to the authors' literary intentions. Deviation from that meant that earlier interpreters looking for authoritative messages had no alternative but to appeal to the authority of the Spirit. They believed such messages to reflect the authority of the text, since the Spirit was the source of the text. In this way, they were not averse to bypassing the human instruments. To put it another way, for them, the authority of the text was associated with the discernment of the message of the Spirit, the divine author, not the discernment of the message of the human author. For them, agency was almost entirely spiritual, whereas today the consensus of interpreters is that there is dual agency—recognizing a level of spiritual agency but assigning much more of what we find in Scripture to human agency. This approach has developed in the recognition of the problem that appeal to authority of the Spirit for an understanding that cannot be found in the human authorship cannot be validated by evidence, only by community consensus.

---

[56]Willemien Otten, "The Long Shadow of Human Sin: Augustine on Adam, Eve and the Fall," in *Out of Paradise: Eve and Adam and Their Interpreters*, ed. Bob Becking and Susanne Hennecke (Sheffield: Sheffield Phoenix, 2011), 29-49, here 39.

[57]This should be understood in the context of the fourfold method of interpretation: literal (related to words of the text), allegorical (related to doctrines), tropological (related to behavior), and anagogical (related to events). See Francis Turretin, *Institutio Theologiae Elencticae*, question 19.

Methodology 59

As to the question of how we could conclude that traditional interpretation could have been misguided for so many centuries, the answer would be that they were pursuing what they believed to be Spirit-given interpretations, which could not in fact stand up to scrutiny by today's standards, though some of those interpretations enjoyed the support of the community over many centuries. Despite this methodological discrepancy, many of those interpretations of the past continue to find support in the church today because they have enjoyed some level of consensus for so long.

Even as today's consensus might still favor maintaining those interpretations, it must be acknowledged that some of them only came to be accepted on the purported authority of the Spirit and cannot be easily defended using only the authority of the author's intentions. For these Christian writers, an essential entailment of the authority of the text was the authority of the Spirit to provide the interpretation. Today, though people in the church routinely make interpretive decisions in that same way, the procedure is fraught. The reason is clear—it leaves too much to private decision making. Once someone claims, "the Spirit told me . . . ," the conversation has nowhere to go.

The fragility of the Spirit-dependent interpretation prioritized by these earlier interpreters is evident in the example of Origen. He insisted that the spiritual level took precedence and published many volumes of his interpretations that were driven by that assumption. The only criterion that could substantiate or denounce his interpretations was found in the disposition of the community.[58] In contrast, appeal to evidence (meanings of words, context of communication, etc.) has an external basis for validation.

Why should this evidential approach be chosen over the spiritualized approaches? First, when people are given so much creative rein,

---

[58]We can also admit that the Spirit may bring important results in our lives even when we are misinterpreting. But that is no excuse to be lax in our efforts to interpret well.

Scripture can be easily abused and turned to our own misguided thinking, which is then attributed to the Spirit. History is sadly filled with examples (the Crusades, Manifest Destiny, antebellum slavery, the Inquisition, etc.). Second, when we pursue these spiritualizing tendencies, Spirit-led or only supposed to be so, the result is that we neglect the actual message in the intentions of the author, consistently believed today to carry authority.[59] The result is that our own ideas (though attributed to the Spirit) replace what God has given the authors. Michael Graves expresses it well: "This religious encounter with the biblical text may be real, but this does not give the individual in question exclusive authority to label their personal insight as the text's 'sense.'"[60]

Even as I, along with many contemporary interpreters, do not claim Spirit-driven interpretation, I want it to be clear that I do not claim that the Spirit has no role in interpretation, only that the Spirit has a different role. The distinction I suggest is that the Spirit does not give us the interpretation of the text—we need to use evidence to find that— but the Spirit helps us to understand the larger spiritual implications of that message that the authors had, convicts us to embrace the truth that the authors give, and transforms us through the power of that truth. In this way, the work of the Spirit is subliminal. It does not override or replace any part of the interpretation process.

Those are all ideas that early interpreters would have endorsed. The difference is that they skipped what I would contend was that important middle step—starting with the intentions of the authors and taking those intentions seriously as the foundation for the interpretation that then serves as the basis for the spiritual application. The long neglect of this middle step was not because they deemed it unimportant. They had no access to the elements that are essential for determining the author's intentions that would enable them to

---

[59]Graves, *Inspiration and Interpretation*, 54.
[60]Graves, *Inspiration and Interpretation*, 54.

Methodology 61

interpret the text in context (especially cultural and linguistic context). Moreover, their own cultural river did not prioritize it.

The methodology I use recognizes the authority of the text as likewise giving space to the power of the Spirit.[61] As was true of the earlier interpreters, we also rely on the consensus of the community, both to validate the use of evidence in the building of the interpretation, and in endorsing the spiritual inferences attributed to the Spirit. In this way, I contend that we can maintain a both/and approach (valuing both evidence *and* Spirit) rather than an either-or approach. At the same time, it cautions us that some long-standing interpretations might need to be reconsidered now that certain types of evidence are available to us that were not previously accessible. "He [Origen] believed that too many texts remain inexplicable, nonsensical or morally repugnant if interpreted literally."[62] I reject such an assessment of the Old Testament, and I am not alone in doing so. Over time we have discovered how seeking out the author's intentions, informed by what Scripture is and how it works, offers us different objectives from those that were long held.

Objectives of interpretation. Evaluation of an Old Testament text on the basis of the author's intentions, whether by me or by anyone else today, will regularly differ from the evaluations found throughout church history. When people interpret Scripture today, they direct their efforts toward determining the author's intentions to the best of their ability using the evidence of language, literature, history, and culture. This is considered sound method and an essential focus even though interpretations may often lead beyond what those investigations can bring.

---

[61]Well articulated by Graves, *Inspiration and Interpretation*, 48. This concept is developed in a book-length treatment by Craig Keener, *Spirit Hermeneutics: Reading Scripture in Light of Pentecost* (Grand Rapids, MI: Eerdmans, 2016). Keener is well known for his extensive knowledge and use of the culture of the NT in his interpretation. He insists that such study on the author's language and culture is the essential building block for interpretation. Then he proceeds from that foundation to call for recognition of the Spirit's involvement as we are energized to have the text come alive in ourselves and our church.

[62]Hall, *Reading Scripture*, 154.

62   New Explorations in the Lost World of Genesis

Throughout the history of Christian interpretation, however, discerning the author's intentions has not generally been the focus, especially in reading the Old Testament. Interpreters of the past were instead primarily interested in practical, devotional, doctrinal, and moral questions. So, for example, the Old Testament narratives were used to provide moral examples to follow, and even very questionable characters (such as Samson) were often scrubbed of their flaws.[63] Such focus reflected the interests in the broader cognitive environment of the early centuries of Christianity. Greek and Roman literature emphasized the imitation of the virtues of great people (for example, in Plutarch's *Great Lives*), so Christians wanted to do the same. By doing so, they were responding to the needs, trends, and inclinations common to their time and to their conversation partners.[64] For them, this was what one was supposed to *do* with Scripture, and they based that on 2 Timothy 3:16—they looked for usefulness and instruction, to provide moral examples and to support doctrine.[65]

Since their objectives were different from ours, it is not odd that we draw conclusions they did not draw and would not have had the inclination to draw. Even if one thinks that they were following an appropriate path of interpretation, they labored under a significant disadvantage. They could not temper their assessments of the Old Testament characters and texts by drawing informative or corrective insights from Hebrew or from an understanding of the ancient world. Consequently, even if they had wanted to do exegetical analysis, they would not have had the tools or the resources to do so.

Their methodology was designed with different objectives. First, the LXX (Septuagint, Greek translation of the Old Testament) was considered authoritative, and Hebrew was largely unknown. Jerome's

---

[63]Graves, *Inspiration and Interpretation*, 32.

[64]Graves, *Inspiration and Interpretation*, 32-33.

[65]For in-depth treatment of 2 Tim 3:16 pertaining to what it says and does not say, and as a reflection of the values that were just referred to, see John H. Walton and D. Brent Sandy, *The Lost World of Scripture* (Downers Grove, IL: InterVarsity Press, 2014), 267-73.

Methodology   63

return to Hebrew for the Vulgate was considered highly questionable. Augustine considered the LXX to be divinely inspired. In fact, Graves notes, "Jerome was the only figure in the early church who regarded the original text of the Old Testament as authoritative over against the Septuagint."[66] Second, early Christian writers were concerned that if they made literal interpretation the focus, they then would have to conclude that Christians must continue the sacrificial rituals of the Jews, a conclusion they wanted to avoid. In that equation, they failed to grasp a contextual approach to interpretation—that those ritual provisions served an important role in the text but not as law that all had to follow. They were neglecting the nuances available when attention is given to genre and to literary, theological, and cultural context. In their approach, they concluded that these rituals were just somehow symbolic in Christ. Since these interpretations went well beyond what is offered in the book of Hebrews, they had to use their imagination more often than not. The alternative solution that we can now offer is that an understanding of Israel's rituals can help us to appreciate how God was making relationship possible even before Christ came. These provisions were not given as universal laws but provided an understanding of how God was working out his plans and purposes even then.

When early interpreters encountered texts that posed difficulties for them, they did not seek to resolve them through exegetical analysis (looking more carefully at the meanings of words or expressions, considering aspects of culture or genre that are not intuitive to us). Instead, they took those difficulties as the Holy Spirit's prompting to take leave of the literal text to propose a higher meaning.[67] To some extent, they had no choice, because the exegetical tools that we are privileged to have at our disposal today were largely unavailable to them. When we encounter a difficulty, we try to dig deeper, not fly higher. The point is,

---

[66]Graves, *Inspiration and Interpretation*, 104.
[67]Graves, *Inspiration and Interpretation*, 52.

we do not use the assumptions and methodologies today that they routinely used then.

Consequently, it should be no surprise that we sometimes come to new and different conclusions. As a result of all of this, it would not serve my purposes well to try to demonstrate how some of the early interpreters came to conclusions similar to mine (e.g., rib, Adam having a vision), because their way of getting there would certainly not be the same as mine.[68] What can be interesting is to show that early interpreters sometimes considered to be questionable what some today consider a given (e.g., seven literal days). I would not validate an interpretation by appealing to such precedents but instead would use them as evidence that there were questions early on and that interpretation was not monolithic. These evidences can then demonstrate that people today who validate their view by claiming "this is how Christians have always thought" can be seen as potentially uninformed. As Andrew Brown points out, "The quest for authoritative ancient precedents for modern interpretive positions is prone to surgical excision and even distortion of the source found."[69]

For example, one cannot simply adopt various statements from Philo about Genesis 1. One must decide whether one is willing to adopt Philo's philosophical perspectives that reflect Middle Platonism, which is not a popular view today.[70] Philo's comments can be understood or used only within that framework. Consequently, nothing he has to say has relevance to the current creation debate unless one intends to reassert Middle Platonic thinking. Furthermore, many early

---

[68]The methodology of using the church fathers to support modern questions is addressed thoroughly in Andrew Brown, *Recruiting the Ancients for the Creation Debate* (Grand Rapids, MI: Eerdmans, 2023). On Adam's rib and his having a vision, see chapter six below, under "Summary of Previous Material" and FAQ 2.

[69]Brown, *Recruiting the Ancients*, 4.

[70]Middle Platonism was a philosophical development that took place toward the end of the first century AD that represented an eclectic merger of Platonic thinking with some later ideas found, for example, in Aristotelian and Stoic philosophies. Plutarch and Philo were among the main advocates of this approach.

Methodology   65

Christian writers were indebted to Philo, which means that statements from them need to be considered in that light as well.

I hear an interesting response from some Protestant readers. They wonder how I can depart from the long-standing Christian interpretations known from the tradition. What is interesting is that for many of them, that tradition is traced back only to the Reformers, who themselves were departing from many long-standing Christian interpretations. If they are tracing tradition back to earlier voices, such as Augustine, we would still be obliged to point out the many ways in which Protestants take a very different position from Augustine. The Reformers were not averse to rejecting opinions voiced in the works of their respected predecessors. As Iain Provan states, "The Reformers were quite happy to rummage through the patristic package to discover what was good and what was not."[71] We must also remember that our hundreds of Protestant denominations testify to how the Reformers themselves so often differed from one another on important points of interpretation. Nevertheless, one might object, what about the points on which all of these agree? My interpretations do not undermine what has been done throughout the history of Christian interpretation. My interpretations sometimes differ because today the objectives of interpretation (adopted by most, not only by me) differ from those that were prominent in the history of interpretation.

Higher sense and figurative interpretation. Many early interpreters therefore were not interested in the plain sense of the text, whereas, in contrast, that is precisely the lost world we are trying to recover. Instead, they sought to develop a "higher sense," whether through allegory or other forms of spiritualization. They used different criteria for interpretation, and their interpretations were validated by their community using a different standard (doctrinal, moral, authoritarian, or inspirational rather than exegetical). They did not just neglect the

---

[71]Provan, *Reformation and the Right Reading*, 299.

66   NEW EXPLORATIONS IN THE LOST WORLD OF GENESIS

author's intentions; they purposefully bypassed them. They validated this procedure by appealing to 2 Corinthians 3:6: "The letter kills, but the Spirit gives life."[72] They therefore assumed a figurative sense, and they not only sought it but prioritized it. Yet, within the early church, some interpreters, such as those referred to as the Antiochenes (best represented by John Chrysostom), opposed Origen as they also sought a higher sense but insisted on basing it on a literal reading.[73] Antiochene interpreters such as Theodore of Mopsuestia (350–428) were inclined to pay more attention to the human authors, to their contexts and intentions. The Antiochene school of interpretation rejected the allegorical techniques of the Alexandrian school, but it still affirmed a higher sense (*theoria*) of the text that could be perceived only by the spiritually minded and was an essential aspect of interpretation. Nevertheless, the Antiochenes believed that this higher sense would be tethered to the literal sense and therefore would be dependent on accurately assessing the literal, historical sense of the text.[74]

Augustine identifies his methodological approach: "Anything in the divine discourse that cannot be related either to good morals or to the true faith should be taken as figurative" (*On Christian Teaching* 3.10.14)—that is, that it must be understood in relation to a higher truth principle.[75] Likewise, Augustine states in *The Literal Meaning of Genesis*, "No Christian will dare say that the narrative must not be taken in a figurative sense."[76] Graves goes on to make the point, "In other words, everyone agrees that the narrative has figurative meaning; the only matter of dispute is whether it has a literal sense."[77]

---

[72]Even this prooftext is taken out of context to demonstrate something Paul was not actually talking about.

[73]Graves, *Inspiration and Interpretation*, 15. Brown questions whether the distinction between Alexandrian and Antiochene methodologies is as straightforward as is usually assumed (*Recruiting the Ancients*, 106).

[74]Hall, *Reading Scripture*, 160-61.

[75]Graves, *Inspiration and Interpretation*, 21.

[76]See Graves, *Inspiration and Interpretation*, 49.

[77]Graves, *Inspiration and Interpretation*, 49.

Methodology 67

What I find interesting here is that many people who disagree with my interpretation of Genesis today will base their disapproval on their assessment that my interpretation is figurative rather than literal. In that, they disagree entirely with Augustine's methodology. Yet, they will turn around and adopt without hesitation Augustine's interpretations concerning original sin, though these are based on that very same methodology they disallowed previously. If Augustine's methods are today considered suspect, then we must be willing to reconsider all of his interpretations.[78]

Early interpreters all accepted as fact that Scripture, being a communication from God, would contain hidden meanings.[79] Little to no value was placed in the literal reading. Jerome, for example, reflecting the expectation of moral value and virtue based on the model of Greek philosophical texts, affirms, "If we were to take all of this literally, what benefits would we derive from such reading?" (*Homilies on the Psalms* 17). This stands in contrast to the Reformers, who insisted on interpreting according to the "plain sense" of Scripture. In the end, the acceptability of an interpretation cannot be based on whether we can find something in the history of Christian interpretation to (purportedly) validate it. It must be based on the evidence of the text.

Looking for Jesus and validations of Christianity. Early Christian writers went to the Old Testament to find Jesus and ideas pertinent to Christianity. They looked to the Old Testament for *Christian* belief. Consider, for example, the role of Proverbs 8 in the Arian controversy. Previous interpretation saw Jesus as the speaker, identified in the text as "Dame Wisdom." They used that to affirm that Jesus existed before eternity and was with God from the very beginning. In contrast, Arius used Proverbs 8 to support his idea that Jesus was a created being. As Graves notes, "It is interesting from a modern perspective to notice

---

[78]For the importance of reading the great Christian writers of the past in their contexts, see Brown, *Recruiting the Ancients*.

[79]Graves, *Inspiration and Interpretation*, 62.

68 NEW EXPLORATIONS IN THE LOST WORLD OF GENESIS

that no one on either side attempted to argue that Proverbs 8 did not speak about Jesus."[80]

Though we still accept many of the interpretations of early Christian writers today, we do not generally endorse their methods. Consider for example, the allegorization of numbers such as three, seven, ten, twelve, and forty (and combinations of them).[81] We do not credit those interpretative methods today even though they are well represented in the history of interpretation in the church. When early Christians paid attention to the details of the text, it was for spiritualized or symbolic meaning (based on a somewhat mystical mathematical logic), not for the lexical-semantic properties of Hebrew or for the cultural background (which are more objectively determined but were not available to them). "There is a long tradition in the church today of people appealing to traditional sources for their own purposes while concealing the points where they are not in harmony with those sources."[82] Such inconsistency is detrimental to productive discourse today.

Although most modern students of Scripture use different methods from Christian writers of the past, which may lead to a different set of interpretive conclusions, we are all dependent on the work that they have done in many ways. All they learned and thought becomes the foundation for whatever innovations we might undertake. Derivation and innovation are complementary, and both play essential roles as they work in tandem. Neither the early Christian writers nor the Reformers are infallible, and attentively reading them reveals their continual disagreements over matters large and small. Even though the Reformers sought to focus attention on the "plain reading" of Scripture as opposed to a mystical or allegorical reading, they still did not always tether themselves to the authors' intentions. They had reinstated the

---

[80]Graves, *Inspiration and Interpretation*, 31.
[81]For examples, see Graves, *Inspiration and Interpretation*, 25.
[82]Graves, *Inspiration and Interpretation*, 133.

Methodology

69

Hebrew text as the foundation for interpretation, but they still had no access to the ancient world, so they could not interpret in light of the ancient Near Eastern culture. Yet, we ignore them and those who preceded them to our peril. Our task is to understand not only their positions (in all their diversity as well as their agreement) but how they arrived at their positions and what values and priorities drove them. We stand on the shoulders of giants, which means that we have no foundation without them but also that we can sometimes see what they could not see. We want neither to underestimate them nor to lionize them. We must listen and learn, yet not be content with stasis. The interconnection between tradition and continuity has always been balanced in the church with new insight and innovation.

In light of all of this, Graves offers sage insight.

The toleration and even appreciation of diverse readings of Scripture provide ample opportunity for Christians to show each other love and humility. To tolerate other interpretations does not mean to agree with them, and toleration does not imply that there is no correct answer. Seeking to understand how others read Scripture demonstrates humility because we recognize that we are not infallible. Since our own knowledge is imperfect, we must be teachable in order to reach the truth. Furthermore, genuinely listening to the opinions of others shows that we love them. If we want others to listen to us, then we should listen to others.[83]

---

[83]Graves, *Inspiration and Interpretation*, 146.

3

Genesis 1

*Creation Account Focused on Function/Order Instead
of Physical/Material Objects*

SUMMARY OF PREVIOUS MATERIAL

The main thrust of the position I developed in *The Lost World of
Genesis One* is that the creation story that the Israelites were telling
and that was of most importance to them was about God causing the
world and everything in it to function according to his purpose. In
doing so, I proposed that we misread the seven-day account when we
read it as describing the material origins of the cosmos. I suggested
that in the ancient world people defined *existence* functionally instead
of materially, that is, that something existed not when it had materiality but when it had functionality—a role and a purpose in an ordered system. I referred to this as a "functional ontology," a perspective
I supported as being present both in the Bible and in the ancient Near
East.

Working through the various aspects of this position, I adopted a
view of Genesis 1:1 that is fairly common among commentators, that
it stands as a literary introduction to the chapter, not as a separate act
of creation.[1] Nothing happens in Genesis 1:1. Rather, it describes what
the situation will be at the end of the seven-day account (heavens and

---

[1]See, e.g., Claus Westermann, *Genesis 1–11* (Minneapolis: Augsburg, 1984), 94; Brevard S.
Childs, *Introduction to the Old Testament as Scripture* (Philadelphia: Fortress, 1979), 145;
Bruce Waltke, *An Old Testament Theology* (Grand Rapids, MI: Zondervan, 2007), 179.

Genesis 1: Creation Account Focused on Function 71

earth created). This is substantiated by the indication in Genesis 2:2 that God's work of creating was done *in* the seven days, thus ruling out some general creative act *before* the seven days (i.e., in Gen 1:1). This is true regardless of one's conclusions about the proper translation of that verse.[2]

I therefore proposed that after that literary introduction concerning what the account is going to be about, the stage is set for the seven days in Genesis 1:2. There we can see that the principal players (earth and sea) are already in place but are nonfunctional. A word study of the descriptive term *tôhû* (often "formless") determined that it refers to something nonfunctional, nonordered, and therefore, in an ancient view, nonexistent.

I then further substantiated the idea that the focus of the account was not material as I discussed how so much of what was happening on the days gave no information about the origination of the elements of the physical world. This is most notable on the first three days, in which material objects are at times manipulated, but none are said to have physically come into existence. So, for example, whether we decide that day one focuses on light, on day and night (i.e., that which was named), or on time, there is nothing material brought into existence. As I considered the days, I made the case that there was so little attention given to material objects being brought into existence and so much emphasis on function that we could infer that the account was more interested in functions than in materiality. Consequently, I concluded that this was a different sort of creation story than would be told in our modern culture. If the narrative interest is on seven days given to establishing functions rather than making objects, then Genesis 1 offers no information by which we might determine the age

---

[2]For a thorough discussion, though perhaps technically inaccessible for some, see Nathan Chambers, *Reconsidering Creation Ex Nihilo* (University Park, PA: Eisenbrauns, 2020), 133-77. See also Robert D. Holmstedt, "The Restrictive Syntax of Genesis i 1," *Vetus Testamentum* 58 (2008): 56-67.

of the earth (a material question). The seven days (regardless of how long they were) do not serve a material purpose but a functional one (more on that in the next chapter).

NEW EXPLORATIONS

Order spectrum. The most important advance in this area of discussion was the decision to adopt a slightly different terminology for the perspective that contrasted to material creation. From the start, some readers found the term *functional* confusing, and critics seized on it for their critiques. I have eventually landed on a descriptor that is far clearer and more defensible, though it was not absent from my original attempts to carve out a new direction. The term is *order*.

In my original work I indicated that *function* pertained to "having a role and a purpose in an ordered system." What I had not yet recognized is that the "ordered" nature of the system was a more fundamental concept in the ancient world than the functioning of the components. Once I made that shift in terminology, many more aspects of the position fell into place, including the ability to posit a new model for how we think about the world. Currently, the primary way of thinking about the world has been dualistic, the two poles represented in the typical terminology of good and evil.[3] This idea appeared as early as the Achaemenid period, with its foundation in Zoroastrianism, and is fundamental to Platonic thinking that served as a basis for much of Hellenism, a cultural movement that influenced Jewish thinking in the Second Temple period. Dualism was not, however, the model used in the ancient world or in the Hebrew Bible. There, instead of the bipartite model of dualism, we find a tripartite model centered on the concept of order. The three component parts of the order spectrum are nonorder (or chaos; Heb *tôhû*), order (best reflected in

---

[3]Much of this information and its development have taken place in conversation with the advanced work of J. Harvey Walton. My ideas have become inseparably interwoven with his research.

Genesis 1: Creation Account Focused on Function

Egyptian *ma'at* and Akkadian *kittu* but also at times expressed in Hebrew terminology such as *ṣdq* [righteous], *mišpāṭ* [justice], *yāṣār* [upright], *ṭôb* [good], *nûaḥ* [rest], and *šālôm* [peace]) and disorder (or evil; Hebrew *ra'*, *'āwel* [injustice], *'āwôn* [sin], *ḥaṭṭā'â* [sin], *nbl* [outrageous], *ḥālal* [profane], or *bəlîya'al* [lawless]).[4]

In the ancient world, creation stories begin with the default condition of nonorder. This default condition is not bad, corrupt, flawed, or damaged, but it is undesirable. Then the creator brings order into the world, though not thereby dispelling all nonorder.[5] This order, which is "good" (= desirable), must be maintained through constant effort or the situation will revert to the default of chaos (that is, nonorder). To the extent that the ideas of ordering and creating are overlapping and interrelated, we could also think of God's continuing work in sustaining and maintaining order as a creation-type activity, though it remains useful to distinguish between the initial establishment of order and the maintenance of that order.[6] We might even consider whether it is appropriate to affirm that God is not just maintaining what he has already done but is continually engaged in bringing new order. Whatever terms we apply to God's continuing interaction with his creation, we affirm that he is actively engaged and has always been so. For those who accept evolutionary models, God's actions can be described in every minute step in the evolutionary process. Regardless of the scientific models one accepts, in God, as in Christ, all creation

---

[4]*Kittu* is translated as "cosmic order" by Beate Pongratz-Leisten, *Religion and Ideology in Assyria*, Studies in Ancient Near Eastern Records (Berlin: de Gruyter, 2017), 299. Also indicated by Dominique Charpin, "Old Babylonian Law and Justice According to Letters and Legal Documents," in *Judicial Decisions in the Ancient Near East*, ed. Sophie Demare-Lafont and Daniel E. Fleming, Writings from the Ancient World (Atlanta: SBL Press, 2023), 147.

[5]Jon D. Levenson states the thesis and then supports it throughout the book. See Levenson, *Creation and the Persistence of Evil* (Princeton, NJ: Princeton University Press, 1994), 12. Note his summary statement, "The confinement of chaos rather than its elimination is the essence of creation" (17).

[6]Terence Fretheim promotes even greater continuity between these divine activities. See Fretheim, *God and the World in the Old Testament: A Relational Theology of Creation* (Nashville: Abingdon, 2005), 4-9.

coheres (Col 1:17). God *makes* each one of us no less than he made Adam, so God's work is more than simple preservation.[7] Yahweh proclaims his remarkable track record and ongoing intentions to do/make "new things" (an important theme in Is 42–48), which focuses on new events and situations.

The third category, disorder, disrupts an ordered system and cannot exist apart from the order it is disrupting. In this tripartite system, the "order spectrum," creation is defined as order bringing. Once this ancient way of thinking is recognized, evidence emerges from all across the primary and secondary literature.

In *The Lost World of Genesis One*, I presented a very limited but representative assortment of ancient texts pertaining to creation from the primary literature. Many more are included (Sumerian, Babylonian, and Egyptian) in the technical monograph, *Genesis 1 as Ancient Cosmology*, and readers can go there to find the larger, yet still only partial selections. In the primary literature, it is evident that, as in Genesis, episodes dealing with creation typically begin with a negative situation (that is, nonorder). Nearly a dozen examples occur in Sumerian accounts, and it is a well-known feature of the great Babylonian work Enuma Elish.[8] More importantly, the transition from that nonordered state to an ordered existence consistently focuses on setting up the ordered world, including both nature and society. It is clear from reading these accounts that the ordering process involves separation, naming, and organizing with a role and a purpose. Some of the listed activities involve the material world: heavens and earth, water boundaries, rivers, and so on. Nevertheless, a greater proportion of ordering activities listed are focused on society: kingship, temples, justice, truth, sleep, summer and winter, dreams, wealth, work,

---

[7]See more extensive discussion in Mark Harris, *The Nature of Creation: Examining the Bible and Science* (Durham, UK: Acumen, 2013), 124-25.

[8]See Jan J. W. Lisman, *Cosmogony, Theogony and Anthropogeny in Sumerian Texts*, AOAT 409 (Münster: Ugarit-Verlag, 2013), 23-81.

Genesis 1: Creation Account Focused on Function

heroism, kindness, and rituals, to name just a few. One of the most extensive Sumerian creation accounts is called Enki and World Order.[9] While these creation accounts include minor references to the manipulation of the physical world, there is almost nothing that could be considered manufacturing of the physical world, for example, terraforming. The gods create animals, but as populations (as in Genesis), not as individual biological units.

Primary literature. In the time since the publication of my previous works, I have continued to catalog texts throughout the corpora of ancient Near Eastern literature, both cosmological texts and other genres. A couple of examples will hopefully be suggestive of the pervasiveness of this perspective.

The Egyptian Memphite Theology speaks of establishing "identity," functioning humanity, the gods, towns, temples, and rituals—all hallmarks of an ordered world.

- Ptah gives life to all the gods (col. 53).
- He pronounces the identity of everything (col. 55).
- "So was made all construction and all craft, the hands' doing, the feets' going, and every limb's movement, according as he governs that which the heart plans" (col. 58).
- "He gave birth to the gods from whom everything emerged—offerings and food, gods' offerings, and every good thing" (col. 58).
- "So has Ptah come to rest after his making everything and every divine speech as well, having given birth to the gods, having made their towns, having founded their nomes, having set the gods in their cult-places, having made sure their bread offerings, having founded their shrines" (col. 60).[10]

---

[9]The Sumerian word translated "world order" is ME. Pongratz-Leisten describes ME as "the institutions, offices, and forms of human behavior that are inherent to and inform the social and cosmic order" (*Religion and Ideology in Assyria*, 201).

[10]Translations by James Allen, in *The Context of Scripture*, ed. William W. Hallo (Leiden: Brill, 1997), 1:22-23.

76   NEW EXPLORATIONS IN THE LOST WORLD OF GENESIS

The Sumerian Disputation Poem, "The Spider Series," is the most materially focused that an ancient account gets. Again, however, we see the focus on temples (the center of order) and civilization (the principal reflection of order).[11]

> When the gods in their assembly created [the universe],
> Brought into being the [S]ky, put tog[ether the Netherworld]
> They brought forth living beings, all creatures,
> Wild animals of the steppe, beasts of the steppe, and all
>   creatures of civilization.
> After t[hey had distribu]ted all sanctuaries to the living beings,
> (And) to the wild animals and creatures of civilization had
>   distributed the temples.[12]

A prayer to Marduk begins with the forming of heaven and earth but quickly moves to fates, temples, offerings, and the role played by rivers and springs.

> The creator, the one who forms the heavens [and the earth . . .
> The lord of cleverness, the wisdom, . [. . .
> The one who determines the fates of [widespread] peo[ple . . .
> The one who designs the plans, the one who assi[gns the share
>   of the heavens and the earth . . .
> The one who lays the foundations of the daises, the one
>   who . . [. . .
> The one who provides cereal offerings to [the Igigi-gods . . .
> The one who promptly sends *taklimu*-offering to [the
>   Anunnaki-gods . . .
> The one who gives the seasonal flood of abundance to [the
>   world . . .

---

[11]Note that the brackets in the translation indicate where the translator has had to deal with some breaks in the text. Often these are defensible from the phrase being repeated in other places or from standard terminology.

[12]Enrique Jiménez, *The Babylonian Disputation Poems* (Leiden: Brill, 2017), 303.

Genesis 1: Creation Account Focused on Function 77

> The one who carves out the rivers in [the mountains/lands . . .
> The one who makes the springs appear in [the mountain
> regions . . .
> The one who clears out the midst of the se[a . . .[13]

In another prayer to Marduk, it is clear that the references to the rivers, springs, and seasonal flood all serve as the basis by which crops grow.

> The one who puts the rivers in order in the midst of the
> mountains.
> The one who opens up spring-wells in the midst of the
> mountain region.
> The one who pours out the seasonal flood of abundance upon
> the entire world.
> [The one] who [supp]lies [gi]fts *from* the broad land—grain.
> [The one who lets] dew fall from the udders of the heavens.
> [The one who *makes*] winds [*carr*]y drizzle over the field.[14]

Last, consider the cosmological/mythological introduction to the great celestial omen series, Enuma Anu Enlil, in which we can see the heavenly bodies in connection to time.

> When Anu, Enlil and Enki, the great gods, in their wisdom,
> Had laid down the plans for heaven and earth,
> Had confided to the hands of the great gods to bring forth the
> day, to start the month for humankind to see,
> They beheld the Sun in the portal of his rising,
> The stars came out faithfully in heaven.[15]

From these we can make several observations. First, we can see the intertwining of elements that we would call (initial) creation with

---

[13]Takayoshi Oshima, *Babylonian Prayers to Marduk* (Tübingen: Mohr Siebeck, 2011), 101.

[14]Oshima, *Babylonian Prayers to Marduk*, 241.

[15]Benjamin R. Foster, *Before the Muses: An Anthology of Akkadian Literature* (Bethesda, MD: CDL, 2005), 495.

those that we would consider sustaining creation and providing for people. For these texts' writers this is a difference without a distinction, since both pertain to order. Second, we can observe the intermixture of what we would call nature with aspects of ritual (e.g., offerings and temples). The inherent connection is found in that for ancient Near Eastern people the temple was the control center for order in the cosmos, and ritual sustained the cosmos by sustaining the god. Third, in comparison, Genesis 1 includes nothing about rituals, though, as I have contended, it suggests a temple context (see chapter four below). Furthermore, though Genesis has a different enumeration of what is created than these pieces do, all the pieces in Genesis can be seen in one place or another throughout the variety of ancient Near Eastern works. I demonstrate this in *Genesis 1 as Ancient Cosmology*. The common ground between Genesis and ancient Near Eastern accounts is not found in the genre of literature, in which gods are being addressed, or in the shape of the account. Nevertheless, we can see from these quotations that the common ground between Genesis and the ancient Near Eastern literature is that creation primarily involves bringing order. As is obvious from these quotations, creation accounts in the ancient world included issues of order such as culture and cult, not the manufacture of the material world.[16] Nathan Chambers states it succinctly: "Material was not a main focus in ancient Near Eastern creation texts."[17] I contend that culture (society and civilization) and cult (temple and ritual) are the prominent interests.

From a very different quarter, note a Jewish example from the Dead Sea Scrolls (4Q416), coming after the end of the Old Testament period. Though the text is fragmentary, its vocabulary indicates that it is elaborating on day four from Genesis 1. It refers to the stars of light, the luminaries, and the hosts of heaven being established for signs and seasons, all fulfilling God's desire: "Season by season,

---

[16]Chambers, *Reconsidering Creation Ex Nihilo*, 40.
[17]Chambers, *Reconsidering Creation Ex Nihilo*, 40.

Genesis 1: Creation Account Focused on Function   79

without ceasing, properly they go according to their host to have dominion for the sake of the kingdom."[18] The text depicts "God's order and rule of the cosmos."[19]

Our last stop is in the book of 4 Ezra (written about AD 100). In 4 Ezra 6:1-6, 38-54, the author makes extensive reference to creation based on Genesis 1. He begins in a similar way to what we have seen as far back as Sumerian cosmologies with a "before creation" statement. In Sumerian literature, these are negations that are going to be addressed by creation. In 4 Ezra the author is making the point that before creation, God already had a plan (4 Ezra 6:6). Nevertheless, it is of interest to observe the aspects of creation to which he refers. Beginning in 4 Ezra 6:38, the author moves systematically through the seven days of Genesis 1, with emphasis on the creative power of the spoken word of God.

> Then the spirit was blowing, and darkness and silence embraced everything; the sound of human voices was not yet there. Then you commanded a ray of light to be brought out from your storechambers, so that your works could be seen. Again, on the second day, you created the spirit of the firmament, and commanded it to divide and separate the waters, so that one part might move upward and the other part remain beneath. On the third day you commanded the waters to be gathered together in the seventh part of the earth; six parts you dried up and kept so that some of them might be planted and cultivated and be of service before you. For your word went forth, and at once the

---

[18] 4Q416, fragment 1, lines 3-4. Translation cited in Jeremy Lyon, *The Genesis Creation Account in the Dead Sea Scrolls* (Eugene, OR: Pickwick, 2019), 104, taken from John Strugnell and Daniel J. Harrington, *DJD XXIV: Sapiential Texts, Part 2, 4QInstruction: 4Q415ff*, Discoveries in the Judaean Desert 34 (Oxford: Clarendon, 1999); see Florentino García Martínez and Eibert J. C. Tigchelaar, *The Dead Sea Scrolls Study Edition* (Leiden: Brill, 1997), 848.

[19] This is the assessment of Lyon, who offers translation and line-by-line commentary in *Genesis Creation Account*, 103-8.

work was done. Immediately fruit came forth in endless abundance and of varied appeal to the taste, and flowers of inimitable color, and odors of inexpressible fragrance. These were made on the third day. On the fourth day you commanded the brightness of the sun, the light of the moon. And the arrangement of the stars to come into being [note: not the objects themselves]; and you commanded them to serve humankind, about to be formed. On the fifth day you commanded the seventh part, where the water had been gathered together, to bring forth living creatures, birds and fishes; and so it was done. The dumb and lifeless water produced living creatures, as it was commanded, so that therefore the nations might declare your wondrous works.[20]

This excerpt is sufficient to demonstrate that there is nothing remotely scientific about this interpretive account. Instead, the author is interested in how things function in God's economy.

In tandem with this evidence that creation accounts focused on order is the evidence that not only do they assign higher value to the issue of order, but they intentionally avoid the physical aspects. A good example of this posture is found in Plato's assertion that the Greeks do not investigate the cosmos, nor have they ever done so, out of respect for the planets (i.e., for religious reasons). The "Athenian stranger" says, "We commonly assert that men ought not enquire concerning the greatest God, and about the universe, nor busy themselves in searching out their causes, since it is actually impious to do so."[21]

---

[20]Translation by Karina Martin Hogan, "4 Ezra," in *Outside the Bible: Ancient Jewish Writings Related to Scripture*, ed. Louis H. Feldman, James L. Kugel, and Lawrence H. Schiffman (Philadelphia: JPS, 2013), 2:1626-27. For insightful discussion, see Joan E. Cook, "Creation in 4 Ezra: The Biblical Theme in Support of Theodicy," in *Creation in the Biblical Traditions*, ed. Richard J. Clifford and John J. Collins (Washington, DC: Catholic Biblical Association of America, 1992), 129-39.

[21]Plato, *Laws*, vol. 2, *Books 7–12*, trans. Robert G. Bury, LCL 192 (Cambridge, MA: Harvard University Press, 1926), §821, p. 111. Some consider the "Athenian stranger" to be a channeled Socrates; others, a persona Plato adopts for presenting his own thinking, finally in his last work taking his own voice; still others, sort of an ideal philosopher.

Genesis 1: Creation Account Focused on Function

Even if Plato himself disagrees with this, it is presented as the common way of thinking.[22]

At this point it is important to note that I am not quoting these texts to suggest that they are right about creation. After all, there are many positions taken by these texts with which none of us would agree. Instead, I quote them as testimony that there was a tradition stretching from ancient times through Second Temple Jewish literature that understood creation in terms of order-bringing activity rather than material manufacturing of objects. In contrast, it is difficult to find any evidence of a material interest. It seems to me that I am therefore justified in suggesting that Genesis may also follow this same trajectory. We will eventually examine the text itself to determine whether this is so, but before that, we should note that focus on order is not an uncommon view among scholars who investigate the literature of the ancient Near East, to whose assessments we now turn.

Secondary literature. The high value of order and its prominence in creation accounts is also evident throughout the secondary literature pertaining to the ancient Near East. Again, a representative selection will have to suffice, but I have drawn from a wide variety of specialists in the ancient Near East (Egypt as well as Mesopotamia), theologians, and biblical scholars.

Renowned Egyptologist James Allen has published and analyzed the Egyptian cosmology texts and concludes that they pertain to order in the cosmos. In a discussion of the Ennead, the nine great gods, he notes that four of them are particularly active in the postcreation world. "Osiris and Isis, Seth and Nephthys represent the opposing but balanced principles of order and disorder, growth and destruction,

---

[22]It is possible that similar thinking is represented in Basil of Caesarea, who warns against delving into the substance of the earth or seeking its foundation. See Craig D. Allert, *Early Christian Readings of Genesis One: Patristic Exegesis and Literal Interpretation* (Downers Grove, IL: InterVarsity Press, 2018), 245.

82 NEW EXPLORATIONS IN THE LOST WORLD OF GENESIS

and the transmission of life."[23] Even a casual reading of Egyptian cosmological texts will make this focus obvious.

Another Egyptologist, Joanna Popielska-Grzybowska, has investigated the concept of god in the Egyptian Pyramid Texts. She draws a contrast between ancient Egyptian thinking about creation and our modern ways: "Therefore, presuming based on the *Pyramid Texts*, organizing or making order seem to be complementary to create wholeness and plenitude based on binary oppositions, so that nothing is missing. It is much more natural or, in other words, an order much more linked to nature, than our modern and European, as it reflects organization of the cosmos."[24]

Assyriologist Marc Van de Mieroop in his tour de force monograph, *Philosophy Before the Greeks: The Pursuit of Truth in Ancient Babylonia*, bluntly states about the Babylonians, "They believed that the gods had created the universe by bringing order into chaos." Concerning Enuma Elish specifically he observes, "Creation in that myth was a work of organization: Marduk did not fashion the universe *ex nihilo*. Rather he created by putting order into the chaos of Tiamat's bodily parts." He expands on that concept by indicating, "Just as [Marduk] ordered the physical world, he organized knowledge and structured it through writing."[25] The latter is no less an act of creation than the former. Accepting that Enuma Elish represents such a view does not demand that Genesis must also do so. I raise these examples to demonstrate that since it was not uncommon for ancient creation accounts to focus on order, it would not be a surprise if that were also

---

[23]James Allen, *Genesis in Egypt* (New Haven, CT: Yale University Press, 1988), 8. It should be noted that Allen is not as inclined to distinguish between material and order as he is to distinguish between concept (in the mind of the creator god) and the reality that emerged from it (46-47). These philosophically complex issues are difficult to unravel but clearly show a different way of thinking about creation from our modern Western concepts.

[24]Joanna Popielska-Grzybowska, *Everything as One: A Linguistic View of the Egyptian Creator in the Pyramid Texts* (Wiesbaden: Harrassowitz, 2020), 315.

[25]Marc Van de Mieroop, *Philosophy Before the Greeks* (Princeton, NJ: Princeton University Press, 2016), 135, 9.

Genesis 1: Creation Account Focused on Function 83

what Genesis is doing. Still, that has to be demonstrated from the text of Genesis.

Arguably the world's leading authority on Mesopotamian celestial divination, Francesca Rochberg has written a remarkable monograph, *Before Nature: Cuneiform Knowledge and the History of Science*. In her thesis statement, she points out that to understand the ancient world, we have to differentiate between *nature* and *science*. In the ancient Near East people were invested at significant levels in the latter but not in terms of the former. As we consider all their efforts in the sciences of astronomy, medicine, and mathematics, we find that they did not investigate those in the context of nature/naturalism. Rochberg observes that their efforts "did not explicitly focus on nature, nor did they require that their objects of inquiry be explained in terms of that separate domain or of what we would consider to be natural causes." She insists, "There have been other ways of doing science besides that which aims to know nature."[26]

Rochberg notes a distinction between how we tend to observe and classify phenomena and how people did so in the ancient world—a difference in focus and interests, which she refers to as a conceptual "scaffolding." "The scaffolding of the cuneiform scribes' world might be described in terms of divine design," but they "do not convey notions of a material essence or an independent rationality apart from divine will."[27]

At one level, even when we can identify what is *not* the case, she recognizes the challenge of describing what *does* constitute the conceptual scaffolding, "because no unified framework served to structure the Assyro-Babylonian world order from a perspective of matter or the 'physical,' such as is provided by the conception of nature." On the basis of these important observations, and getting to the point of my work, she suggests alternatively that "conceptions of order, norms, and

---

[26]Francesca Rochberg, *Before Nature* (Chicago: University of Chicago Press, 2016), 7, 34.
[27]Rochberg, *Before Nature*, 29.

84 New Explorations in the Lost World of Genesis

schemata based upon such norms were central features of the scholarly corpus of texts dealing with the phenomena, and consequently of what was deemed in those texts to be knowable and significant." From these observations, she draws our attention to a basic idea: "The very notion of physical phenomena being subject to laws is a profoundly cultural claim."[28]

Turning to Persian thought, professor of Iranian studies Antonio Panaino sees the same emphasis on ordering in Persian Zoroastrianism, the religion of the Achaemenid Empire when many books of the Old Testament began taking final shape and transitioning to canonical status. "It is improbable that Ahura Mazdā was conceived as a divinity who had created the world from 'nothing' as in a kind of *creatio ex nihilo*. Rather, he put in order the whole universe, establishing a general harmony in a primordial state."[29] This would not be something that was derived from Zoroastrianism by the Israelites since it is observable as early as Sumerian and Egyptian documents. It rather shows how pervasive this way of thinking was in the ancient world.

Richard Clifford combines scholarship on the Old Testament and the ancient Near East. He provides an analysis of ancient Near Eastern and biblical creation accounts, one of the most accessible works of its kind, which I used extensively in my early work.[30] He has also served as coeditor of a volume of collected essays on the topic.[31] As early as 1985, however, he published an article on the theology of creation where he discussed similarities and differences between the ancient and modern ideas of creation. He cites four categories of differences,

---

[28]Rochberg, *Before Nature*, 85, 176.

[29]Antonio Panaino, "Cosmologies and Astrology," in *The Wiley Blackwell Companion to Zoroastrianism*, ed. Anna T. M. Stausberg and Yuhan Sohrab-Dinshaw Vevaina (Hoboken, NJ: Wiley-Blackwell, 2015), 235.

[30]Richard J. Clifford, *Creation Accounts in the Ancient Near East and in the Bible* (Washington, DC: Catholic Biblical Association of America, 1994).

[31]Clifford and Collins, *Creation in the Biblical Traditions*.

Genesis 1: Creation Account Focused on Function

and the second one, the issue of what emerges from creative activity, is of most interest to us. "To the ancients, human society organized in a particular place was the emergent. To moderns, on the other hand, creation issues in the physical world, typically the planet fixed in the solar system. Community and culture do not come into consideration."[32] After giving examples, he concludes, "Ancient cosmogonies were primarily interested in the emergence of a particular society, organized with patron gods and worship systems, divinely appointed king (or some other kind of leader), and kinship systems." The object of creation, he indicates, "is not the mere physical universe but the 'world' of men and women."[33]

Before leaving Clifford's work, a final observation that he makes in his fourth difference, the criterion for truth, is worth noting. "We expect a creation theory with its empirical reference to be able to explain all the data, to be compatible with other verified theories and data." In contrast, he notes a distinctly different criterion for ancient cosmologies, which he identifies as its "dramatic plausibility." He then comments, "In one sense it is no less empirical than the scientific account, but its verisimilitude is measured differently. Drama selects, omits, concentrates; it need not render a complete account. The story can be about a single aspect and leave others out of consideration."[34] This is similar to what I propose in my view that Genesis 1 concentrates its attention on ordering of the cosmos with a particular perspective in mind and has therefore left out discussions of the material creation

---

[32]Richard J. Clifford, "The Hebrew Scriptures and the Theology of Creation," *Theological Studies* 46 (1985): 507-23, here 509. Bruce Waltke does not use the word *order* but cites Clifford's four categories favorably. See Waltke, *An Old Testament Theology* (Grand Rapids, MI: Zondervan, 2007), 200-201. He turns away from the material view of the cosmos when he indicates, "These ancient cosmogonies—including that of Genesis 1—do not ask or attempt to answer scientific questions of origins: the material, manner, or date of the origin of the world and of its species. . . . How closely this cosmology coincides with the material reality cannot be known from the genre of an ancient Near Eastern cosmology, which does not attempt to answer that question" (202).

[33]Clifford, "Hebrew Scriptures and the Theology," 510-11.

[34]Clifford, "Hebrew Scriptures and the Theology," 511-12.

86   NEW EXPLORATIONS IN THE LOST WORLD OF GENESIS

out of nothing. This is its prerogative to do so, and we need to be attentive readers, taking the text on its own terms.

Israeli biblical scholar and comparativist Meir Malul, after noting that *tôhû wābôhû* pertains to chaos "from a structural rather than physical or ontological point of view," observes, "Imposing order on disorder does structurally bring it into existence, but ontologically it just makes known that which has been unknown by imposing its own frame of reference." By *structure* he refers to the structure of world order. Later in the book, he explains that everything called *tôhû wābôhû* ("chaos") "was perceived as either nonexistent or as in disarray and disorder. Existence and order are, of course, defined from the point of view of cosmos, i.e., civilization." He offers a concluding observation, "What is interesting to realize here is the fact that an entity—real and material in the physical world—as long as it did not fall within the classificatory rules of society, could be deemed nonexistent and related to as though it did not exist."[35]

Old Testament theologian Walter Brueggemann refers to Genesis 1–2 as a "liturgical narrative." As such, in his opinion, it stands as an account in which God uses both utterances and acts "to create a life-world of order, vitality, and fruitfulness that makes life possible and that, in the end, is judged by God to be 'very good.'" Regardless of whether one accepts his label of liturgical narrative or his proposal that this ordered world stands in contrast to Israel's experience in exile, his observation remains astute, that Israel's interest in creation pertains to "the practicalities of living faithfully in the world."[36]

Old Testament theologian Jon Levenson offers an extensive analysis in his book *Creation and the Persistence of Evil*. His main focus is on the idea that chaos continues to exist even in the wake of creation.

---

[35]Meir Malul, *Knowledge, Control and Sex: Studies in Biblical Thought, Culture and Worldview* (Tel Aviv: Archaeological Center, 2002), 285-86, 464.

[36]Walter Brueggemann, *Theology of the Old Testament* (Minneapolis: Fortress, 1997), 153-54. Note Fretheim's agreement with this perspective in *God and the World*, 32.

Genesis 1: Creation Account Focused on Function 87

God's creation is a demonstration of his mastery in defeating forces of chaos. In his view, "the point of creation is not the production of matter out of nothing, but rather the emergence of a stable community in a benevolent and life-sustaining order."[37]

As a final example, theologian Mark Harris offers an extensive analysis of *creatio ex nihilo* versus *creatio continua*.[38] On the basis of that analysis, he offers the straightforward conclusion, "An important function of the first section of Genesis 1 (vv. 1-10) is to describe the *ordering* of the pre-existent chaotic waters, by God's imposition of boundaries upon them, rather than a *making* from nothing."[39] Harris continues, however, to propose that Genesis 1 is compatible with an *ex nihilo* view and that if pressed to consider the question, ancient Israelites would have affirmed it. In effect, the *ex nihilo* question is anachronistically applied to the Old Testament, as it represents conversations that did not arise until centuries later. It is a legitimate biblical doctrine and an important one; it is just not the story that Genesis is telling. I affirm Harris's statement that "*creatio ex nihilo* is incipient in the creation accounts, simply by virtue of the over-arching and transcendent presence of God described therein, and the trust and dependence on God expressed throughout the Bible."[40] The argument starts with the conviction that God is not a contingent being and proceeds to the logical conclusion that there is nothing that was not created by him and nothing that coexists with him. The inevitable conclusion of that is that he therefore created out of nothing. But, I reiterate, my claim is that that is not the concern of the Genesis account—it is not the story that Genesis is telling. Moreover, the conversation about *creatio ex nihilo* is theologically and metaphysically fraught with more modern questions and issues.

---

[37]Levenson, *Creation and the Persistence*, 12.
[38]Harris, *Nature of Creation*, 120-30.
[39]Harris, *Nature of Creation*, 122 (emphasis original).
[40]Harris, *Nature of Creation*, 123.

I should note that these many primary and secondary texts would not have been so easily invoked as supporting my position when I was using the term *function* because they do not use that terminology. But once I shifted to the use of the concept of *order*, a very closely related idea in my perception, the supporting statements were manifold. This slight shift in perspective therefore brought my position into line with ideas that have been articulated from all directions for the last generation and hopefully brings some clarification to those readers who might have found the label "function" to be confusing or unclear. These examples from primary and secondary literature demonstrate that seeing creation as order bringing is the primary perspective represented in the ancient world and that modern scholarship has recognized it as such. I am not alone in reaching these conclusions.

Illustrations. *House and home.* Absent from *The Lost World of Genesis One* but included already in *The Lost World of Adam and Eve* is what I have found to be the very useful illustration of the distinction between house and home, and subsequently the distinction between a creation account that is a "house story" and one that is a "home story."[41] Since it is presented in *The Lost World of Adam and Eve* at length, I will only offer a quick summary here. Both building a house and making a house a home are arguably creative activities. The former pertains to material, physical construction: foundation, framing, and roof, as well as electricity, plumbing, and heating/cooling. In contrast, making a home pertains to organization (cabinets, closets), furnishing, decorating, and room use. But even that enumeration understates the idea of home. Home has to do with our identity, our personality, and our story.

When we talk about creation in our cultural river, we tend to tell a house story. Science provides the plot for that story, and it is what has become of most interest to us. It is a legitimate way to talk about

---

[41]*LWAE*, 44-52. I am grateful to Leith Anderson for suggesting this direction of thought in personal conversation.

Genesis 1: Creation Account Focused on Function

89

creation. I contend that, in contrast, what interested people in the ancient world the most concerning creation was the home story. Their grounding was in the order of the cosmos, not in its material stuff. Whether Egyptian, Babylonian, or Israelite, such an approach is contingent on the idea of the gods as the ones who bring order for their purposes—that is what was of most importance to them. This would also explain why cosmic order and social order merged in their thinking.

Computer. To expand briefly on an illustration I have used in the past, consider how you talk about your electronic devices. For most people, such a conversation would inevitably focus on software, not hardware (i.e., function over material). We are much more interested in our apps than in the chips; we care more about the programs than we do about the polymers (that make up the monitor). The way we describe our computers reflects what is of most importance to us. It is true that the apps will not work without the chips, but that does not mean that a discussion of apps should also be considered a discussion of chips or that any discussion of computers must include chips.

How did the play begin? Imagine that you are attending a play in the city, but due to contrary circumstances of weather, traffic jams, accidents, construction, and parking, you do not arrive until the first act is nearly done. No sooner do you find your seat than the lights come up for intermission. You might turn to those around you and ask, "How did the play begin?" One person speaks up to inform you about when the script was written. Though you protest that that is not what you meant, he insists that there could not be a play without a script, so that is surely the right answer. Another helpful person begins to recount when the theater was built and the set constructed. Obviously, they contend, the play would not exist without theater and set. Of course, you cannot disagree, but you continue to object that your question is not being answered. A third party chimes in with information about the selection of the cast—after all, without the cast, there could be no play—the play began with the choosing of the actors. Again, you reply that as true as that is, that is not what you wanted to know. Finally, in exasperation, you blurt out your more precise question: "What has happened since the curtain opened?"

The value of this illustration is that all the answers are correct and true. Each one offers a defensible perspective on how the play began and, indeed, supplies a factor on which the existence of the play is contingent. Nevertheless, as we can see, not every right answer addresses what was of most interest to the questioner.

In similar manner, when we ask, "How did the world begin?" we must realize that there are several right answers that offer true perspectives. In our cultural river, we are most interested in the theater and the set perspective. But we should not insist that that is the only way to answer the question or that other people of other times must be interested in the same question and answer that we are. We do an injustice to the literature if we impose our perspectives on their texts rather than let the texts speak for themselves. For those who pride themselves in reading literally, the hallmark of such a strategy is to let the text speak for itself.

Image of God. Many in-depth analyses of the image of God have been published, and I have benefited from all of them.[42] The topic is treated, albeit briefly, in both *The Lost World of Genesis One* and *The Lost World of Adam and Eve*. In the former I used "subdue and rule" as indication that the main aspect of the image of God was the function

---

[42]Zainab Bahrani, *The Graven Image* (Philadelphia: University of Pennsylvania Press, 2003); Edward Curtis, "Man as the Image of God in Genesis in the Light of Ancient Near Eastern Parallels" (PhD diss., University of Pennsylvania, 1984); W. Randall Garr, *In His Own Image and Likeness: Humanity, Divinity, and Monotheism* (Leiden: Brill, 2003); Stephen L. Herring, *Divine Substitution: Humanity as the Manifestation of Deity in the Hebrew Bible and the Ancient Near East* (Göttingen: Vandenhoeck & Ruprecht, 2013); Catherine McDowell, *The "Image of God" in Eden: The Creation of Mankind in Genesis 2:5–3:24 in Light of the* mis pi, pit pi *and* wpt-r *Rituals of Mesopotamia and Ancient Egypt* (Winona Lake, IN: Eisenbrauns, 2015); J. Richard Middleton, *The Liberating Image* (Grand Rapids, MI: Brazos, 2005); Ryan S. Peterson, *The* Imago Dei *as Human Identity: A Theological Interpretation* (Winona Lake, IN: Eisenbrauns, 2016).

Genesis 1: Creation Account Focused on Function   91

as stewards, and in the latter I added the elements of substitute for God, identity, and relationship with God to the derivable aspects.

Applying the order spectrum to this discussion, we can see that the image of God designates humanity as order bringers. Subduing (or subjugating; see below in this chapter) and ruling not only are functions but give us the status of working alongside God, participating in what he is doing as we bring order in his name. This implies relationship. It moves beyond a function to an objective, even a calling or a commission. When Iain Provan discusses the image of God, he describes the image as vocational, as it uses royal imagery. He elaborates, "The vocation of kings in the ancient world involved not only ruling and subduing, but also looking after the welfare of their subjects and ensuring justice for all."[43] Brent Strawn likewise adopts the royal imagery and further elaborates on humankind in the role of viceroy, "the Divine Sovereign's stand-in within the created world . . . God's own re-presence."[44] Paul-Alain Beaulieu insightfully adds his observation that the Image of God pertains to "acting with the authority of the god in a given role."[45]

I previously drew attention to the biblical democratization of the image of God in that, instead of just being a designation pertinent to the king (as in Mesopotamia), in Genesis it was now pertinent to all humanity. Now I can take what is a logical next step by recognizing that the image is not only applied across the human spectrum but is corporate rather than individual. To put it another way, in Mesopotamia the image was attached to an institution, kingship, and only circumstantially to the individual who happened to be on the throne.

---

[43]Iain Provan, "Before Moses: Genesis Among the Christians," in *The Cambridge Companion to Genesis*, ed. Bill T. Arnold (Cambridge: Cambridge University Press, 2022), 341-60, here 345.

[44]Brent Strawn, "From *Imago* to *Imagines*: The Image(s) of God in Genesis," in Arnold, *Cambridge Companion to Genesis*, 211-35, here 216-17.

[45]Paul-Alain Beaulieu, "The God List CT 24 50 as Theological Postscript to Enūma Eliš," in *Des polytheismes aux monotheismes: Melanges d'assyriologie offerts a Marcel Sigrist*, ed. Uri Gabbay and Jean Jacques Pérennès (Leuven: Peeters, 2020), 109-28, here 117-18.

In Genesis, the image is attached not to an institution but to a corporate entity, humanity as a whole, with no individual representative.[46] We are all together the image of God; no single one of us can claim to be the image of God. This corporate identity is also reflected in the Christian concept of the body of Christ. No individual can claim to be the body of Christ; it is a corporate designation. Yet, each Christ-follower participates in and contributes to both the body of Christ and the image of God. This will force some rethinking of some issues that we address by referring to the image of God (such as abortion, euthanasia, severe genetic conditions). We are not human (i.e., having dignity and worth) because we are the image of God; we are the image of God because we are human (not zebras or turtles). In the end, that need not change one's position on these issues, but it may change how one makes one's argument.

These ideas find an interesting counterpart in the very familiar New Testament verses, Ephesians 2:8-10. Ephesians 2:8-9 is the more familiar for its contrast between works and grace/faith. But in Ephesians 2:10 we find Paul turning his attention to Genesis 1 as he develops a parallel between human creation there and new creation in Christ experienced by Christians.[47] Creation of humanity in Genesis 1 was the work of God, not of human effort, and the same is true for new creation in Christ in Ephesians 2. Nevertheless, as Klyne Snodgrass points out, new creation, like the first creation, "is not from works, but it surely is *for* works."[48] This presents a further parallel to

---

[46]Strawn, "From *Imago* to *Imagines*," 217.

[47]Ephesians commentators are unanimous that Paul is referring to new creation ("creation in Christ"). For a sampling, see Clinton Arnold, *Ephesians*, Zondervan Exegetical Commentary on the New Testament (Grand Rapids, MI: Zondervan, 2010), 140-41; Harold Hoehner, *Ephesians: An Exegetical Commentary* (Grand Rapids, MI: Baker, 2002), 347; Andrew Lincoln, *Ephesians*, Word Biblical Commentary (Dallas, TX: Word, 1990), 113; Klyne Snodgrass, *Ephesians*, NIV Application Commentary (Grand Rapids, MI: Zondervan, 1996), 106-7; Frank Thielman, *Ephesians*, Baker Exegetical Commentary on the New Testament (Grand Rapids, MI: Baker, 2010), 144-45.

[48]Snodgrass, *Ephesians*, 107.

Genesis 1: Creation Account Focused on Function 93

Genesis 1 that can now be recognized once we apply the order spectrum to our interpretation. Humankind was created for the work of participating in God's plans and purposes for the ordering of creation.

In Genesis 1, I have noted, people are created to be image bearers and order bringers. Bringing order results in good (throughout the days of Gen 1). In Ephesians 2, people are seen as being in Christ; that is, our identity is found in him who is the very image of God (Col 1:15)—the true image of God. As new creation (2 Cor 5:17), we assume our roles as the image of God as God intended (now in Christ)—the role for which we were created. In that role we now can serve as order bringers in the way God always intended. We have been created in Christ for good works, taking up the role as order bringers. That is what the church is supposed to do and be as a result of being in Christ. I maintain that this does not simply refer to doing acts of mercy and being channels of grace, though those would be included. Far more, we are working as God's agents in the world to bring about the order of his kingdom. This role was prepared for us in advance, that is, ever since the creation in Genesis 1, now finding its fulfillment in that we have become a new creation.

Minor issues. I will conclude this section by turning attention to a few minor issues and how they have developed in recent years.

It was good. In *The Lost World of Genesis One*, I made the distinction that the assessment of being "good" pertained to function rather than material workmanship or moral quality. Now, based on the order spectrum, I can extend that idea.[49] Order (though defined differently by different cultures) is the ultimate good in the value system of the ancient world. It is the desirable state and is brought about by God (or the gods in polytheistic societies). In Genesis, beyond functioning the way that God intended, something that is good has been incorporated

---

[49]On "good" being relative, see Provan, "Before Moses," 344; see also Iain Provan, *Discovering Genesis: Content, Interpretation, Reception* (London: SPCK, 2015), 63-64.

into the ordered system. Something that is not good is either not yet ordered (Gen 3:18) or has been seriously disrupted and is therefore disordered/evil (the situation prior to the flood).

Subdue = subjugating (land; Gen 1:28) and ruling (animals; Gen 1:29). Rule over the animals would be understood to give people access to the animals as food (see the next section). Domesticated animals provided a variety of raw materials (e.g., their hides, wool, and milk), but certainly domestication also provided food. That is one of the reasons domestication took place.

The Hebrew root *kbš* (most often translated "subdue" in Gen 1:28) occurs fourteen times and, based on the nuances present in English usage, is more appropriately translated "subjugate" rather than "subdue."[50] One country could subdue another without subjugating it. Subduing involves bringing calm to a threatening situation. Subjugation pertains to putting something under one's authority, control, or rule.[51] One might be able to subdue an angry crowd through calming words, but the crowd has not been subjugated. A lion tamer subdues his subject but does not subjugate the lion. Subduing vegetation could be accomplished by weeding or pruning; subjugation would involve planting and harvesting. Furthermore, we can see that this posture of subjugating is not inherently abusive or exploitative from 1 Chronicles 22:18, which talks about how the inhabitants of the land are subject to the Lord. Subjugating is viewed as a positive way to bring order. Consequently, while people are called to subjugate the land, that does not mean that every form of subjugation is approved. Some subjugation would also be classified as exploitation. The pertinent question is whether any particular subjugation is bringing God's order or is simply bringing profit.

---

[50]Eight in the *qal* stem (including Gen 1), five in the *niphal* stem, once in *piel*. Most are in the context of warfare (*piel*) or slavery (*qal*). Exceptions: Esther 7:8; Mic 7:19; 1 Chron 22:18.

[51]Numerous translations reflect this by choosing "master it" (CEB, GW, NCV), or "put it under your control" (CEV, ERV, GNT, NIrV). NLT translates "govern." Wycliffe's translation says to "make it subject," and the AMP actually renders it "subjugate."

Food allotment (commensality). In Genesis 1:29, God gives plants for food, which will become available to them as they are able to subjugate the earth. This has often raised questions about whether this suggests that prior to the flood, humans were supposed to be vegetarian. Rather than thinking of this provision as a restrictive grant, we can reconsider it in terms of *commensality*, defined as positive social interactions that are associated with parties eating together in contexts that define relationships.[52] It is therefore logical that food is included in the discussion.

This food allowance creates a commensal relationship between God and humankind that makes them beholden to God even as they are given the high position of being his image bearers and serving as order bringers alongside him. Consequently, their subjugating must always align with *his* concept of order. It does not therefore give freedom for exploitation for our own selfish desires—our self-centered sense of order. Commensality reflects indebtedness rather than obligation in some contexts, though "feeling obliged" could work as an alternative to an obligation that implies being under compulsion. A commensal relationship *could* involve compulsion, but it could just mean that one is beholden to another in any number of vague ways. It is incumbent on people to serve as functioning images. The blessing (not commands) of these verses includes *benefits* (having the capacity and permission to be fruitful, multiply, and fill), indication of a *vocation* (subjugate and rule) and providing *supply* (a type of perquisite) as they are given food. All three of these offer insight into the image of God.

Seven days that are not chronologically sequential. If the days are about God bringing order to the cosmos, there is no reason to think

---

[52]Note that the provision of food unquestioningly implies that their bodies were made to process food and its nutrients, and therefore they needed food and its nutrients. One of my students, Raymond Hanus, raised a very provocative question in light of those observations: What would happen if they refused to eat? Of course, the inevitable response is that they would die for lack of those needed nutrients; therefore, death before the fall was not impossible.

that they would be in chronological order. Alternatively, the priorities of order in the cosmos could be reflected in the sequence. Others have pointed out that such alternative options for the seven days have long been available once it was recognized that the account was literarily structured (day 1 // day 4; day 2 // day 5; day 3 // day 6). Even for those who are not inclined to agree with my emphasis on ordering the cosmos, this structure (the framework hypothesis) would suggest a literary prioritizing, not a chronological sequence.[53]

Further insights from the ancient Near East. In the iconography of the ancient Near East, we find many examples of a god or heroic figure grasping wild animals in each hand ("master/mistress of animals" motif).[54] "The Master of animals manifests royal power and the maintenance of order in the cosmos through nature."[55] Similarly, iconography shows humans in scenes with grains and domesticated animals. These are both used to convey the idea of humans ruling by bringing order in the world. Again, these connections become much more meaningful once we make the transition from function to order. As art historian Irene Winter observes, these positive representations reflect an ideal world order.[56] In the context of these interests, we can appreciate the inclusion of subjugating and ruling in the creation account of Genesis.

---

[53]Provan, "Before Moses," 344-45. This provides easy resolution to the "problem" of light before the sun—the problem only exists if one holds the unwarranted assumption that the account is chronological.

[54]Michael J. Chan and Maria Metzler, "Lions and Leopards and Bears, O My: Re-reading Isaiah 11:6-9 in Light of Comparative Iconographic and Literary Evidence," in *Image, Text, Exegesis: Iconographic Interpretation and the Hebrew Bible*, ed. Izaak J. de Hulster and Joel M. LeMon (London: T&T Clark, 2014), 196-225.

[55]Stéphanie Anthonioz, "The Lion, the Shepherd, and the Master of Animals: Metaphorical Interactions and Governance Representations in Mesopotamian and Levantine Sources," in *Researching Metaphor in the Ancient Near East*, ed. Marta Pallavidini and Ludovico Portuese (Wiesbaden: Harrassowitz, 2020), 15-28, here 16.

[56]Irene J. Winter, "Representing Abundance: A Visual Dimension of the Agrarian State," in *On Art in the Ancient Near East*, vol. 2, *From the Third Millennium B.C.E.*, Culture and History of the Ancient Near East 34.2 (Leiden, Brill, 2010), 199-226.

Genesis 1: Creation Account Focused on Function 97

Finally, with regard to understanding the "spirit of God" in Genesis 1:2, a stimulating article that has advanced my thinking pertains to the four winds in ancient Mesopotamia.[57] The four winds are deified in Mesopotamia, and the Southwind is of particular interest because its very name (Akkadian *šūtu > ša'u*) refers to flying about, fluttering. It is referred to as the "breeze of [the god] Ea." This Akkadian term is also used of birds to describe them as circling, swooping, or soaring. In Genesis 1:2, the difficult-to-translate verb describing the activity of the spirit is also used of birds in Deuteronomy 32:11, as is its cognate in Ugaritic texts. Furthermore, the Southwind in Mesopotamia also leads kings into battle, just as the spirit of the Lord does in Judges and Kings. Just as the spirit is in the vanguard of military campaigns, the spirit is here seen in the vanguard of creation. This stands as another example of how details from ancient Near Eastern texts can bring welcome insight to biblical texts and offer resolution to some of the persistent problems of interpretation.

ANSWERS TO FREQUENTLY ASKED QUESTIONS

1. Why can't Genesis 1 include both origination of material objects and establishment of order (that is, both a house story and a home story)? Of course, an account focused on order assumes in part the manipulation of physical aspects of the cosmos. The question is whether any given account is *interested* in discussing material origination. Certainly, any creation account *could* potentially concern origination of both the physical universe and order in the cosmos, but we must let each account speak for itself. A material focus cannot automatically be adopted as the default position; that perspective would have to be demonstrated. When we look through the seven-day account in Genesis day by day, we see almost nothing that could be

---

[57]Franz A. M. Wiggermann, "The Four Winds and the Origins of Pazazu," in *Das geistige Erfassen der Welt im Alten Orient*, ed. Claus Wilcke (Wiesbaden: Harrassowitz, 2007), 125-65.

98   NEW EXPLORATIONS IN THE LOST WORLD OF GENESIS

considered a material focus, while, in contrast, we see a thoroughgoing treatment of ordering and organizing. From a methodological standpoint, finding a random statement or two that may refer to material would not prove that it is a materially focused account.

We can therefore proceed by asking what, in the wording of the text, comes into existence on each day? That question is best answered through the verbs and modifiers rather than through the nouns (light, *rāqîaʾ*, birds, etc.). What has changed in the perspective of the text after each day?

Day 1: What now exists is day and night (named/designated), and a time-oriented *separation* between them as they alternate. Light is only the medium/mechanism. No material origination is specified, but time is the most basic element of order in our lives. Here we also already see an anthropocentric focus.

Day 2: What now exists is a (space-oriented) *separation* (named/designated) between the waters (the existence of the waters is not new). No material origination is designated except perhaps the *rāqîaʾ*, but in my view, this is simply the space between the waters that people inhabit, not a material object. Even for those who consider the *rāqîaʾ* a material object, it is the separation of the waters that is the focus.

Day 3: What now exists is a *process* of fecundity according to kinds (existence of sea and dry land is not new). The land is productive. No material origination is specified, but order is set up so that we can have food.[58]

Day 4: What now exists is *dominion* of the heavenly realm by lights (themselves only mechanisms). Israel does not know they are objects, so it is not new objects that they now believe exist—God made *lights*, but more importantly, he assigned them dominion.[59] This is not a reference

---

[58]Note the pattern that order, even cosmic order, is anthropocentric in focus.

[59]It does not matter what *we* know about the sun, moon, and stars. We are interested in what sort of account Israelites believed this to be, so we have to work with their understanding.

Genesis 1: Creation Account Focused on Function   99

to material origination, since lights are not material in any ancient understanding. The "lights" bring order to our lives as they mark the signs, festivals, days, and years—the specific explanation of the text.

Day 5: What now exists are *filled arenas* (sea and sky) populated by self-multiplying, swarming, and teeming creatures. The text does not indicate that God *made* them, only that he populated the sea and sky with them. No explicit material origination is stated, but in terms of order, God furnishes our home with these creatures.

Day 6: What now exists are *kinds* of living creatures and *image bearers to subjugate and rule*. The first topic of day six uses the same language as day three: the grammatical subject is land/earth, the verb expresses causing something to come forth (i.e., producing), and the result is "kinds" pertaining to populations. These are the only two occurrences in the Old Testament of "land" being the subject of this verb. We should first note that the author chose "land" (*ʾereṣ*) rather than "earth" (*ʾădāmâ*). The latter would have been more likely to designate substance, while the former is more suited to refer to domain or territory. On day three we could easily have thought about the *ʾereṣ* being generative (i.e., the ground from which the growing plants spring), but that would have more likely used *ʾădāmâ*. Regardless, that is not an option in day six; both we and they know that animals do not spring from the ground. The alternative to the ground being identified as "generative" is that it is being identified as "productive," for example, "may the land [*ʾereṣ*] be abundantly producing plants and animals." This speaks about the bounty of the land, comparable to the description later in the Old Testament of a land flowing with milk and honey. The abundance is indicated by the reference to "kinds"—the varieties of living creatures. It speaks of the productivity of the land: a land rich in diversity, containing all sorts of animals. In this way, it is very similar to birds and fish in day five. So, "Let the *ʾereṣ* [land] produce living creatures after their kind" means that what now exists is variety in abundance in the land.

100 NEW EXPLORATIONS IN THE LOST WORLD OF GENESIS

Is there material origination? Day six is the only day when the verb *ʿāśâ* ("make") is used with a direct object that Israelites would have understood to be material objects. Yet even here we have to be attentive to the qualifiers: "God made the wild animals according to their kind." First, it is still talking about a population, not individual beasts, and second, the qualifier indicates that the focus is the taxonomy: he sorted them into groups.[60] Third, we have seen in days two and four the willingness of the author to use *ʿāśâ* ("make") even when material origination is not in view. We could hardly then insist that this occurrence of that same verb must be understood materially.

So much for the animals, but people are also brought into the picture on day six. Here we again encounter the verb *ʿāśâ*, but again it has a significant qualifier. The NET version shows it clearly: "Let us make humankind in our image, after our likeness, so they may rule over the fish of the sea and the birds of the air, over the cattle, and over all the earth, and over all the creatures that move on the earth." Often readers have read "making humans" as material origination, but there are multiple qualifiers here. God makes humans his image/likeness. When a board of trustees says, "Let's make Carol our president of the company and put her in charge of all daily operations," there is no material origination. Rather, an identity is being made as well as a task (elements of order and function). In like manner, God is giving humanity an identity and a commission.

Given this analysis of the six days, we can observe that most days do not have any possible material origination connected to them, and the few random statements that may suggest otherwise are isolated and can be explained otherwise. In contrast, every day has a clear outcome with regard to order. This alone would suggest that Genesis is not offering an account of origins of both material and order. To claim that it is an account of material origination would be

---

[60]Even if in this one instance readers might see a material origination, one stray example would be insufficient to conclude that the entire account is one of material origination.

Genesis 1: Creation Account Focused on Function

a case of special pleading. For an indication of how a material account would be framed, see question four below. The Old Testament does make comments about material creation, but Genesis 1 is not that sort of account.

Thus far, we have discussed only the six days. Day seven comes at the climax of the account and must not be neglected. Yet, it almost always is because interpreters assume that Genesis is telling a house story, and it is clear that nothing material is brought into existence on this day. That should tell us something. Our full treatment of day seven is the topic of the next chapter, but here it should be noted that when we view the account in terms of order, day seven regains its climactic position as the main point. God has completed ordering the cosmos and is now ready to take up his rule as he continues to bring additional order and maintain that which he has already brought.

So, "Can't it be both?" is the wrong question. Instead, we must ask, "*Is* it both?" The analysis above suggests that it is not. This is not a new observation. Even the early Jewish and Christian writers noticed that there was little material production going on in the seven days. They therefore posited theories wherein the material creation took place in Genesis 1:1 and that the six days were spent organizing and setting up the cosmos.[61] Nathan Chambers indicates that this was "the predominant view in the early and medieval church."[62] At the same time, we have to exercise caution. Andrew Brown summarizes, for example,

The creation hermeneutic of the Cappadocian Fathers, Ambrose, and Augustine hovered on the boundary of the physical

---

[61]This is sometimes referred to as two-stage creation. Paul Copan and William Lane Craig address it and point to medieval Jewish commentator Ramban. See Copan and Craig, *Creation Out of Nothing: A Biblical, Philosophical, and Scientific Exploration* (Grand Rapids, MI: Baker, 2004), 60-64. Allert refers to a similar notion in Ephrem the Syrian (second–third century), and Augustine also differentiates between the simultaneous creation of all things (Gen 1:1) and then the administration of creation represented by the days (Allert, *Early Christian Readings*, 223, 290).

[62]Chambers, *Reconsidering Creation Ex Nihilo*, 211.

and the metaphysical, the historical and the ontological, what becomes and what is, because that is how they saw the very nature of the first day. It was a one-way portal from eternity into time. That is why, in both Hexaemeron 1.6 and 2.8, Basil wants to expound it carefully, combining temporal and atemporal senses, and is comfortable with accepting multiple meanings of the same biblical text.[63]

This idea that the seven days pertain to ordering and organizing is very similar to mine, except that I have interpreted Genesis 1:1 as a literary introduction rather than a general material creation. In contrast to those early writers, my claim is that the text, in line with creation accounts of its day, simply does not recount material origination—that is not an issue in which the ancient world was interested.

2. Does Genesis 1 affirm creation out of nothing?[64] In the last segment I noted some of the important results of the creative process in the days of Genesis that can help us reply to this question. For example, pertaining to day one, how does one create time out of nothing? Day and night out of nothing? Lights? Those statements have no meaning. People who argue for creation out of nothing desire to maintain that God created material out of nonmaterial—a worthy point to make. I have no objection to that affirmation and would even be willing to grant that the theology of creation out of nothing could be defended as a biblical idea. Nevertheless, we must differentiate between the concept of a biblical idea (which may have support in other biblical passages) and the determination of what the Genesis story is (that is, house or home?). If the Genesis 1 account is not about material origination, and my contention is that it is not, then creation out of

---

[63] Andrew Brown, *Recruiting the Ancients for the Creation Debate* (Grand Rapids, MI: Eerdmans, 2023), 145.

[64] Two recent and thorough discussions of this topic are Copan and Craig, *Creation Out of Nothing*, and Chambers, *Reconsidering Creation Ex Nihilo*. For a more concise yet very helpful discussion, see Allert, *Early Christian Readings*, 203-28.

Genesis 1: Creation Account Focused on Function 103

nothing does not apply *to this text*. The *ex nihilo* conversation assumes that Genesis 1 is a material account—a house story. As important as a house story can be, that is not the story Genesis wishes to tell.

A common refrain in these discussions is that the verb translated "create" (*bārā³*) never mentions material that is being used in the process. Analysts therefore conclude that there was no material used and that the verb therefore represents creation out of nothing. Another reason, however, for material not being mentioned is that it is not an account of material origination—that *bārā³* does not have a material orientation. If analysis suggests that Genesis 1 is about order, not about material, and *bārā³* can easily be used for bringing order (which study of its usage provided in *LWG1* demonstrates), then there is no reason to think that *bārā³* in Genesis 1 is material, and it is therefore no surprise that no material is mentioned. The oft-noted fact that only God is the subject of the verb does not make it material. God is also the only true bringer of order.

The question about *ex nihilo* creation ultimately concerns the question of contingency—that is, is all matter created by God (and therefore contingent on him), or does matter (pre)exist eternally independent of God? I do not question that the entire universe is contingent on God. I fully agree that only God is eternal. I fully believe that God is ontologically distinct from his creation (thereby rejecting some forms of panentheism and implications of ancient Near East polytheism). Those philosophical-theological questions are not the ones at issue in Genesis. I am not of the opinion that the question of creation out of nothing is essentially an anachronistic one, though it may often be framed within anachronistic assumptions. In that regard, Chambers addresses the commonly expressed modern position that the *ex nihilo* conversation today pertains to philosophical questions that were not part of the conversation in Old Testament times.[65] Be

---

[65]Chambers (*Reconsidering Creation Ex Nihilo*, 9-10) mentions Bernard F. Batto, *In the Beginning: Essays on Creation Motifs in the Ancient Near East and the Bible* (Winona Lake,

104 NEW EXPLORATIONS IN THE LOST WORLD OF GENESIS

that as it may, that is not the argument that I am making. I am trying to discern what aspect of creation Genesis seeks to recount (compare the illustration concerning "How did the play begin?").[66] In quest of that answer, I stand firmly against those who believe that Genesis 1 is an account of material creation out of nothing and reject the idea that *bārāʾ* provides support for an *ex nihilo* view. Nevertheless, I believe that God is the Creator of the material world, and that, when he did so, he created out of nothing. But I repeat, that is not the story Genesis wishes to tell.

As a final note, some contend that even some ancient Near Eastern accounts can be read as presenting creation out of nothing, particularly in Egypt.[67] Note, however, that when an Egyptian text talks about the nonexistent, we have to recall that in Egyptian thinking, something that is "nonexistent" is not necessarily nonmaterial. For the Egyptians, the cosmic waters were nonexistent. Moreover, the question of preexistent matter was not a question on the table for Egyptians.[68]

IN: Eisenbrauns, 2013); Othmar Keel and Silvia Schroer, *Creation: Biblical Theologies in the Context of the Ancient Near East* (Winona Lake, IN: Eisenbrauns, 2015); Joseph Blenkinsopp, *Creation, Un-creation, Re-creation: A Discursive Commentary on Genesis 1–11* (Edinburgh: T&T Clark, 2011); and Levenson, *Creation and the Persistence*, as a representative group. The list could be expanded exponentially, for this enjoys a consensus in critical scholarship.

[66]It is tangentially of interest that in Copan and Craig's defense of creation out of nothing, they interact at some length with E. J. Young, *Studies in Genesis 1* (Philadelphia: P&R, 1964), who draws the distinction (with which they seem to agree) that Gen 1:2 depicts a "first stage in the creation of the present well-ordered earth" (Copan and Craig, *Creation Out of Nothing*, 62). Young contrasts this to a situation that was "confused and out of order." Though I would find it easy to agree, perhaps the most important distinction between this view and mine is that the order spectrum is tripartite, whereas Young as well as Copan and Craig are applying a dualistic, bipartite model. Nevertheless, Young, whom Copan and Craig again quote, indicates that the purpose of Gen 1 is "to show how God brought this world from its primitive condition of desolation and waste to become an earth, fully equipped to receive man and be his home" (Copan and Craig, *Creation Out of Nothing*, 62). This looks strikingly similar to the focus on order I have been proposing.

[67]See discussion regarding the Memphite Theology in Chambers, *Reconsidering Creation Ex Nihilo*, 24-26.

[68]Chambers, *Reconsidering Creation Ex Nihilo*, 37.

Genesis 1: Creation Account Focused on Function

3. If throughout the history of the church people have thought of the creation account in Genesis in material terms, why should we think differently now? In chapter two I addressed the issue of the history of interpretation and its limitations. The answer to this question follows similar lines. In Michael Graves's book *The Inspiration and Interpretation of Scripture: What the Early Church Can Teach Us*, he summarizes some of the early interpretation of Genesis 1, demonstrating that it was not much interested in material origination (though some arguably would have seen material origination as involved).[69] Consequently, the premise for this question is flawed—church history does not show that a material view is monolithic. A quick survey will clarify the diversity and perspectives evident in the early Christian literature.

Origen, pointing out the problems of days one through three without sun, considers the account purely spiritual. Basil contests the allegorical approach and wants to take the six days literally, but his focus is less on materiality and more on natural philosophy and the beauty and abundance of the natural world. John Chrysostom, always one for reading Scripture in its plain sense, nevertheless focuses on moral exhortation. Ambrose believes that Genesis 1 corrects pagan views (but the only pagan views he knew were Greek views, not ANE views). He believes that Genesis is compatible with the science of his day (though that is far different from the science of our day). Augustine, who writes profusely on this topic, argues for coherence between Genesis and natural philosophy, yet his interpretation of the details is metaphorical. He asserts that if Scripture seems to oppose

---

[69]Michael Graves, *The Inspiration and Interpretation of Scripture: What the Early Church Can Teach Us* (Grand Rapids, MI: Eerdmans, 2014), 95-99. See further Peter C. Bouteneff, *Beginnings: Ancient Christian Readings of the Biblical Creation Narratives* (Grand Rapids, MI: Baker, 2008), especially 170-73. A good overview of the variety of positions can be found in Andrew Louth, *Genesis 1-11*, Ancient Christian Commentary on Scripture (Downers Grove, IL: InterVarsity Press, 2001). For detailed analysis, see Allert, *Early Christian Readings.*

what we find in the natural world, then we are reading Scripture incorrectly. Graves writes, "Augustine is clear that reason and the facts of nature can redirect how Christians interpret Scripture." A long, oft-quoted statement from Augustine says that Christians should not bring themselves to shame by suggesting that Scripture makes claims that "any pagan" would recognize as patently ridiculous. Graves summarizes it well: "If a human theory about the natural world conflicts with a presumed teaching of Scripture, and 'reason should prove that this theory is unquestionably true,' then 'this teaching was never in Holy Scripture but was an opinion proposed by man in his ignorance.'"[70] Furthermore, Augustine famously believed that the seven-day structure of Genesis 1 was only a concession to our human understanding, not in any sense the process or time frame that God actually used.[71]

The point of all of this is not to say that since I can find statements in the early Christian writings that do not focus on the material aspects, Genesis 1 is therefore not material.[72] Rather, my point is that we cannot reasonably claim that the church has maintained throughout its history a monolithic material perspective on Genesis 1.[73] Even those who were committed to reading literally did not necessarily read with a material emphasis. Furthermore, reading the account as pertaining to order, as I do, is not a figurative, symbolic, or allegorical reading; the account is about God bringing order, which he actually did.

Before leaving this question, it is also important to point out that the question of whether the focus is on material or on order is a

---

[70]Graves, *Inspiration and Interpretation*, 97-98.

[71]Allert, *Early Christian Readings*, 274-75.

[72]Brown, *Recruiting the Ancients*, 279, warns us, "Until we read ancient writers with motivations that transcend the quest for self confirmation, our understanding of them will often be shallow and deficient."

[73]Note Allert's similar concern (*Early Christian Readings*, 54), echoing the same in the work he cites by D. H. Williams.

Genesis 1: Creation Account Focused on Function 107

different question from that which asks whether the days are seven literal days. Early Christian writers can be seen to exhibit diversity on both of those questions, but the question of literal reading differs in both. For example, someone could conclude that God ordered the world in seven literal days, even though the material origination of the cosmos was not taking place in those days. If the author intended to provide an account of God ordering the world, then someone reading literally would interpret the account accordingly.

4. If we were to find a creation account that explained material origins, what would we expect it to look like? What would we need to see to conclude that Genesis or another ancient creation text is about material creation? I would expect such an account to use the same kind of language that is used in the rest of the Bible when it *is* talking about the material world:

- Yahweh made the sea and the dry land (Jon 1:9)—these are already present in Genesis 1:2
- Yahweh laid the foundations of the earth (Ps 104:5; Job 38:4)—along with its dimensions, footings
- Yahweh stretches out the heavens (Ps 104:2)
- Yahweh forms the mountains (Amos 4:13)—Note the contrasting neglect of terraforming the geophysical features of the landscape in Genesis 1. Genesis does not report that he makes rivers or lakes or mountains or deserts. It does not even report him making water.
- Yahweh knit/wove together, fearfully made; frame and sinews (Ps 139:13-15)

These passages talk about what God has done and in my view pertain to the material/physical world, but they are not *creation accounts*. I might also note that even many of these pay more attention to order/function. I am not trying to build a theology of creation (for either the

108 NEW EXPLORATIONS IN THE LOST WORLD OF GENESIS

writers of the OT or for us) but trying to understand a particular piece of literature (Gen 1).

5. Isn't there evidence that people in the ancient Near East did think of creation in material terms? Some have read the cosmological literature from the ancient Near East and have noted references to what appear to be material aspects of the cosmos. In light of these observations, it would be natural to question whether my approach might be an oversimplification when I suggest that ancient Near East cosmologies did not conceive of creation in material terms. As an example, we can consider the great Babylonian hymn to Marduk, Enuma Elish, which is the most familiar cosmological text from ancient Babylon. Not only do the opening lines mention that the gods had not been formed or destinies decreed (lines 7-8), but material things are also cited as lacking, for example, heavens and earth in the first two lines. We should note, however, that the text explains that heaven and earth did not exist because they had not been given names. In other words, their role and function in the ordered universe had not yet been established. Some have noted that by the time Marduk comes on the scene as creator, the physical universe has already been created, and he is just (re)organizing it. While I would claim that comparing his organizing to the act of creating is a difference without a distinction, we could still ask what the original creation looks like in Enuma Elish. The text in fact has nothing to say about that. The initial creative act is in line 9, where the gods are created.

When Marduk does his creative work in tablet V, he begins by establishing the constellations, the stations for the great gods, and the phases of the moon (lines 1-36). He then sets up days and years (lines 37-46). His next acts bring about the winds, the clouds, the Tigris and Euphrates, and other terrain features, all connected to parts of Tiamat's body (lines 47-64). This is as close as it gets to material terraforming, though it might be considered cosmic planning more than anything we would consider material origination. After all, the

Genesis 1: Creation Account Focused on Function

creation is related to the body of a slain mythical creature—hardly the sort of material ontology that would interest either Genesis or us.

In another example, in the creation description in a bilingual text, KAR 4, heaven and earth (its faithful companion) were separated, gods and goddesses were made; "heaven was set up and earth was made." This is clarified as the text continues to talk about the designs completed as waterways were dug, from canals and irrigation ditches to the Tigris and Euphrates.[74] This is reference to some (very general) material aspects but not with materiality in focus.

In another text called the Founding of Eridu are these lines:

He created animals, the creatures in the open country,
He created the Tigris and Euphrates and put them in place,
Benevolently he assigned names to them,
He created canes, sedges, marshes, reeds and canebrakes, he
    created vegetation of the open country,
But the lands were marshes and reed-beds.
The cow, the calf, the bull, the ewe, the lamb, the breeding ram.
There were palm groves and forests.
The wild sheep and the antelope were standing at his service.[75]

This excerpt clearly deals with items we would call material. Yet we note that it is prefaced by an indication that it is going to describe Marduk's intention "that the gods should be settled in a dwelling of their pleasure."[76] These elements all have to do in some way with making the temples of the gods—ultimately a home story. After the quoted lines, the text proceeds to talk about creating the brick mold and the cities with their shrines.

These are just a few of many examples that provide a glimpse of the emphasis on a home-story approach to accounts of creation by ancient

---

[74]Wilfred G. Lambert, *Babylonian Creation Epics* (Winona Lake, IN: Eisenbrauns, 2013), 353.
[75]Lambert, *Babylonian Creation Epics*, 373.
[76]Lambert, *Babylonian Creation Epics*, 373.

110　　New Explorations in the Lost World of Genesis

Near Eastern writers. In the end, however, the question is not whether readers can find some isolated lines that refer to material aspects of the cosmos;[77] the question is what the overarching interest in ancient cosmologies is. One would scour the Egyptian, Babylonian, and Sumerian sources in vain trying to identify an indisputable interest in material origination. Order in the cosmos is the highest value, and it is what these accounts discuss; it is what the gods bring about in the creation activity.

6. Aren't there many examples of bārāʾ *referring to material objects?* In *The Lost World of Genesis One*, I presented a full analysis of *bārāʾ* ("create").[78] Someone perusing those data may find examples that look like they may refer to material creation. As I mentioned there, however, the question is not whether they are material objects; the question is whether the author is objectifying them (that is, treating them as material objects). When we say something like, "The sun glowed on the horizon, setting ablaze everything it touched in the radiance of its final gasp before disappearing below the horizon," the sun's materiality (and even the specific fact that it *is* a burning ball of gas) is not the point. Instead, the aesthetic beauty of the sunset is being celebrated.

Nevertheless, I have not contended that *bārāʾ cannot* be material or that it never is. What my analysis demonstrates is that it is not always material and in fact often is not. Instead, the verb frequently makes a statement relative to the order spectrum. Perhaps one could attempt to make the case that the verb is never objectively material, but I do not need to make that case. Once we know that it does not have to be material and that it often pertains to order, we can ask whether it is being used in a context that is patently material or

---

[77]Note that in the piece called The First Brick, one line says, "He created mountains and seas," which sounds material, but the next line is telling: "to make all things abound" (Lambert, *Babylonian Creation Epics*, 381).

[78]*LWG1*, 36-45, chart of all occurrences on 40-41.

Genesis 1: Creation Account Focused on Function

dealing with order. My answer to question one above has already provided that information.

In the end, the question is not what we mean by our terms but what Israelites meant by their terms. Theological inquiries must be set aside while doing the lexical-semantic work needed to understand what they were asserting through the words they chose.

4

Genesis 1

Cosmic Temple and Rest

SUMMARY OF PREVIOUS MATERIAL

After the proposal that the seven-day account was focused on order (function) rather than material, the second major pillar of the Lost World proposal was that the significance of the seventh day had been underestimated.[1] Based on the work of numerous earlier scholars, I proposed that the seventh day, far from being what amounted to a liturgical footnote, was actually the climax of the account.[2] This conclusion was based on several observations:

---

[1]See *LWG1*, 71-106, propositions 7-11.

[2]Jon Levenson, "The Temple and the World," *Journal of Religion* 64 (1984): 275-98; John M. Lundquist, "What Is a Temple? A Preliminary Typology," in *The Quest for the Kingdom of God*, ed. Herbert B. Huffmon, Frank A. Spina, and Alberto R. W. Green (Winona Lake, IN: Eisenbrauns: 1983), 205-20; Michael Fishbane, "Genesis 1:1–2:4a / Creation," in *Text and Texture: Close Reading of Selected Biblical Texts* (New York: Schocken, 1979), 3-16; Jon C. Laansma, *"I Will Give You Rest"* (Tübingen: Mohr Siebeck, 1997), 17-76; Gordon J. Wenham, "Sanctuary Symbolism in the Garden of Eden Story," in *I Studied Inscriptions from Before the Flood*, ed. Richard S. Hess and David Toshio Tsumura, Sources for Biblical and Theological Study 4 (Winona Lake, IN: Eisenbrauns, 1994), 399-404; Moshe Weinfeld, "Sabbath, Temple and the Enthronement of the Lord—The Problem of the Sitz im Leben of Genesis 1:1–2:3," in *Mélanges bibliques et orientaux en l'honneur de M. Henri Cazelles*, ed. André Caquot and Mathias Delcor, AOAT 212 (Kevelaer: Butzon & Bercker; Neukirchen-Vluyn: Neukirchener Verlag, 1981), 501-12; Victor Hurowitz, *I Have Built You an Exalted House*, Journal for the Study of the Old Testament Supplement Series 115 (Sheffield: JSOT Press, 1992), appendix 5, 330-31. This is widely supported by other scholars as well. See, e.g., Jon D. Levenson, *Creation and the Persistence of Evil* (Princeton, NJ: Princeton University Press, 1994), 100. This is affirmed by Matthijs de Jong, "The Seventh Day in Genesis 2:2-3 and the Change from Kingship to Sabbath," in *Congress Volume Aberdeen 2019*, ed. Grant Macaskill,

Genesis 1: Cosmic Temple and Rest

- Divine rest in the ancient Near East was centered on temples as the place where the gods rested
- Rest pertains to stability rather than relaxation ("engagement without obstacles rather than disengagement without responsibilities")[3]
- Seven-day temple dedication ceremonies gave explanation for the seven-day structure of the Genesis account
- A common homology exists between temple and cosmos in ancient thinking
- Creation accounts in the ancient Near East conclude with temple building

NEW EXPLORATIONS

A number of monographs have been published in the interim supporting various of these ideas and expanding on them.[4] The data from the ancient Near East continue to support the basic concepts of divine rest, the connection between temple building and creation, the temple as the control center of the cosmos, and the interconnections between temple, creation, rest, and order. As one example, Michael Hundley aptly summarizes, "As in Egypt, the temple [in Mesopotamia] was structurally and conceptually connected to the moment of creation, thereby representing the ordering of the world and, in its

---

Christi Maier, and Joachim Schaper (Leiden: Brill, 2022), 17-49, here 22, who provides additional supporting sources.

[3]*LWG1*, 72.

[4]Michael Morales, *The Tabernacle Pre-figured: Cosmic Mountain Ideology in Genesis and Exodus* (Leuven: Peeters, 2012), 76-83; Michael Hundley, *Gods in Dwellings* (Atlanta: Society of Biblical Literature, 2013); Daniel Kim, *Rest in Mesopotamian and Israelite Literature* (Piscataway, NJ: Gorgias, 2019); G. K. Beale, *The Temple and the Church's Mission* (Downers Grove, IL: InterVarsity Press, 2004). I also subsequently developed the ideas in *GIAC*, 100-119, under the categories of the cosmic role of the temple in the ancient world, the building of temples described in cosmic terms, the cosmic functions of temples, temples as models of the cosmos with cosmic symbolism, the connection between cosmic origins and temple building, the cosmos as a temple, and divine rest and temples in cosmologies.

contemporary context, connoting an ordered world that functioned as originally intended."[5] Again, once I identified *order* as the operative word (replacing *function*), all the pieces fell more neatly into place. As Daniel Kim observes, "Rest is a sign that the cosmos over which [the gods] rule is stable and peaceful." He states simply, "Rest is a symbol of divine rule."[6]

Modification in terminology. At the same time, I recognized some slight modifications were necessary. My initial discussions, following those who had previously discussed the relationships between cosmos and temple, focused on the idea that the cosmos was being portrayed as a temple or at least in temple terms.[7] Jon Levenson had spoken of a homology between temple and cosmos. Nevertheless, it soon became clear that the analogy eventually broke down (as analogies tend to do). My colleague Daniel Block brought to my attention the basic problem: Temples, by definition, delineate an outside and an inside; sacred space is secluded from profane space. If the cosmos is defined as a temple, where is the "outside" that is differentiated from the sacred space "inside"?[8] The homology idea was simply built on the nature of the space (temple or cosmos) as inhabited by divine presence. Nevertheless, the homology broke down if interrogated in light of the temple as differentiating sacred and mundane space—an aspect the homology left out of consideration.

The objection, however, though not without merit, is easily mitigated by focusing on what was always the central point. The cosmos was being prepared to be sacred space by virtue of God's stepping into it to dwell among people in the same way that the temple was sacred space where God dwelt among people. The adjustment, then, is that rather than talking about "cosmic temple," I am now inclined to talk

---

[5]Hundley, *Gods in Dwellings*, 79-80.

[6]Kim, *Rest in Mesopotamian and Israelite Literature*, 18.

[7]Nathan Chambers, *Reconsidering Creation Ex Nihilo in Genesis 1* (University Park, PA: Eisenbrauns, 2020), 183, refers to this as the "now prevalent interpretation."

[8]In ANE thinking, the "outside" would be the cosmic ocean.

Genesis 1: Cosmic Temple and Rest 115

about "cosmos as sacred space," thereby restricting the homology to a certain aspect of the temple.[9]

To be fair, Levenson's position never intended to bring differentiated space into the picture. This is evident in the summary he offers:

> Collectively, the function of these correspondences is to underscore the depiction of the sanctuary as a world, that is, an ordered, supportive, and obedient environment, and the depiction of the world as a sanctuary, that is, as a place in which the reign of God is visible and unchallenged, and his holiness is palpable, unthreatened, and pervasive.[10]

He concludes by observing that the sanctuary was conceived in Priestly circles "as a macro-temple, the palace of God in which all are obedient to his commands."[11] Here the idea of order is prominent, and the focus is on God's rule. As I have stated it, God's rest is God's rule over the cosmos, which he has ordered to be his dwelling place. This concept is supported by Hundley: "Temples in particular were cosmic centers, the hearts of the ordered world, where the gods and their representative the king ruled."[12]

Extension of order rather than of sacred space. A second area in which I have made slight modifications is in relation to the concept that the human task was to expand sacred space. G. K. Beale developed this idea into what he identified as the mission of the church.[13] It seemed a logical idea when I was first piecing everything together,

---

[9]In a later article, Block considers this possibility and says, "We may indeed view the world as originally created and Eden in particular as sacred space." He then provides the caveat, which I accept, "This does not mean that either the cosmos or Eden was a temple." Daniel I. Block, "Eden: A Temple? A Reassessment of the Biblical Evidence," in *From Creation to New Creation: Biblical Theology and Exegesis*, ed. Daniel Gurtner and Benjamin Gladd (Peabody, MA: Hendrickson, 2013), 3-29, here 22.

[10]Levenson, "Temple and the World," 86.

[11]Levenson, "Temple and the World," 86.

[12]Hundley, *Gods in Dwellings*, 80.

[13]Beale, *Temple and the Church's Mission.*

especially in light of all space being sacred space in the new creation in Revelation 21. Nevertheless, the support from the biblical text for expansion being the human commission was not as easily identified, especially in the Old Testament.

Again, however, a small reorientation of terminology presents a clearer picture, and it is again the result of the switch from *function* to *order*. I would now maintain that it is not sacred space that is to be extended but God's order. People were created in his image to be order bringers alongside him. To be sure, sacred space is the center of order, but I would now say that it is order that is expanded in the human world, not sacred space per se. This remains aligned with some of Beale's most central tenets: "God's rest both at the conclusion of creation in Genesis 1–2 and later in Israel's temple indicates not mere inactivity but that he had demonstrated his sovereignty over the forces of chaos (e.g., the enemies of Israel) and now has assumed a position of kingly rest further revealing his sovereign power."[14]

Support in early Christian and Jewish literature. Further research has also elaborated the connection between cosmos and temple as recognized in early Christian and Jewish texts. Hindy Najman observes, "A correspondence between divine creation of the world and the human construction of the Temple is nowhere explicitly mentioned in the Hebrew Bible. But it is hinted at or assumed, and it is explicitly discussed in many para-biblical, early Christian, and rabbinic texts. The topography of Eden seems to correspond implicitly in various details with that of Solomon's Temple." A few pages later, she continues, "There is a heavenly Temple, prepared before creation in Eden, which will ultimately be revealed on earth. This can be described as an edenic paradigm of the ultimate heavenly temple. Some of the aforementioned texts associate the heavenly Temple with Eden—an

---

[14]Beale, *Temple and the Church's Mission*, 62. Beale discusses the relationship between creation, temple, and rest on 60-66.

Genesis 1: Cosmic Temple and Rest   117

association that, as we have seen, is implicit in biblical traditions."[15] These Second Temple texts, like some parallel ideas in Christianity, still have to be recognized as anachronistic and therefore require caution when we interpret Genesis.

ANSWERS TO FREQUENTLY ASKED QUESTIONS

1. How can the seventh day be about a temple when there is no mention of a temple? Block raises this question particularly when he observes, "The narratives of Gen 1–3 are silent on either the earth or Eden as a dwelling place for God."[16] I consider this to be a case in which the connection between rest and temple would have been so plain to the ancient reader that it did not need to be said. That is, that it was self-evident within the cultural context does not mean that the temple identification is the focus of the Genesis account. Other passages (Ex 20:8-11; Ps 132:13-14) provide further elaboration of the connection. Furthermore, the well-known interconnections between temple, cosmos, and order both in Israel and in the ancient world would have evoked the inference of a temple inauguration. In this case, the seven days do not carry any significance for the age of the earth. Instead of viewing the seven days as the time period over which all of the material universe was created, they may be viewed as the days of inauguration of sacred space.

As a final observation, scholars note close parallels between Genesis 1 and the construction of the tabernacle in Exodus 39–40.[17] Levenson moves beyond the shared terminology and narrative arc to suggest that the instructions regarding the tabernacle in Exodus 25–31 occur in seven speeches, of which the last has to do with Sabbath and specifically refers back to the seventh day of the creation account

---

[15]Hindy Najman, *Losing the Temple and Recovering the Future: An Analysis of 4 Ezra* (Cambridge: Cambridge University Press, 2014), 106, 118.

[16]Block, "Eden: A Temple?," 22.

[17]De Jong, "Seventh Day in Genesis 2:2-3," 28-29.

118   NEW EXPLORATIONS IN THE LOST WORLD OF GENESIS

(Ex 31:17).[18] It would seem apparent, then, that Exodus reflects an understanding that the seventh day was intrinsically associated with the sanctuary.

2. Do any ancient Near Eastern creation accounts use a seven-day period? No, there are no extant creation accounts in the ancient world that depict creation as having taken place in seven days. There are numerous accounts (as I have previously noted) that connect creation and temple building, and there are examples of temple dedications taking place over a seven-day period.[19] The most prominent use of a seven-day temple dedication outside the Bible is in the cylinders describing Gudea's temple building and dedication (about a millennium before Solomon). Another use of seven days is found in the Baal Epic, where Baal builds his house (temple) in seven days. But none of these specifically depicts creation as taking place in seven days.[20]

3. Granting that the seven-day structure has a literary rather than chronological purpose and that it mirrors the seven-day temple inaugurations, what is the significance of the number seven that it

---

[18]Levenson, *Creation and the Persistence*, 83-86, following Peter Kearney, "Creation and Liturgy: The P-Redaction of Exodus 25-30," *Zeitschrift für die alttestamentliche Wissenschaft* 89 (1977): 375-87. The seven speeches are Ex 25:1–30:10; 30:11-16, 17-21, 22-33, 34-37; 31:1-11, 12-17.

[19]See *LWG1*, 180-81n1: Levenson, "Temple and the World," 288-89; Hurowitz, *I Have Built You*, 260-61, 275-76. The number seven is prevalent, though there are variations (e.g., Esarhaddon's dedication of the temple in Assur over three days and Assurnasirpal's dedication of Kalhu over ten days). Hurowitz's appendix on 280-82 provides the entire list of over forty texts. Another striking seven-day festival is an Old Babylonian ritual from Larsa. See Edwin C. Kingsbury, "A Seven Day Ritual in the Old Babylonian Cult at Larsa," *Hebrew Union College Annual* 34 (1963): 1-34. There is no evidence that this is a temple dedication ritual; in fact, each day focuses on a different god. Intriguingly, the rituals for each new day also begin in the evening (26). Kingsbury lists several other seven-day rituals (27).

[20]Amar Annus, "On the Origin of Watchers: A Comparative Study of the Antediluvian Wisdom in Mesopotamian and Jewish Traditions," *Journal for the Study of the Pseudepigrapha* 19 (2010): 277-320, here 287, notes that the seven antediluvian sages tasked with bringing order by instructing humankind in the arts of civilization are sometimes presented in the literature as having names beginning with UD (= "day"). They represent the golden age, the days of splendor. As intriguing as this is, it would be quite a stretch to find in these a reference to seven days.

Genesis 1: Cosmic Temple and Rest

should be used in these contexts? One of the most complicated aspects of ancient cultures to penetrate is their rhetorical use of symbolic language, because those ideas are inherent in a culture and rarely explained. The rhetorical or symbolic use of numbers is no exception; in fact, it stands as one of the primary examples of the principle. Regarding the number seven, Gina Konstantopoulos observes, "When considering the appearances of iterations of seven, on the whole the number signifies transition and liminality. Within texts, it serves as a marker of both spatial and temporal distances and works to move a particular character, and the audience of the text along with them, from one state or location to another."[21] This is pertinent to the Genesis account since the seven days represent a transition from the non-ordered (liminal) condition to the ordered condition that eventuates from God's creative activity, as well as the transition of God's presence into the cosmos. Seven is the appropriate number to symbolize that transition both with regard to the temple inauguration and to the acts of creation.

Denise Flanders adds further observations as she analyzes the use of numbers in the Hebrew Bible. She indicates that both Hebrew and Ugaritic literature use seven-day time periods in connection to "intervals of activity under divine supervision and power."[22]

---

[21]Gina Konstantopoulos, *The Divine/Demonic Seven and the Place of Demons in Mesopotamia*, Ancient Magic and Divination 20 (Leiden: Brill, 2023), 26.

[22]Denise C. Flanders, *The Rhetorical Use of Numbers in the Deuteronomistic History* (Leiden: Brill, 2023), 99. She is citing Daniel Fleming, "The Seven-Day Siege of Jericho," in *Ki Baruch Hu: Ancient Near Eastern, Biblical, and Judaic Studies in Honor of Baruch A. Levine*, ed. Robert Chazan, William W. Hallo, and Lawrence Schiffman (Winona Lake, IN: Eisenbrauns, 1999), 209-22, here 213. Barry G. Webb observes that the number seven is regularly associated with cultic festivals. See Webb, *The Book of Judges*, New International Commentary on the Old Testament (Grand Rapids, MI: Eerdmans, 2012), 371n65. In another study, Adele Berlin does not discuss the number seven except to indicate that it is a "symbolic or sacral number" but offers a nicely nuanced examination of the ways numbers are used. See Berlin, "When Five Is Not 5: The Bible's Nonliteral Use of Numbers," in *Ve-'Ed Ya'aleh (Gen 2:6): Essays in Biblical and Ancient Near Eastern Studies Presented to Edward L. Greenstein*, ed. Peter Machinist, Robert A. Harris, Joshua A. Berman, Nili Samet, and Noga Ayali-Darshan (Atlanta: SBL Press, 2021), 177-88.

120   New Explorations in the Lost World of Genesis

4. Divine rest in the ancient Near East is often in temples but also often involves sleep. Is the idea of the god resting on a throne in the temple found in the ancient Near East? Andrew George has published a gazetteer of temple names from ancient Mesopotamia with almost fifteen hundred names documented.[23] These names stand as one of the best contemporary sources for understanding the ideology and conceptions of the temples, so that is where we would expect to find information about divine rest in temples being on a throne. The following give a sampling of names that make very clear the idea that the temples featured the throne from which the deities ruled and from which they decreed destinies:

- "Long Side, Place of the Chosen Throne" (no. 24), a chamber in the Esagil temple of Babylon
- "House of the Throne" (no. 92), temple of Gula at Larak
- "Throne, Pure Place" (no. 93), shrine in the Ekur temple at Nippur
- "House, Dais of the Throne" (no. 110), temple of Ishtar at Nippur
- "Dais of Kingship" (no. 115), seat of Anu in a cella in Uruk
- "Pure Mound" (no. 179), shrine of Enlil in the Ekur at Nippur. This name features in numbers 178-84, and George describes it as referring to "the cosmic seat of the king of the gods in the divine assembly, whence destinies are determined."[24]
- "House of Decisions of Heaven and the Underworld (no. 256), seat of Shamash, sun-god of justice in the Esagil temple in Babylon (similar names in nos. 257-61)
- "House of the Throne" (no. 432)
- "House of the Director of Heaven and the Underworld" (no. 1049), cella of Nabu in the Ezida temple in Borsippa

---

[23]Andrew R. George, *House Most High: The Temples of Ancient Mesopotamia* (Winona Lake, IN: Eisenbrauns, 1993). Concerning sleep, for example, Gudea Cyl B xiv 21-22 refers to the bedroom provided in the temple as the resting place of the house.

[24]George, *House Most High*, 77.

Genesis 1: Cosmic Temple and Rest 121

These and others like them offer overwhelming evidence that the temples were considered the places where the gods had their thrones and from which they ruled.[25] Admittedly, the temples did also include bedchambers, and they are also occasionally referred to in the names, but temples were not built so that the gods would have places to sleep (compare the American White House, which, though it includes residential quarters and bedrooms, has significance as the place from where the president rules the country).[26] The question is whether their rest in the temples refers to their sleeping in the beds or to their sitting on their thrones.[27] Enuma Elish, the Babylonian Epic of Creation and Hymn of Praise for Marduk, portrays the building of the temple in which the gods can rest. Enuma Elish VI:51-54 uses *pašaḫu* to refer to the gods settling in to an ordered cosmos after the work is complete. In this sort of context, it does not pertain to either sleep or ruling.[28]

In the end, however, the question of sleep or rule may be a difference without a distinction. Bernard Batto develops the motif of the sleeping gods but even so establishes that their sleeping is indicative of their rule (which is sufficiently secure that they can rest at ease).[29] As summarized by Kim, "Rest is a sign that the cosmos over which

---

[25]Numerous names refer to crowns as well as to the *mes*, the governing principles bringing order to the cosmos and society (nos. 747-60, 774-76, 1193; etc.).

[26]No. 210, "Pleasant House"; no. 345, "House, Sacred Boudoir"; no. 539, "House of the Sacred Bed-Chamber"; no. 665, "Pure House, Bed-Chamber," but the ceremonial bedrooms in the temples were the sites for the sacred marriage ceremonies, not just a place to sleep/rest, e.g., "Giparu House," no. 377; the *giparu* is the chamber for the ritual of the sacred marriage.

[27]No. 627, "Restful Abode," a name for a shrine in the Esagil temple in Babylon, does not provide sufficient information to determine what it was used for; similarly, no. 859, "House Which Gives Rest"; no. 870, "House of Pleasant Rest," the temple of Sin in Babylon. All these clarify the previous point that temples were the places where the gods rested.

[28]The Epic of Erra and Ishum similarly refers to the stability that eventuates after the chaos of warfare.

[29]Bernard F. Batto, "The Sleeping God: An Ancient Near Eastern Motif of Divine Sovereignty," in *In the Beginning: Essays on Creation Motifs in the Ancient Near East and the Bible* (Winona Lake, IN: Eisenbrauns, 2013), 139-57.

122 NEW EXPLORATIONS IN THE LOST WORLD OF GENESIS

they rule is stable and peaceful."[30] This same concept can be seen as Israel enjoys rest from its enemies.

5. If the seventh day is more interested in God ruling than in relaxing, what does Sabbath observance look like for humans? I broached this subject briefly in *The Lost World of Genesis One* and addressed it at somewhat greater length in *Old Testament Theology for Christians*.[31] In both, I make the point that Sabbath observance comprised acknowledging God's rule and *participating* in God's order rather than *imitating* God by relaxing. Sabbath is not the sort of thing that should have to be regulated by rules. If we must be reminded, commanded, or coerced to observe it, it ceases to serve its function. It is the way we acknowledge that God is on the throne, that this world is his world, that our time and goods are his gift to us. This is the thrust of Isaiah 58:13-14.

> "If you keep your feet from breaking the Sabbath and from doing as you please on my holy day, if you call the Sabbath a delight and the LORD's holy day honorable, and if you honor it by not going your own way and not doing as you please or speaking idle words, then you will find your joy in the LORD, and I will cause you to ride in triumph on the heights of the land and to feast on the inheritance of your father Jacob." For the mouth of the LORD has spoken.

When combined with the instructions about fasting in the earlier part of Isaiah's chapter, we may infer a humanitarian focus, which could also be the focus of some important New Testament statements, though the New Testament treatments may or may not shed light on Israelite perceptions or on Old Testament texts. Nevertheless, for comparison, in Mark 2:27 Jesus states, "The Sabbath was made for

---

[30]Kim, *Rest in Mesopotamian and Israelite Literature*, 18. All of these are dealt with in detail in my later monograph, *GIAC*, 110-19.

[31]*LWG1*, 145-56; John H. Walton, *Old Testament Theology for Christians* (Downers Grove, IL: InterVarsity Press, 2017), 170-71.

Genesis 1: Cosmic Temple and Rest　　　　　　　　　　　　　　123

man, not man for the Sabbath." One possible reading in light of the issues discussed above is that humankind was not made to be enslaved by the Sabbath regulations (after all, it celebrated their freedom from slavery), but the Sabbath was meant to serve humanitarian purposes. That is, it is not for the benefit of the one who is observing the Sabbath ("God knows we need a break and some leisure time"— psychological benefit) but for the benefit of those whom the Sabbath observer might serve. In Luke 6:5, when Jesus asserts, "The Son of Man is Lord of the Sabbath," he then would be identifying himself as the ultimate humanitarian.

It has been relatively easy over the centuries to make the adjustment from "doing my work" over six days to on the Sabbath "*not* doing my work." It is significantly harder to make the adjustment from "not doing *my* work" on the Sabbath to "doing *his* work." In terms of application (now no longer dealing with OT text-in-context), I would urge that we consider the following if we seek to implement Sabbath observance into Christian worship based on Genesis, the Decalogue, and Deuteronomy:

1. stepping back from our own attempts to control our lives (through our "work" especially) and instead engaging in activities that acknowledge God as the one truly in control (as he demonstrated at creation and in the exodus)

2. turning our attention to active acknowledgment of God (worship) and kingdom work (service in his name)[32]

3. consciously extending the Sabbath ideology to all parts of life as we give God his due, treat others the way he has treated us (by being gracious managers[33] and being a source of goods and freedom), and recognize and protect the rights of others

---

[32]Again, I acknowledge that this does not represent an ancient Israelite view. No rituals or worship are implied for their Sabbath observance, and their view of kingdom would be that attached to covenant, at least until the latest stages of the OT.

[33]This explains why animals and servants are also not to work.

If we would desire to be Sabbath observers, there are three questions we can use week by week as we examine our commitment:

- Who is in control of our lives and our world, and the ultimate bringer of order?
- Is God worth it?
- How is my kingdom work coming?

6. Isn't God's throne in heaven? How can it be on earth? Again, I think we are asking twenty-first-century questions rather than thinking within the ancient cultural context. Ancient people viewed the temple as the linchpin between heaven and earth, present in both simultaneously. Hundley states succinctly the idea that building a temple was a way of bringing heaven on earth: "More than simply bringing heaven to earth (and ontologically belonging to a different sphere of existence), the temple created heaven on earth."[34] Moreover, God's presence in either temple (heavenly or earthly) does not suggest that he is present only there. The presence of God was manifest in his temple, yet at the same time he was present everywhere. Similarly, in the ancient Near East, the deity could be simultaneously present in a crafted image and in an astral manifestation.[35] The answer to the question whether God's throne is on earth or in heaven, then, is yes—a both/and, not an either-or, but more importantly a moot point.

7. Did God need a home? God has no needs, and he did not need to provide a place for himself, and neither did he need Israel to provide a home for him.[36] Yet, this is no reason to say that God therefore is not creating the cosmos as his home or that he did not commission the building of the temple for that purpose. It is not that God needed a home; it is that he desired to dwell among people in relationship with them (Ps 132:13-14). God's presence is all about his will, not his need.

---

[34]Hundley, *Gods in Dwellings*, 135; see extensive discussions throughout.
[35]See Hundley, *Gods in Dwellings*, 368-69.
[36]A point ably made by Block, "Eden: A Temple?," 34.

Genesis 1: Cosmic Temple and Rest

8. Would the Israelites in the Old Testament, including those who penned Scripture, have considered the seventh day to be about God's rule? To some extent this question has already been answered indirectly. If Israelites would have understood the connections between rest and temple and between temple and rule, then rest and rule would have been intrinsic to their thinking, even if undeveloped in the Genesis account.

From another perspective, this connection finds support in the proposal by Matthijs de Jong that Sabbath is particularly used in Genesis as a replacement for kingship (an idea notably absent in the early chapters of Genesis).[37] He observes that in the ancient Near East, "kingship is the linchpin of order—it holds the world together—kingship brings order and order requires kingship."[38] Though humankind, when described as God's image, is given royal status of sorts, the very democratization of the concept subverts the concept inherent in ancient kingship.[39] In the Babylonian creation account, creation brings order and is climaxed by Marduk being declared king of the gods. In Genesis, creation also brings order, and the climax is God resting, which I have suggested implies his ruling. De Jong extends this concept from God's rest to Israel's Sabbath observance when he notes, "The Sabbath brings order, order requires the Sabbath"—pertaining exclusively to Israel, as Sabbath is a covenant feature and the sign of the covenant.[40] The covenant conceptually takes the place

---

[37]De Jong, "Seventh Day in Genesis 2:2-3."

[38]De Jong, "Seventh Day in Genesis 2:2-3," 17.

[39]Brent Strawn, "From *Imago* to *Imagines*: The Image(s) of God in Genesis," in *The Cambridge Companion to Genesis*, ed. Bill T. Arnold (Cambridge: Cambridge University Press, 2022), 211-35, here 217.

[40]De Jong, "Seventh Day in Genesis 2:2-3," 18. In fairness, it should be noted that de Jong is more interested in the Sabbath observance derived from the seventh day as playing this role and ties these ideas to the Priestly writer.

We cannot draw conclusions about whether Sabbath understanding was drawn from Genesis or shaped Genesis because, of course, when Genesis was written, Israelites were already observing the Sabbath. I am inclined to the view that Israel saw the foundation of Sabbath thinking as going all the way back to creation and framed the account in Genesis with that in mind.

126   NEW EXPLORATIONS IN THE LOST WORLD OF GENESIS

of kingship; and Sabbath, as the sign of the covenant, indicates the centrality of the concept of rule rather than relaxation. De Jong considers this to encapsulate the theology of the writers of the Old Testament, not to be just a later idea.

In the ancient world, kingship was a gift from heaven to bring order on earth. Kingship is not viewed that way in the Old Testament, but Sabbath is given that role for Israel. Covenant defines order for Israel, and the Sabbath is the sign of the covenant (Ex 31:13-17). The idea that Sabbath is the centerpiece of order stands as yet another piece of evidence that order is the focus of the work of creation. The interconnections of order, rest, and temple are the basis for seeing the idea of God's rule as an intrinsic part of this ideological construct.

9. It appears that Jewish interpretation, as evidenced in the New Testament and in the Mishnah, focuses entirely on resting from work. Did the Jews outside the Old Testament ever understand the seventh day in terms of God's rule? Among the Dead Sea Scrolls were several fragments of a work designated the Songs of the Sabbath Sacrifice (4Q400–407). In these liturgical pieces, the focus is consistently on God's rule, his kingdom, and his administration of his kingdom.[41] The emphasis on rule in connection to Sabbath liturgy is suggestive, but these songs make no reference to God's rest or to human rest, so one must connect the dots because it is not explicit. Another work, the Damascus Document, contains a lengthy description of behavior related to Sabbath (CD VI–VII) and focuses attention on doing justice (thus reflecting the concerns of Is 58) but also has sections detailing what activities are and are not acceptable (CD X–XII).[42] In line with the latter, the Mishnah's attention is primarily on the sorts of work that

---

[41]Note particularly 4Q401:1, "praises of your kingship"; 4Q401:3, "recount the splendour of his kingdom"; 4Q403:31, "magnify the King of glory"; 4Q403:34, God of gods, king of kings. Translations from Florentino García Martínez and Eibert J. C. Tigchelaar, *The Dead Sea Scrolls Study Edition* (Grand Rapids, MI: Eerdmans, 1998), 2:807-37.

[42]Translations in Martínez and Tigchelaar, *Dead Sea Scrolls Study Edition*, 1:559-61, 567-71. The latter is also the focus of Jubilees (chap. 2).

Genesis 1: Cosmic Temple and Rest

cannot be done.[43] I have not been able to find much that moved beyond that focus in Jewish thought, with the more recent exception of Rabbi Samuel Hirsch's view that Sabbath was intended for humans to acknowledge God as Creator and to accede to his authority. "On each Sabbath man restores the world to God, as it were, and thus proclaims that he enjoys only a borrowed authority."[44]

10. *The term* šabbāt *is widely recognized to refer to ceasing, and that is the only term for divine resting in the seven-day account. What is the support for divine rest in Genesis being connected to divine rule?* I addressed this question briefly in *The Lost World of Genesis One*, but it calls for more attention.[45] My contention is that the rest on the seventh day in Genesis, while it explicitly represents only *disengagement* (i.e., ceasing) from the process of inaugurating order (whether through conflict with other deities or not), is more importantly an expression of *engagement* as the deity takes his place at the helm to maintain an ordered, secure, and stable cosmos.

Discussion must begin with the seventh day of the creation week, on which God ceased (*šabbāt*) his ordering of creation (Gen 2:1-3), but it cannot end there. Genesis 1–2:4 neither explains the significance of God's rest nor offers an explicit connection to God's rule or to Sabbath as a religious observance. Though these therefore cannot figure prominently in the rhetorical strategy of Genesis, we soon learn that cessation is not the only aspect of God's rest on the seventh day. We discover from Exodus 20:8-11 that when God ceased, he also rested (*nwḥ*) by taking up his residence. The next piece is added in Psalm 132:14, where we find that God rests (*nwḥ*) in the temple, and it is specified that rest is indicative of his rule. God's rest is therefore not in a bed but on his

---

[43]Efraim Gottlieb, "Sabbath," in *Encyclopedia Judaica*, 2nd ed. (Jerusalem: Keter, 2007), 17:618. See also Lawrence Schiffmann, "Sabbath," in *Encyclopedia of the Dead Sea Scrolls* (Oxford: Oxford University Press, 2000), 2:805-7. For a helpful summary through the ages, see Ezra Millgram, *Sabbath: The Day of Delight* (Philadelphia: JPS, 1944), 211-56.

[44]Gottlieb, "Sabbath," 619. Rabbi Hirsch was a nineteenth-century philosopher.

[45]*LWGI*, 73.

128 NEW EXPLORATIONS IN THE LOST WORLD OF GENESIS

throne.[46] We can thereby infer that God has created the world with the intention of ruling over it and dwelling within it in the midst of his people (Ps 132:14—"I have desired it"). All of this demonstrates that Sabbath rest is misunderstood if it is only considered in terms of disengagement (*šabbāt*). God disengages from the ordering of creation because he is ready to take up his rule as he maintains order in the cosmos and among humanity. He is the source and center of order.

We might even consider whether the verb *šbt* might have a further nuance.[47] Rather than simply "ceasing," which would have meaning in relation to a previous activity, a translation like "pausing" would recognize it as a transitionary reflection of a temporary posture that implies resumption at a later time.[48] If this is viewed in the context of order bringing, God pauses on the seventh day as he takes up his rest and then continues bringing and sustaining order. This idea of *šbt* would make good sense of Genesis 8:22, where the main features of order will never again pause as they did in the flood, when order was temporarily suspended.[49]

Two observations can be made about such pauses that highlight why humans might have considered them to be problematic. First, during such pauses in order bringing, no advances are being made. When people pause from their work, for example, they are pausing

---

[46]Since Gen 2:1-3 speaks only of God ceasing, it is not interested in the question of where he rests. That is a question that arises when the verb *nwḥ* is introduced. I continue to maintain that the deeply ingrained cultural concepts would have naturally implied a temple imagery when the rest of God was noted.

[47]For an extensive discussion of the semantic elements of *šbt* in connection with both Hebrew *nwḥ* and Akkadian *šabattu*, see Jon D. Levenson, *Israel's Day of Light and Joy* (University Park, PA: Eisenbrauns, 2024), 17-48.

[48]Hebrew usage shows both permanent and temporary cessation as contextual possibilities. In most of the seventy-one occurrences, the stoppage is temporary, since resumption is anticipated, but in some it is clearly permanent (e.g., 2 Kings 23:11; Is 13:11; 17:3). Perhaps the pausing on the seventh day is more like a teaser left to be picked up in Exodus.

[49]Suggested to me by J. Harvey Walton. We might compare how modern races that take place over several days are managed (such as the Iditarod or the Tour de France). At the end of each day, there is a pause, during which time no one can advance as the status quo is maintained.

Genesis 1: Cosmic Temple and Rest 129

from their normal order-bringing activities. The ancient Israelites would have viewed work as order-bringing activity, and pausing, particularly in the agricultural work, could be disruptive rather than a welcome relief. That is, pursuing God's order may at times require some sacrifice regarding our own pursuits of order that brings our own benefit.

The second observation is based on the premise that order must be actively maintained. Consequently, when order bringing pauses, there is danger of collapse into a liminal state (nonorder). For example, in the sabbatical year the land is given rest. During that year, it is not producing a planted crop. This not only maintains a status quo but also represents the collapse into a liminal state—the land is not producing food (Ex 23:10; Lev 25:1-7). This is particularly the case with regard to the land lying fallow during the exile to make up the neglected sabbatical years (2 Chron 36:21). Yet, the sabbatical year is designed to bring order for others—again showing a humanitarian focus.

Returning to Genesis 8:22, the flood brought a return to the liminal state when order was suspended. Given these observations, we may consider the idea that *šbt* represents a pause at a particular juncture. The status quo provides no advancement of order, and there is danger of a lapse into nonorder. All of these show that disregarding order-bringing activities that we pursue for our personal benefit can bring a certain level of jeopardy, but that is the very point as people are called to give up their own benefits to pursue benefits for others and for God's kingdom.

It is therefore not surprising that God provides rest (*hēnîaḥ* > *nwḥ*, "stability, security"; Deut 3:20; Josh 1:13; 21:44; 2 Sam 7:1; 1 Kings 5:4) for his people (rather than people depending on themselves to provide for themselves). In similar fashion, this is not the provision of disengagement (leisure, relaxation, sleep), but their rest gives freedom to engage in life under God's protection and provision. Consequently, we might infer that Sabbath theology was intended to turn the Israelites'

130 New Explorations in the Lost World of Genesis

attention away from their natural impulse to try to work to preserve order in their lives and instead focus on God as the source and center of order.

11. How should we think about Sabbath as we factor in the New Testament and think about application today? One of the first payoffs of understanding rest as indicative that a desired level of order has been achieved is that when we read of Jesus' offer of rest in Matthew 11:28, we can now understand better what he was talking about. The rest he offers is not about relaxation (obvious from "take my yoke upon you") but about the stability and security of ordered kingdom life. We can also understand the discussion of Hebrews 3–4 as referring to the yet-to-be-established full order of the kingdom that will characterize new creation.[50] Rest is all about order.

This approach also tracks well with the comments about the Sabbath made by Jesus in the discussion in the grain fields. "The Sabbath was made for man" can be seen as referring to the opportunity it offered for readjusting our perspective on God as the source and center of order in our lives. Jesus' identification as Lord of the Sabbath is indicative of how he, as God incarnate, is the source and center of order. In fact, all things cohere in him (Col 1). In accordance with Deuteronomy 5, Jesus indicates that the Sabbath stands for freedom, not slavery.

When Jesus heals on the Sabbath, it is justified, since these are actions that bring God's order into play.[51] Consequently, doing good on the Sabbath is most appropriate (again, Is 58), and the Father is always at work maintaining his order in the cosmos. His rest is his rule as he maintains order. We do not imitate his rest/rule; we participate in it rather than in pursuing our own order.

I am therefore not convinced by those who think of the seven-day account only as part of a pattern for the human workweek. Likewise,

---

[50]I have been appreciably informed and instructed by the work of Jon Laansma.

[51]Man with a shriveled hand (Mt 12:9-14; Mk 3:1-6; Lk 6:6-11); woman crippled by a spirit (Lk 13:10-17); man with swelling (Lk 14:1-5); pool of Bethesda (Jn 5:1-18).

Genesis 1: Cosmic Temple and Rest 131

I find inadequate the view that Sabbath rest reflects God's understanding that we all need downtime, since that becomes simply practical psychology with no obvious theological aspect.[52] Furthermore, it is misguided to focus our attention only on questions such as whether we are *required* to observe the Sabbath. We should not be approaching it in regard to legal entailments. Instead, we should be incorporating the very ideas underlying the Sabbath into our thinking about God's role in our lives. We unfortunately follow the Pharisees when we consider only what we are allowed or not allowed to do on the Sabbath. As noted earlier, Sabbath observance means stepping back from our own attempts to control our lives (through our "work" especially) as a means to acknowledging that God is the one truly in control (as he demonstrated at creation and in the exodus). It involves turning our attention to active acknowledgment of God (worship) and kingdom work (service in his name). It addresses the important question of who is in control of our lives and our world. In that way, I agree with Mark Buchanan: "We resist that which six days of coming and going, pushing and pulling, dodging and weaving, fighting and defending have bred into us. What we deny ourselves is all our well-trained impulses to get and to spend and to make and to master."[53]

The application question, then, is not about what we are allowed or not allowed to do. It is a question of whether God is worthy of our focused attention, and it gives us an opportunity to consider how our kingdom work is doing. It is about God being with us and about our looking to God as the one who brings order rather than our own efforts. This sense of order—this rest—has a positive sense to it. Buchanan points to a line from J. R. R. Tolkien that describes Rivendell, where for the hobbits, "all fear and anxiety was lifted from their minds.

---

[52]J. Harvey Walton (personal communication) offered the additional perspective that in an agro-pastoral society, taking a day off when the harvest clock is ticking is undesirable and could jeopardize the harvest. There is a reason why they had to be coerced and threatened to do it.

[53]Mark Buchanan, *The Rest of God* (Nashville: Nelson, 2006), 12.

The future, good or ill, was not forgotten, but ceased to have power over the present."[54]

The theology I have derived from the Old Testament provides the basis for helping us to understand the New Testament, not the other way around. That is, if we had only the New Testament, we could not use that to reconstruct the Sabbath theology that I have drawn from the Old Testament. Moreover, we can now see that it plays a significant role in the overarching theology I earlier proposed. God's rest is among us, and his rule is over us. It is the foundation of what I call an Immanuel theology, as it expresses the significance of God's presence with us.[55]

---

[54]Buchanan, *Rest of God*, 125.

[55]For my sermon explaining Immanuel theology, see "Immanuel Theology: What God Has Always Wanted- Dr. John Walton," YouTube, March 14, 2019, 40:49, www.youtube.com /watch?v=knyUtOf_O6s. For a published summary, see John H. Walton, *Old Testament Theology for Christians*, 27-28, or John Walton and Kim Walton, *Bible Story Handbook* (Wheaton, IL: Crossway, 2010), 28-30.

5

Genesis 2

The Garden and the Trees

SUMMARY OF PREVIOUS MATERIAL

I gave little attention to the garden and the trees in *The Lost World of Adam and Eve*. Proposition 13 discussed the garden as sacred space, that is, a place of God's presence, and the source of fertility. For the former, the most important information derives from the widely recognized use of Eden imagery in the tabernacle, as well as the recognition that gardens are connected to sacred space in the ancient Near East. I offered documentation both in modern scholarship and in earliest interpretations. Such evidence could be multiplied exponentially. For example, in the Dead Sea Scrolls, 4Q265:14 already anticipates the references I mentioned in Jubilees as it indicates that the Garden of Eden is holy as well as every shoot in it.[1]

In early Christian interpretation, Ephrem the Syrian (fourth century) also spoke of the Garden of Eden as a tabernacle and Adam and Eve as priests.[2] This shows that similar ideas occurred early in

---

[1]Similar statements in Jubilees 3:12. See Jeremy D. Lyon, *The Genesis Creation Account in the Dead Sea Scrolls* (Eugene, OR: Pickwick, 2019), 166-67. Note, however, that these sorts of statements are generally tied to primordial perfection, a concept I will reject.

[2]Ephrem the Syrian, *Hymns of Paradise* 3.16; C. Rebecca Rine, "Interpretations of Genesis 1–2 Among the Nicene and Post-Nicene Fathers," in *Since the Beginning: Interpreting Genesis 1 and 2 Through the Ages*, ed. Kyle R. Greenwood (Grand Rapids, MI: Baker, 2018), 121-45, here 139; Gary A. Anderson, *The Genesis of Perfection: Adam and Eve in Jewish and Christian Imagination* (Louisville, KY: Westminster John Knox, 2001), 56-57.

Christian history. I am not suggesting that since a respected theologian such as Ephrem said it, it must be right. That is not how we validate interpretation. One could find numerous other points that Ephrem made that we would not find acceptable. For example, he extended the comparison between Eden and the tabernacle by indicating that the tree of the knowledge of good and evil should be understood as a gate to the inner court and that the fruit should be considered as the veil of the temple, and further that the special trees of Eden were the cross. It is clear, then, that Ephrem was using interpretive methods that most scholars would be uncomfortable with today, so citing him in support of some ideas we might happen to share superficially is not a method that has integrity.

I also presented evidence of the significance of gardens connected to temple and palace in the ancient world, with archaeological and literary evidence presented. This included discussion of sacred trees found in ancient Near Eastern literature and iconography, particularly the Neo-Assyrian motif of (presumably) a date palm flanked by genies, which I proposed represented world order. In the Garden of Eden, however, these trees find a different significance in that they represent the presence of God by symbolizing those aspects of order that are characteristic of deity.

Since I had suggested that Adam and Eve were not referred to in Genesis 1 (where corporate humanity was the topic of discussion), and that therefore Adam and Eve were not necessarily presented as the first and only of their species, I had to address the question of what significance Adam and Eve had (if not biological). In light of the recognition that the Garden of Eden was sacred space, parallel to the later tabernacle and temple, I proposed that Adam was given the task of serving as a priest in sacred space (with Eve later to join him in that task). I gave evidence for this in analysis of the verbs in Genesis 2:15. I further discussed the problem of Eve in a priestly role since Israel did not permit women to be priests. For a model, I turned instead to the idea

Genesis 2: The Garden and the Trees

of Israel (men and women alike) as a kingdom of priests. I suggested that when the text said it was not good for man to be alone, the focus was neither psychological nor biological but pertained to the monumental task of caring for sacred space. My conclusion, therefore, was that the reason Adam and Eve became the topic of discussion was not that they were the first and only of their species (biological criterion) but that they represented people now in relationship to God, serving in his presence (theological criterion).

New Explorations

Garden as sacred space. In 2013, my friend and colleague Daniel Block published an article debating whether Eden could be identified as a temple.[3] He conceded that the tabernacle and temple were characterized by Edenic features but was not willing to accept that Eden should therefore be considered sacred space. He proposed that the design of the tabernacle and temple were built on the platform of creation theology but rejected the conclusion that the creation account in Genesis was therefore built on the platform of temple theology. He objected to reading Genesis in light of later texts,[4] but, of course, one could legitimately question whether these *are* later texts. His position therefore depends on a particular dating of the texts, which remains debatable.

Nevertheless, Block's analysis rightly identified some of the more questionable connections that scholars have at times made between Eden and the tabernacle/temple. Some of these were tenuous to begin with (and not connections that I had accepted), and, as Block pointed out in detail, they do not stand up to scrutiny. Yet, at the same time, even as weak links can be recognized for what they are and discarded, that does not mean the whole theory would collapse. Demonstrating

---

[3]Daniel I. Block, "Eden: A Temple? A Reassessment of the Biblical Evidence," in *From Creation to New Creation: Biblical Theology and Exegesis*, ed. Daniel Gurtner and Benjamin Gladd (Peabody, MA: Hendrickson, 2013), 3-29.

[4]Block, "Eden: A Temple?," 20-21, 26. He refers to the comparison of Eden to sacred space as a "nonreciprocating equation."

that some of the individual pieces of evidence can each be questioned, and some rejected, is not the same thing as proving that Eden is not considered a temple. The strongest evidence for Eden's sacred status is the four rivers flowing from it.[5] Furthermore, I find the ancient Near East evidence that I presented in *The Lost World of Adam and Eve*, which he does not address, to have a significant contribution to make to the question of whether the garden can be identified as sacred space of some sort. In the end, I welcome the way that Block's critique can bring further nuancing, but I do not find his objections convincing enough to discard the identification of Eden as sacred space in Genesis.

Additional and extensive refinements are called for in response to the research of J. Harvey Walton.[6] Rather than viewing the garden as sacred space in which God dwells in the human realm, he suggests that the garden represents the converse, that is, humans dwelling in the divine realm, which is located at the source of the four rivers.[7] Here is his summary:

---

[5]I discussed this in detail in *LWAE*, proposition 13; see also Ezek 47. Block addresses it briefly in "Eden: A Temple?," 12-13, but does not really offer a different reading.

[6]J. Harvey Walton, "Knowing Good and Evil: Values and Presentation in Genesis 2–4" (PhD diss., University of St Andrews, 2023), http://hdl.handle.net/10023/27738.

[7]Walton, "Knowing Good and Evil," 76-79. Both El in the Ugaritic epics and the flood hero in Gilgamesh, Ūta-napišti, dwell at the mouth of the rivers in the divine realm. As a *liminal* divine realm, it should not be confused with the heavenly dwelling of God. It is remote and isolated but not solely in the spiritual realm. Therefore it is not contradictory that known rivers (Tigris and Euphrates) should flow from it.

EXCURSUS 2: THE RELATIONSHIP BETWEEN THE DIVINE REALM AND HUMAN ORDER

J. HARVEY WALTON

Christian theology is frequently inclined to define *order* as more or less synonymous with the divine experience of the world. Order exists where God lives and manifests when God's will is carried out. Nonorder or disorder, in this way of thinking, needs to originate through sources of agency other than God, whether human or demonic. This theocentric conception of order leads directly to the idea that the place where the gods live—the divine realm in heaven or the temple on earth—is a place of consummate order and a place in which any order-seeking human would desire to live. In this way of thinking, access to such spaces is a blessing that is limited to a highly privileged few but that

Genesis 2: The Garden and the Trees

anyone would want and would do anything in their power to receive.

In both the ancient Near East and the Old Testament, however, order is anthropocentric, not theocentric; it is defined by the *human* experience of the *human* world. The gods are the source of the world order and are actively involved in sustaining it, but they can also act in ways that are contrary or antithetical to order. Gods, including Yahweh, can and do serve as agents of chaos.[1] The human order is defined in social and political terms, usually founded on a city (i.e., Jerusalem or Babylon), usually at the center of an empire, and usually involving an ethnic distinction (i.e., the "black-headed people" in Assyria or the descendants of Jacob in Israel). These social and political structures are what order-seeking humans desire and what they will do anything in their power to gain or retain.

The temple is the throne of the god on earth and the source from which order radiates, but the temple itself is not a place of human order. Things and places that are *holy*—or, in the polytheistic ancient Near East, things or places that have qualities of divinity—are effectively *removed from* the order of the human world, forbidden from human use or interaction. Because the temple is outside the human world, it is a dangerous place and not somewhere that order-seeking humans would desire to live. The interior of the temple—a large building with tiny windows set high on the walls (1 Kings 6:4)—is an alien region of darkness and smoke (e.g., Ps 97:2), hostile and inhospitable to human life. Humans do desire *access* to the presence of God, to present offerings and receive blessings (the meaning of, e.g., Ps 27:4; 84:4), but they do not want to take up residence in the temple's holy place and live with God as a roommate.

Because the divine realm is removed from the social and political realms of human order, as far as humans are concerned it is a place of nonorder, comparable to the wilderness, the sea, the mountains, or the netherworld. A human who is translated into the divine realm, such as Enoch, Elijah, or the Mesopotamian flood hero Uta-napišti, has to leave the human world behind, just as a human who is exiled or dies must also. Because the human world is the place where humans experience their ideal state of being—in other words, where they experience order—leaving that place behind is always an undesirable experience, regardless of where they go after they leave. Even if the place they wind up in is not objectively unpleasant—as seen in the netherworld in Egypt, Uta-napišti's island in Gilgamesh, or Yahweh's audience chamber in Exodus 24:9-11—it still lacks the ordered structures of the human world and is therefore less desirable than the human world.

Human order is found in human social and political structure, not in manifested divine will and not in pleasant or tolerable human experience. When the people of Israel are exiled to Babylon at the will of the deity, they are suffering a state of nonorder, which is a cause for lament, even if they are objectively doing well for themselves (e.g., Nehemiah). A human in the divine realm, even if they were to enjoy a comfortable or privileged existence there, would feel the same. A human in the divine realm does not become a participant in some kind of theocentric frame of the world order; they are simply removed from their proper place and lose the ability to participate in and benefit from the anthropocentric order to which they belong. The divine realm is not where human order can be found or the desirable state of human existence can be achieved.

---

[1] Note examples such as the flood or the exile.

In this view, the garden represents a liminal place for humans.[8] This shift offers a significant challenge for interpreters who not only adopt the idea that Eden should be equated with the tabernacle/temple but then extrapolate other ideas from that. Specifically, such interpreters contend if Eden is sacred space, there are implications of covenant stipulations and the characteristic emphasis on holiness. I had not proposed such extrapolation, and the text of Genesis is silent on those issues.[9]

Still, this shift from God dwelling in the human realm to humans dwelling in the divine realm calls for some revision in the position as I articulated it. We can begin with Walton's description of how this change affects our understanding of the significance of the garden scenario. That is, it is precisely the understanding that Eden is in the divine realm that leads to the recognition that Israelite readers would have considered the divine realm to not be a place for humans to find order.

> Human visitors to the divine realm include the elders of Israel in Exodus 24:9-11, Isaiah in Isaiah 6:1-4, and Moses and Elijah in Exodus 19 and 1 Kings 19, respectively. All of them are there for an audience with God, and the venture is depicted as somewhat hazardous (Exod 19:21-25; 24:11; Isa 6:5). Humans do not desire the divine realm because the divine realm is not *safe* for them.[10]

The upshot of this discussion is that if Eden represents humans situated in the divine realm rather than God dwelling in the human realm, a priestly role for Adam and Eve that I previously had proposed becomes less plausible, because priests have a role only in the latter

---

[8]Ziony Zevit, *What Really Happened in the Garden of Eden?* (New Haven, CT: Yale University Press, 2013), 118; Walton, "Knowing Good and Evil," 74.

[9]Walton, "Knowing Good and Evil," 75.

[10]Walton, "Knowing Good and Evil," 133. Besides these biblical examples, he points out that in ANE literature, neither Gilgamesh nor Adapa wishes to remain in the divine realm—they find it an uncomfortable and unnatural place.

Genesis 2: The Garden and the Trees

model.[11] Furthermore, once this shift is made, we see an alternative to the general assumption that Eden represents a pristine, desirable place for humans to live. Christian traditions have treated it as just that as well as a state to which we long to return (for further discussion see below, "Is Eden paradise?"). Walton takes a contrasting position, maintaining that the very point of the narrative is that life in the divine realm, with its concomitant immortality, does not bring order conducive to humans. Given this revision, we are compelled to reconsider the role and significance of Adam and Eve.

We can still think of the garden as sacred space in the general sense that it is in the divine realm. That two of the named rivers are known geographically (Tigris and Euphrates) does not resolve the question whether the garden is in the divine realm or the human realm. The differentiating line between the two realms is not as clear cut in the ancient world. For example, in Gilgamesh, Uta-napišti is dwelling in the divine realm, yet Gilgamesh can get to it and it has connections to features of terrestrial geography. It is a liminal divine realm and not the place where the gods dwelt. The important aspect of the discussion is not about actually locating it but in characterizing it. Is it idyllic or undesirable? What are the human roles? As I become more inclined to view the garden as in the divine realm, it is therefore important to turn attention to those human roles. If the significance of Adam and Eve is not found in a priestly role, what is it?

The role of Adam and Eve in the garden. Since I have maintained that Adam and Eve are not important biologically, that is, not the first and only of the species from whom all humans biologically descend, I have considered the question of why they are important in the text. Why are they singled out for attention? As noted at the beginning of

---

[11]This should be qualified as true in the ANE. By the Hellenistic period, Jews imagined a functioning priesthood in heaven represented in individuals such as Melchizedek or Enoch. The first evidence of this concept is in the third century BC, so I would not assume it as being reflected in Genesis.

140   NEW EXPLORATIONS IN THE LOST WORLD OF GENESIS

this chapter and in my past work (*LWAE*, proposition 12), I had previously proposed that it was because of the priestly role that they were given, serving in sacred space, Eden.

In contrast, Walton addresses this question by raising the issue of whether we should view Eden as a temple garden, as I had proposed, or, alternatively, as a monumental garden adjoining a royal palace.[12] Both are restricted space in their own way, but they should not be conflated.[13] He reasons that if Eden is in the divine realm, then the garden is more like a palace garden, "intended to represent royal imagery rather than sacred imagery." He adds the distinction, "Temples are the residences of the gods in the *human* world." In his view, "Eden is in the divine realm, and the residences of gods in the divine realm are palaces, not temples."[14] Palace gardens must also be cared for and served—the job of wardens.[15] These are order-bringing and order-maintaining activities. He additionally concludes, "The fertility of the garden is symbolic of the order and stability that the king causes to flourish throughout the empire. . . . Planting a garden is thus symbolic of establishing and sustaining the royal order of empire."[16]

What advance does this represent in our interpretation of Eden and the human role in it? If the garden is being presented in connection with royal imagery and is located in the divine realm, then

---

[12]Biblical references to palace gardens occur in 1 Kings 21:2; 2 Kings 21:18, 26; 25:4; Neh 3:15; Jer 39:4; 52:7. There are no biblical references to temple gardens.

[13]We might well wonder whether at times a single garden would be shared in some way by palace and temple, but Walton notes that they have different symbolic significances: a temple garden provides food for the gods; a palace garden is a monument to honor the king.

[14]Walton, "Knowing Good and Evil," 77.

[15]Neh 2:8 identifies Asaph as the keeper (using the same term, *šmr*, as in Gen 2:15) of the king's garden—and, as Walton points out, he is not a priest ("Knowing Good and Evil," 78).

[16]Walton, "Knowing Good and Evil," 78. His research is supported by Terje Stordalen, *Echoes of Eden: Genesis 2–3 and Symbolism of the Eden Garden in Biblical Hebrew* (Leuven: Peeters, 2000), 95, 97, 101; Mirko Novák, "The Artificial Paradise: Programme and Ideology of Royal Gardens," in *Sex and Gender in the Ancient Near East: Proceedings of the 47th Rencontre Assyriologique Internationale*, ed. Simo Parpola and Robert M. Whiting (Helsinki: Neo-Assyrian Text Corpus Project, 2022), 443-60, here 452.

Genesis 2: The Garden and the Trees   141

adjustments must be made in how we view the role of humans in Genesis 2. We therefore now have two alternative roles before us: priests or wardens (see Asaph, Neh 2:8). These roles differ in their particulars even though they share some overlapping similarities. Priests preserve the sanctity of God's dwelling among humans by preserving integrity to the rituals and maintaining the required order, which, if violated, may cause the deity to remove his presence. No threats of defilement or abandonment would exist if Eden were in the divine realm, and no such threat is apparent in Genesis, thus making the need for a priestly role unnecessary.[17] Our alternative category, warden, is an administrative role (potentially reflected in the task of naming the animals in Gen 2), not servitude, but it also does not assume a threat to order as a priest's role might. Priests protect against defilement; Genesis 2–3 contains no language related to defilement. A human warden in the divine realm would be serving in an order-bringing capacity.[18]

The verbs that define the human task in Genesis 2:15 can be explained in either model, but perhaps the point is not the role that Adam and Eve had but the idea that they were placed *there* (in the divine realm, outside the human realm). That is, the focus may not be on *what* the humans are doing and *why*, but *where* they are doing it, in which case, perhaps our attempts to identify the human role are misguided—simply asking the wrong question.[19] It does not matter what role they play—their significance is not found in their role.

Let us begin by returning to the identification of Adam and Eve as archetypes. If they truly function in the text to represent all humanity,

---

[17]Priests could still be seen as playing the role of mediator for the worship being given to the deity. This is the role that heavenly priests played in the Hellenistic period, but there is no sense of this in Genesis in general, and it is not reflected in the verbs of Gen 2:15.

[18]In Neo-Assyrian texts, the overseer of royal/temple property is the *rab bani*, who serves as the administrator of temple property, especially orchards. See A. Leo Oppenheim et al., eds., *The Assyrian Dictionary of the Oriental Institute of the University of Chicago* (Chicago: Oriental Institute, 1956–2010), vol. R, p. 4.

[19]J. Harvey Walton, personal communication.

as I have previously suggested, then they are not being presented as individuals who are singled out—they are more like conglomerates or aggregates. That is, as they are archetypes representing corporate humanity, the text is not interested in them as individuals (regardless of whether they are individuals or not). They are instead personifications of the human collective. What they are and do, humanity is and does. Genesis does not focus on their individual story—it is interested in giving our story. If that is the case, their role is no different from the role of all of us. J. Harvey Walton clarifies, "His name is 'human,' so his archetype is ontological, not social. Genesis 2 is placing 'human' in a cosmic hierarchy with gods and animals, not a social hierarchy with other kinds of humans and their respective duties."[20] Even when "Adam knew Eve his wife" (Gen 4:1 KJV), we could understand the text as saying, "humanity procreated"—that, after all, was the blessing bestowed on corporate humanity in Genesis 1.

The advantage of this view, that their individual role is insignificant to the passage, is that it overcomes two inherent problems that existed in my original support of a priestly role for Adam and Eve: (1) that priestly representation is different from archetypal representation, in which case I had to address two very different categories of representation; and (2) the disconnect found in that women could not be priests in Israel. The view as order-sustaining wardens in the divine realm currently strikes me as more sustainable, but the warden role would be incidental, not theologically significant. The alternative that Walton suggests is that their archetypal role conveys the idea that humanity is not suited to dwelling in the divine realm, that is, that the human search for order for themselves will not find resolution in the divine realm.[21] Their significance is not in their individuality, nor in their role, but in that they were there and that being there did not provide resolution. In this case, it is not a story of what

---

[20]J. Harvey Walton, personal communication.
[21]Walton, "Knowing Good and Evil," 133-34.

Genesis 2: The Garden and the Trees 143

humanity once had and lost. It is a vignette about where we belong (or not).

Herein lies the most important exegetical payoff. If their role were considered priestly in nature, as I previously maintained, it would have been a role that they had as *individuals* representing others in their service in sacred space. In the warden model, their significance is not as individuals but as archetypes, as elsewhere in the chapter. They are not distinct from other humans but archetypally represent humanity as the texts explore what is good for humanity (desirable, ordered).

Following that idea to the next logical step, if everything about Adam and Eve in Genesis 2–3 is about all of us in general and not about them in particular, then nothing depends on their being individuals who made one choice or another, who lived here or there. Some would claim that even if their individualism is not found in Genesis 2–3, it can be seen in Genesis 4–5, where they take a position in the genealogy. Yet, even there we could understand the genealogies as going back to the category of humanity (that is, humanity, or the human line, produced [named individuals]).[22] Most importantly, in Genesis 2–3, where the theology is generally located, their individualism is immaterial. What they do and experience, we all do and experience. Their ontology and destiny is our ontology and destiny.[23] The role that Adam is given is only to locate humanity in the divine realm in a subservient position to the deity. When he is driven out, it is not because he failed as a priest; it is because humanity finds the experience of dwelling in the divine realm unnatural and not a place where they will be able to find order. As Walton puts it, "living in the divine realm isn't really a privilege for humans. Genesis 2 is not a desirable condition."[24] This archetypal role will continue to have significance when we deal with Genesis 3 below.

---

[22]As an archetype, Adam is a generic human. That differs from an allegory, where he would represent an abstraction such as humanity.

[23]J. Harvey Walton, personal communication.

[24]J. Harvey Walton, personal communication. See Walton, "Knowing Good and Evil," 144.

144   NEW EXPLORATIONS IN THE LOST WORLD OF GENESIS

To conclude this discussion, Genesis 2 concerns issues of human *identity* (dust, rib) and considers the idea of human *location* in the divine realm.[25] The text is interested in the location as the divine realm (Gen 2:8-14) and in the naming of the animals (Gen 2:19-20). Aside from the general concepts of serving and keeping, no attempt is made to define the human role.

Tree of the knowledge of good and evil. In my publications, both in my Genesis commentary and in *The Lost World of Adam and Eve*, I made the case that this tree could be construed as a wisdom tree, based on the use of the terminology elsewhere (Deut 1:39; Is 7:15-16; 2 Sam 19:35; 1 Kings 3:9). Wisdom can be understood as the pathway to order, so the fruit of this tree was viewed as giving humans the autonomy to pursue order on their own terms rather than serving as order bringers working toward God's order.[26] I suggested that the "good and evil" pair reflected the idea of knowing what was desirable and undesirable for bringing order.

In Walton's dissertation, he offers a refinement that continues to associate the tree with order, but he chooses not to use the word *wisdom*. After all, the text could have called it a wisdom tree. Furthermore, when Eve identifies the fruit as desirable to make one wise, she does not use what may have been the expected word for wisdom (*ḥākam*) but instead uses a word usually associated with insight (*hiphil* stem of *śkl*).

Interacting with the information from the Gilgamesh Epic, Walton observes that the characteristic that transforms Enkidu from an uncivilized companion of animals to a true human, like a god, is reflected in the Akkadian term *ṭēmu*, often translated (inadequately) as

---

[25]On dust and Adam's rib, see chapter six below, under "Summary of Previous Material" and FAQ 2.

[26]Bendt Alster, *Wisdom of Ancient Sumer* (Bethesda, MD: CDL, 2005), 24, does not use the term *order* but encapsulates it well when he describes ancient wisdom as "the means by which to make the best out of life." Zevit cites wisdom as what helps people "gain mastery over their lives" (*What Really Happened*, 163).

Genesis 2: The Garden and the Trees   145

"intelligence." Following Tzvi Abusch, Walton offers a more suitable, expanded definition:

> "Intelligence" (*ṭēmu*) represents, not the esoteric wisdom of sages given to elites, but rather the capacity to design and execute complex strategies, and is not only common to all humanity but is arguably their defining feature. . . . *Ṭēmu* essentially represents the ability to establish order on the earth; it is the property that separates humans from animals, and also the property that separates civilized humans from the chaotic barbarians, both demonstrated by the transformation of Enkidu.[27]

He therefore opts to retain the word *knowledge* for the tree in Genesis, with the additional descriptors of *awareness* and *intelligence*, as he concludes that it is equivalent to *ṭēmu* as "the capacity to know what constitutes order in a manner appropriate to one's sphere of being."[28] The tree in Genesis that provides knowledge of what is good and bad therefore provides "awareness of which things are conducive to order and which things are not." Walton continues with an additional insight that offers important balance to how Genesis 2–3 is often treated:

> There is no need to try to establish "knowing good and evil" as belonging specifically to the moral sphere, the judicial sphere, the ritual sphere, the cultural sphere, or the sexual sphere; the concept is generic enough to be relevant and applicable to any or all of them. In Genesis 3, the specific context is "knowing how to put the world the way it ought to be" (the literal meaning of *ṭēmu*), and this context is established by the opening of the eyes,

---

[27]Walton, "Knowing Good and Evil," 148. He derives this definition from the extensive analysis of Tzvi Abusch, "Ghost and God: Some Observations on a Babylonian Understanding of Human Nature," in *Self, Soul and Body in Religious Experience*, ed. Albert I. Baumgarten, Jan Assmann, and Guy G. Stroumsa (Leiden: Brill, 1998), 363-83; see also Takayoshi M. Oshima, *Babylonian Poems of Pious Sufferers* (Tübingen: Mohr Siebeck, 2014), 246.
[28]Walton, "Knowing Good and Evil," 149.

146　New Explorations in the Lost World of Genesis

correcting nakedness, and becoming like [a] god, as seen also for Enkidu.[29]

Though his treatment is more nuanced and more connected to the ancient Near Eastern texts, the bottom line differs little from what I had previously suggested about the tree representing wisdom—a pathway to order. Moreover, he takes the logic one step further to suggest that Genesis is not a story that offers "an explanation for an undesirable state" (that is, how sin came into the world; see more in chapter 7, FAQ 4), instead offering "a devaluation of cultural ideals."[30] His proposal is that the ideals for bringing order that were elevated in Mesopotamian thinking are being systematically deconstructed in Genesis. Humanity has gained something that is positive—the knowledge that makes them "like god" (Gen 3:22). Following Ziony Zevit, Walton summarizes,

> It is godlikeness, not chaos and/or death, that is the concept that forms the subject of the narrative. But the literary focus is still not on the actions and events that produced godlikeness at some point in the past; the focus is instead on the relative value and utility of godlikeness, specifically its inability to produce order in the human world.[31]

God tells them that if they eat of the fruit, they will die. He does not threaten to drive them from the garden, though that is what he does to withhold the tree of life from them.[32] Most importantly for the narrator, they learn that they do not belong there; order for humans is not to be found by dwelling in the divine realm. At the same time, they gain godlikeness, yet also find that neither can that bring the sought-after order.

---

[29]Walton, "Knowing Good and Evil," 150.

[30]Walton, "Knowing Good and Evil," 168.

[31]Walton, "Knowing Good and Evil," 168; see Zevit, *What Really Happened*, 264.

[32]Ūta-napišti was granted eternal life in the realm of the gods, though there is no mention of a tree. Adam and Eve have access to the tree of life in the divine realm of the garden, and that could potentially be the source of immortality.

Genesis 2: The Garden and the Trees 147

Answers to Frequently Asked Questions

1. Should we consider the garden to be a pristine paradise? First, it needs to be understood that the Hebrew word used to refer to the Garden of Eden is *gān* ("garden"). The author does not use the late Hebrew word *pardēs*, which is a loanword from Old Persian (Avestan) and refers to a walled-off pleasure garden (see Eccles 2:5; Song 4:13; Neh 2:8).[33]

To understand how the idea of the Garden of Eden as paradise developed, we need to examine the etymology of the word *paradise*.[34] In the translation of Genesis 2 in the Septuagint, the word *paradeisos* was chosen to speak of the Garden of Eden. That is the Greek version of the same loanword from Old Persian, and it retains the same Persian meaning.[35] The English word *paradise*, taken from the Greek, took on additional meaning beyond the usage in Persian, Hebrew, Classical Greek, and Septuagint Greek and is epitomized in Dante's *Paradise* and Milton's *Paradise Lost*.

The extended meaning of *paradeisos* to *paradise* began appearing in the Hellenistic Greek of Second Temple Jewish literature (such as 2 Enoch 8:1-3; Jubilees 17:26; 1QH 8; 4 Ezra 8:52). It became prominent in the Roman Greek of the patristic literature, where it is used as a term for heaven, the dwelling place of God, and therefore also as a place of life after death.[36] That both Greek and Latin translations use

---

[33]One of many sources that provide this information is Bob Becking, "Once in a Garden: Some Remarks on the Construction of the Identity of Woman and Man in Genesis 2–3," in *Out of Paradise: Eve and Adam and Their Interpreters*, ed. Bob Becking and Susanne Hennecke (Sheffield: Sheffield Phoenix, 2011), 1-13, here 4-5.

[34]Note the caveat that even as we identify the etymology, lexical-semantic methodology maintains that etymology is an unreliable guide to meaning, since usage shifts over time.

[35]Also borrowed into Latin and used by Jerome in the Vulgate in Gen 2–3.

[36]G. W. H. Lampe, *Patristic Greek Lexicon* (Oxford: Clarendon, 1961), 1010-13, list hundreds of references that trace the evolving definition. Summaries of the development can be found in standard reference works such as Hugh Pyper, "Paradeisos," in *The Oxford Companion to Christian Thought*, ed. Adrian Hastings, Alistair Mason, and Hugh Pyper (Oxford: Oxford University Press, 2000), 514-15; and James Charlesworth, "Paradeisos," in *The Anchor Bible Dictionary*, ed. David Noel Freedman (New York: Doubleday, 1992), 5:154-55.

it for the Garden of Eden allows easy conflation that results in Eden being seen not only as a place of divine dwelling, or even the divine realm, but as a place of perfection, corresponding to the Greek idea of a primordial golden age.[37]

This summary demonstrates that the concept of paradise reflected in our modern picture of the Garden of Eden was a later development—a product of the Hellenistic world. Consequently, no evidence or logic supports the idea that Eden had this meaning in Genesis. The importance of this is that many of the theological assumptions that are made about Eden as being a place of perfection throughout the history of Christian interpretation cannot be sustained from the viewpoint of Genesis. While thinkers such as Augustine considered paradise to represent the ideal, it is more likely that Genesis, on the reading I have been offering, considered Eden to represent the divine realm, foreign and unnatural for human habitation.[38] If we are going to maintain a commitment to authors' intentions and the biblical context, Eden should not be viewed in an idealistic way.[39]

2. Are we heading back to Eden? This question follows immediately on the heels of the one just considered. One common theological perspective considers Eden and new creation to be bookends of history. This approach draws firm connections between protology (the study of the initial state) and eschatology (the study of the end times and the final state). Since the new creation is an ideal, pristine, or perfect state, this view considers Eden to be the same—a state to which humanity is being restored (derived from a doctrine of recapitulation). One of its primary advocates in early Christianity is Irenaeus in the second

---

[37]Rev 2:7 draws a connection between eschatology and protology, linking the Garden of Eden with the final state.

[38]This statement about Augustine is based on the sharp dichotomy drawn between the two cities in *City of God* (e.g., 14.28). See Willemien Otten, "The Long Shadow of Human Sin: Augustine on Adam, Eve and the Fall," in Becking and Hennecke, *Out of Paradise*, 29-49, here 45.

[39]Walton, "Knowing Good and Evil," 70-74.

Genesis 2: The Garden and the Trees 149

century. "According to Irenaeus' protological orientation, the desire for a comprehensive understanding of what *happened* in Jesus Christ, what *is* presently happening, and what *will* happen in the future, compels a re-reading and re-appropriation of the texts which attest to the *beginning*."[40]

I would contend that while we may legitimately see some parallels between the beginning and the end, beginning perhaps as early as Isaiah 51:3 and further developed in Revelation 21–22, they do not suggest that Eden represents a perfect state to which we will return.[41] We do well to observe recapitulating features, but that does not require the end to represent a return to the same state as the beginning. Moreover, we therefore cannot extrapolate from the end scenario (new creation) for defining the beginning scenario (Eden). Finally, it is important to note that conflating a supposed beginning with some future ideal end is not part of the philosophy/cosmology of the ancient Near East. Order is cyclical, not progressive, so there is no meaningful concept of end. Beginnings are chaotic, not pristine, and the closest concept of end they had in the ancient Near East was a return to chaos—for example, when kingship collapses.[42]

---

[40]*Against Heresies*. See Thomas Holsinger-Friesen, *Irenaeus and Genesis: A Study of Competition in Early Christian Hermeneutics* (Winona Lake, IN: Eisenbrauns, 2009), 33.

[41]In this I follow J. Richard Middleton, *A New Heaven and a New Earth: Reclaiming Biblical Eschatology* (Grand Rapids, MI: Baker, 2014), 171-72, 233-35.

[42]J. Harvey Walton, personal communication.

6

Genesis 2

Adam and Eve

SUMMARY OF PREVIOUS MATERIAL

In *The Lost World of Adam and Eve*, the main focus was developing the idea that Adam and Eve were to be understood as archetypes—that is, that what was important about them was not how they might be *different* from the rest of us (for example, in their activities or material origins) but in how they were the *same* as the rest of us. They were presented as representatives of humanity, as their names indicate. I further developed this in chapter five above. Their archetypal role does not settle the question of whether they were real people in a real past, and I am not trying to resolve that.

Major points made in connection with this included, first of all, that we have no reason to conclude that the humans created on day six in Genesis 1 were Adam and Eve. Genesis 1 is talking about the human race (a population, just as the birds, fish, and animals are populations) and does not specify that there are only two or what their names are. The literary divider in Genesis 2:4 offers ample reason to make a distinction between the seven-day account and Adam and Eve.[1]

A second aspect of the proposal was that once Adam and Eve are seen in isolation from day six, it is not clear that they were the only

---

[1] This is an observation that proceeds from the structure of the book, not from any theory of sources, which would be a different discussion.

Genesis 2: Adam and Eve 151

humans around. Several long-recognized elements in the text leave space for the possibility that others already existed (Cain's wife, Cain's fear that others would kill him, and that Cain builds a city—something one does not do for oneself). If others existed outside the garden, then Adam and Eve are not presented as the first and only members of the biological species.

This possibility opens up a third area of investigation introduced last chapter: If Adam and Eve were not the first and only members of the species, then what is their significance? This determination must be made from Genesis (as opposed to, say, from Romans), since that is the text we are dealing with. As it is, we are startled to find that Adam is clearly referred to only in passing in the rest of the Old Testament (leading off the genealogy in 1 Chronicles). Nothing else about him becomes a topic for conversation in the Old Testament.[2] The New Testament has more to say about Adam and Eve, and the various passages were treated in *The Lost World of Adam and Eve* to determine what they actually say and do not say. Regardless, there is no indication that Genesis has the same interest in Adam and Eve that the New Testament does. Any distinctive role of Adam (and presumably of Eve as his partner) pertains to their responsibility with regard to the garden (Gen 2:15). On the premise that the garden be considered sacred space, I suggested that their significance was in their role (see further discussion in chapter five above), which I had identified as priestly—serving sacred space and guarding its sanctity. Beyond that, the text focuses on the family (community) as an order-bringing institution. The text has no interest in whether Adam and Eve are the first and only of their species or whether there are other people around. It is just not a question that the text is addressing.

---

[2]Some believe that Hos 6:7 makes reference to him, but I agree with the majority of interpreters, who view Adam as a place name in that context.

A third investigation focused on the details of the formation of Adam and Eve respectively. Dust was interpreted to pertain to human mortality, not chemical composition or biological origins, and was therefore understood to represent an important aspect of Adam's archetypal role. He is dust, as all of us are (Ps 103:14 shows that Gen 3:19 does not refer just to Adam). Understanding of Eve is developed not through a surgical event (removal of a rib) but through a vision Adam has that clarifies her ontology. He sees himself cut in two, with one half becoming Eve. He therefore understands that they are ontological equals (bone of my bone, flesh of my flesh). It is not simply the removal of a rib. I addressed this through careful lexical analysis.

I drew conclusions in a number of areas. Regarding theology, I proposed that according to the Genesis account, people were created mortal (the significance of dust). This viewpoint is not contradictory to Paul's assertion in Romans 5:12. He indicates that humans are subject to death because of sin, but that does not imply that sin transformed people from immortal to mortal. Rather, we are subject to death because of sin, since the inevitability of death was the result of having been driven from the garden and being deprived access to the tree of life. Immortal people would have had no use for a tree of life, but mortal people would have their life sustained by it. Once it became inaccessible, natural mortality took its course, and death became inevitable—all because of sin, according to Paul's view.

A second conclusion pertained to the way we think about Genesis and science, particularly models of evolution. If Genesis is not offering a scientific account of human origins, then it cannot be making a truth claim that is incompatible with evolutionary theory. This posture does not attempt to defend the scientific viability of biological evolution; it merely addresses the question of whether Genesis could be seen as compatible with an evolutionary model.[3] This is an important question

---

[3]More on this in Gijsbert van den Brink, *Reformed Theology and Evolutionary Theory* (Grand Rapids, MI: Eerdmans, 2020).

Genesis 2: Adam and Eve   153

because evolution is the reigning scientific paradigm for biological origins. If dust is functioning archetypally to convey human mortality rather than offering a scientific view of human origins, then Genesis is not weighing in on scientific mechanisms. As long as God is seen as the Creator (even if evolution proposes how his work of creation proceeds), then those who feel compelled by the scientific evidence supporting biological evolution can also adopt the affirmations of Scripture. Such a decision would not require the choice between science and Scripture that many propose. There is no war between them and never was.[4]

Finally, the special creation of humanity can still be affirmed, not from Genesis 2 but harking back to Genesis 1. If, as suggested in previous chapters, creation is viewed as establishing order and connected to roles and functions, then giving humans the role of image bearers and order bringers is the most significant part of human creation. These related roles are not something that evolve; they can only be given by God. Giving them is the ultimate act of human creation, therefore representing an act of special creation.

New Explorations

Understanding of the negations. When reading the account in Genesis 2, it is striking that it begins with a deficiency, a negation.[5] In this way it parallels Genesis 1:2, which also begins with a deficiency that the rest of Genesis 1 resolves. The seven-day acts of bringing order indicate the power of creation as God brings order into a nonordered condition. In Genesis 2:5-6, the negation does not pertain to order in the cosmos but to terrestrial order, specifically the absence of agriculture and, more significantly, the absence of humanity.

---

[4]See more in chapter nine, FAQ 9. For a thoroughgoing investigation of the history of a supposed war between the Bible and science, see Derrick Peterson, *Flat Earths and Fake Footnotes: The Strange Tale of How the Conflict of Science and Christianity Was Written into History* (Eugene, OR: Cascade, 2021).

[5]These do not represent broken or disrupted order but areas where order has yet to be established.

154   New Explorations in the Lost World of Genesis

In Sumerian creation accounts, agriculture is one of the first gifts that the gods give to humankind.[6] If that represents how people commonly thought in the ancient world, this would be a logical progression in Genesis as elements of order are being considered in various areas. The absence of order in general was redressed in the seven days of Genesis 1, but now in Genesis 2 and following, a variety of negations circumscribe a discussion of what are the components of order in the terrestrial realm—the realm where people, as image bearers, have been given the role of order bringers. The first arena to be addressed is agriculture. Genesis 2–3 rectifies the deficiency noted in Genesis 2:5-6 by putting humans in place.[7]

Agriculture is only the first of a number of deficiencies that are identified in the text and for which remedies are then offered. These include:

- Not good for man to be alone (Gen 2:18): resolved by family/community[8]

- Naked and unashamed (suggesting lack of civilization; Gen 2:25): resolved by shame (which motivates civilized behavior associated with order) and clothing[9]

- Not being like God (Gen 3:5): resolved (see Gen 3:22) but inadequate for bringing order[10]

---

[6]Examples include the Royal Chronicle of Lagaš and the Dispute Between Ewe and Wheat, translations in Jan J. W. Lisman, *Cosmogony, Theogony and Anthropogony in Sumerian Texts* (Münster: Ugarit-Verlag, 2013). See discussion in Frans A. M. Wiggermann, "Agriculture as Civilization: Sages, Farmers, and Barbarians," in *The Oxford Handbook of Cuneiform Culture*, ed. Karen Radner and Eleanor Robson (Oxford: Oxford University Press, 2011), 663-89.

[7]This line of thinking has been developed in detail by J. Harvey Walton, "Knowing Good and Evil: Values and Presentation in Genesis 2–4" (PhD diss., University of St Andrews, 2023), http://hdl.handle.net/10023/27738.

[8]Note that "not good" is not the same as "evil" (Hebrew *raʿ*). The former indicates nonorder, while the latter pertains to disorder.

[9]Being naked and unashamed is characteristically a negative situation expressing the absence of civilized sensibilities. See Enkidu in the Gilgamesh Epic as an example.

[10]Becoming like God is a pursuit in a number of ANE epics, particularly Gilgamesh, Atrahasis, and Adapa. Adam and Eve are like God in the sense of being order bringers, but the

Genesis 2: Adam and Eve 155

Other Genesis contexts do not begin with a negation but consider ideas for order bringing that were popular ways of thinking in the ancient world, such as city building (Gen 4:17), developing the arts of civilization (Gen 4:20-21), and attempting to procure divine presence (Gen 11:1-9). Since these need to be developed, they imply that they were missing. J. Harvey Walton proposes that Genesis is subverting purportedly tried and true values, not by suggesting they are wrong but affirming that they are inadequate. He observes that this approach is similar to the subversion of values that characterizes Ecclesiastes (see excursus 1 in chapter one above).

Consequently, the negations, deficiencies, and ways that order is lacking provide an explicit guide to what the author of Genesis is seeking to communicate. It has been common in Christian interpretation to understand Genesis 1–11 as presenting various offenses. In contrast, I accept the view that the narrator is discussing where the highest form of order can be found as he is in conversation with the standard values of the ancient world. As each remedy is deemed inadequate, a void grows that is eventually to be filled with the covenant, God's ultimate mechanism for human order and identity.

The absent preposition in the Hebrew of Genesis 2:7 that is generally added in translations. In the discussion of human origins, it would not be an exaggeration to suggest that Genesis 2:7 is the centerpiece of modern debates between science and the Bible. This verse is used by those who contend for a special creation of Adam in their claim that the text portrays God as a craftsman forming the first human out of dust. This direct, hands-on activity of God is therefore seen as contradictory to the scientific evidence that humanity evolved, by ruling out that they emerged from a line of preexisting hominids. In this special-creation view, proponents think that the text is making a scientific affirmation concerning human origins, an affirmation that,

---

text clearly shows that they were not as much like God as they desired to be and as much as the fruit of the tree provided.

156   NEW EXPLORATIONS IN THE LOST WORLD OF GENESIS

while not couched in scientific terminology, is nevertheless biological or chemical in nature. In their view, the verse is seen as requiring biological discontinuity from any potential ancestors as it affirms what is understood to be a de novo (quick and complete) creation of humanity—no predecessors or processes. Genesis 2:7 thereby holds pride of place among arguments against evolution and is therefore central in the supposed conflict between the Bible and science regarding human origins.

According to Kathleen Crowther, this concept of God as craftsman became preeminent only in the Reformation period.

In the sixteenth century, both Lutheran and Catholic writers and artists began imagining God as a craftsman, shaping raw material into the perfect form of the human body. In contrast, their medieval counterparts had imagined God as an architect, a designer who carefully planned the measurements and proportions of the human body but did not get His hands dirty in the act of creation.[11]

In *The Lost World of Adam and Eve*, I presented information from the ancient Near East to contend that the focus of a statement such as Genesis 2:7 was human identity, not scientific human origins of a material nature. I am now able to advance that argument further from the details of the Hebrew text. Specifically, the Hebrew text does not have a preposition preceding the word *dust*. English translations have wavered between supplying "from" (NIV, NLT, NRSV) and "of"/"out of" (KJV, ESV, HCSB) as prepositions. Scholars who have grappled with the admitted absence of the preposition suggest that it is implied.[12] However, a detailed study of the intricacies of

---

[11]Kathleen Crowther, *Adam and Eve in the Protestant Reformation* (Cambridge: Cambridge University Press, 2010), 98.

[12]Bruce Waltke and Michael O'Connor, *Introduction to Biblical Hebrew Syntax* (Winona Lake, IN: Eisenbrauns, 1990), 174 (§10.2.3c, nos. 11-14), suggest that Gen 2:7 is a case of double accusatives that need to be translated with a preposition. Similar assessment can

Genesis 2: Adam and Eve 157

Hebrew grammar provides evidence that the more accurate translation would be, "The LORD God formed (the identity) of the (archetypal) human—dust of the earth."[13] It is appropriate at this point to note further that the early Greek translations have "And God formed man, dust from the earth."[14]

Consequently, there is another question that must be addressed. If the text does not indicate that man was created "from" the dust, then Genesis 2:7 cannot be a statement of special creation from a material point of view. It is rather a statement of identity. It is juxtaposed to the image of God identity given in Genesis 1, in that here it draws out the lowly mortality of humanity, which stands in contrast to the high calling of humanity's identity as image bearers.[15]

Some worry that the continuity of species inherent in evolutionary theory eliminates human particularism—that is, an ontological differentiation between humans and animals. They see this aspect as preserved in the idea that humanity is the result of special creation, a de novo act with no predecessors or continuity with previous lines of hominids. This often features prominently in arguments against evolutionary theory.[16]

---

be found in Paul Joüon and Takamitsu Muraoka, *Grammar of Biblical Hebrew* (Rome: Gregorian and Biblical Press, 2011), 423-24, §125v. Nevertheless, the syntax of Gen 2:7 is different from the other examples in that here both accusatives follow the verb, whereas in the other examples, the verb comes between the accusatives. Other options are shown in Waltke and O'Connor, *Introduction to Biblical Hebrew Syntax*, §10.2.3e, nos. 35-39. The only syntactically comparable example in which the verb is followed by the two nouns is Gen 42:25.

[13]The presence of a disjunctive accent over the word *ʾādām* suggests that instead of implying a preposition between two accusatives (*man* and *dust*), the phrase "dust from the earth" should be viewed as appositional. The various appositional functions are discussed in Joüon and Muraoka, *Grammar of Biblical Hebrew*, §131. Concerning the identity: "forming" (Hebrew root *yṣr*) is often more interested in identity than in shape. See Ps 103:14; Zech 12:2; and discussion in *LWAE*, 71-72.

[14]NET translation of *kai eplasen ho theos ton anthrōpon choun apo tēs gēs.*

[15]This is a similar contrast to that which is expressed in Ps 8.

[16]These are, of course, all modern issues and modern questions—ones that would not have occurred to people in the ancient world.

If we rule out Genesis 2:7 as an act of special creation (materially speaking), we can still find an act of special creation and human particularism in another passage. Here I refer to Genesis 1:26-28. The image of God was addressed above in chapter three, but here I pick up another thread of that discussion. It is undebated that the image of God distinguishes people from animals (evident in both Gen 1 and Gen 9). As noted earlier, some might consider the image to pertain to mental faculties that characteristically differentiate humans from animals (for example, self-awareness). Alternatively, I proposed that the image does not comprise such faculties; instead, it is defined by the role that humans are given—that of order bringers. This is a unique role of humanity and can only be given by God. Ability to bring order could potentially be seen as an evolved trait, but Genesis makes the point that this is a commissioning from God. Furthermore, such an endowment of role and purpose can now be understood as an act of creation. If, as I have maintained, creation pertains most importantly to ordering with a role and a purpose, then such ordering is what brings something into existence. As such, the designation as image of God is a special act of creation by God that defines human particularism.

Even for those who adopt an evolutionary model, such a perspective on human creation sees God as having a specific role in the essential creation of humans that evolution does not address—we were given a role by God that defines our identity and our purpose in his economy. That could be maintained even within a view of evolution of human species in biological continuity with previous species. Genesis 2:7 therefore does not offer an alternative view to evolutionary models.

It is now evident how important a role a simple preposition or its absence can play. This is a good example of the significance of the intricacies of Hebrew grammar. Something this small can influence how a biblical text is interpreted and its wider applications to the

Genesis 2: Adam and Eve 159

issues of our day. The lack of the preposition here means this passage cannot be used to support special material creation. On the other hand, however, it supports the idea of identity, which is a stronger theme throughout the opening chapters of Genesis.

Adam and Adapa. Above I suggested that the significance of Adam and Eve was not in their being the first and only of the species from whom all are genetically descended but in their archetypal role.[17] When we examine Mesopotamian literature, another perspective can be factored into our consideration: the concept of rhetorical ancestors. Even in modern times, we reflect a rhetorical understanding of ancestry when we speak of America's founding fathers. When we turn attention to Mesopotamian traditions, we find examples of this concept in stories of sages sent from the gods in primeval times to instruct humankind in the arts of civilization.[18] They are called the *apkallu*.[19] The first and most famous of the *apkallu* was Adapa, also known as one who lost human's chance for immortality.[20] Amar Annus has brought attention to the fact that Assyrian king Ashurbanipal portrayed himself as a descendant of

---

[17]S. Joshua Swamidass, *The Genealogical Adam and Eve: The Surprising Science of Universal Ancestry* (Downers Grove, IL: InterVarsity Press, 2019), has used population genetics to propose that all modern humans can be biological descendants of a single more recent couple, not the first of the species. I can neither affirm nor contest his findings, technical as they are, but they reflect a conviction that the Bible claims that all humans must be biological descendants of a single couple, a conviction I do not hold.

[18]In one broken text from Qumran (4Q530, column 2, line 7) that preserves a section of the book of Enoch (Book of Giants), the Watchers are portrayed as gardeners. This sort of activity is reflected in the Neo-Assyrian reliefs of the *apkallu* caring for the sacred tree—a symbol of world order. See Amar Annus, "On the Origin of Watchers: A Comparative Study of the Antediluvian Wisdom in Mesopotamian and Jewish Traditions," *Journal for the Study of the Pseudepigrapha* 19 (2010): 277-320, here 293.

[19]This tradition is discussed in relation to the sons of God in Gen 6 in *LWF*, 126-28. In Enoch, the *apkallu* tradition is preserved in the Watchers, who are equated by Enoch with the sons of God in Gen 6.

[20]Adapa's full name is Uanadapa; he is known in Hellenistic traditions preserved by Berossus as Oannes. For a full discussion, see Shlomo Izre'el, *Adapa and the South Wind* (Winona Lake, IN: Eisenbrauns, 2001). For comparison to Genesis, see Tryggve N. D. Mettinger, *The Eden Narrative: A Literary and Religio-historical Study of Genesis 2–3* (Winona Lake, IN: Eisenbrauns, 2007), 100-109.

Adapa.[21] This is a rhetorical claim of ancestry, not a biological one. Similarly, Nebuchadnezzar called himself the "offspring of Enmeduranki" (a well-known ancient king).[22] Such examples illustrate that in the ancient world, a primordial, archetypal figure could be rhetorically placed as the ancestor of kings. When we recall that in Genesis 1–11, royal imagery is used for humanity as a whole (particularly the image of God), it would be no surprise that Israelites at some point in time would place archetypal Adam as the rhetorical ancestor of humanity. If this is the case, biological claims are not being made.

Finally, based on the work of J. Harvey Walton, we can now give further definition to how Adam and Eve serve as archetypes. He provides a summary in this excursus.

---

[21] Annus, "On the Origin of Watchers," 294, referring to the text in Simo Parpola, *Letters from Assyrian and Babylonian Scholars*, State Archives of Assyria 10 (Helsinki: Helsinki University Press, 1993), text 174, line 8. Further discussion and examples of how kings related themselves to the *apkallu* (primarily in terms of their wisdom) can be found in Beate Pongratz-Leisten, *Herrschaftswissen in Mesopotamien*, State Archives of Assyria 10 (Helsinki: Neo-Assyrian Text Corpus Project, 1999), 309-19. For the text, see Martti Nissinen, *Prophets and Prophecy in the Ancient Near East*, 2nd ed. (Atlanta: SBL Press, 2019), 118f.7-9 (p. 199).

[22] Annus, "On the Origin of Watchers," 295.

EXCURSUS 3: WHAT ARE ADAM AND EVE ARCHETYPES OF?

J. HARVEY WALTON

An *archetype* is a character whose literary presentation is intended to represent an entire group of people. Biblical archetypes include Noah (a righteous servant of God), the Pharisees (religious hypocrites), Judas Iscariot (a betrayer), Stephen (a martyr), or Job (a righteous sufferer). Because Genesis 2–3 has historically been read as an etiology of gender roles, Adam and Eve are usually seen as archetypes of human males and females, respectively. The presentation of the characters in the text itself, however, indicates that this may have not been the original author's intent.

In the destiny of Genesis 3:17-19, Adam (alone, with no mention of Eve) is decreed painful toil and an eventual return to dust. In Genesis 3:22-24, it is Adam (alone, also with no mention of Eve) who has become like God and who is banished from the garden and the tree of life. If Adam represented human males, then the destiny of death and labor would fall to males alone, but this is obviously not the case. Further,

Genesis 2: Adam and Eve

in Genesis 2:7, Adam (alone) is created to fill the void of having no human to work the ground (Gen 2:5). Both male and female humans share the task of agriculture, just as both male and female humans share the destiny that makes the task more difficult. Adam's character does not archetypally represent human males; his character archetypally represents all humans, male and female, who try to overcome the wasteland by working the ground.

If Adam's character represents both male and female humans, his helper (Gen 2:18) probably does too. There is no reason to assume that the need of a human alone requires a female to fill the void any more than the need of the ground required a male to fill the void. Solitude, isolation, and alterity (read: being alone) is a nonordered state that both males and females can experience, and it is resolved by companionship and community, which *can* include a spouse (the social role eventually assigned to Eve's character in Gen 2:23-25) but can also include other kinds of relationships involving people of both sexes. The avoidance of the word *wife* in Genesis

2:18, and the avoidance of any of the normal words for marriage, sex, or procreation in Genesis 2:24, indicate that Eve's role as "helper" is more generic than a simple romantic or reproductive partner. All of this suggests that Eve's character archetypally represents all humans, male and female, who try to overcome solitude and isolation through community.

Adam's character represents both male and female humans acting in a particular capacity (working the ground), and the destiny addressed to Adam alone is directly related to that vocation. If Eve's character also represents both male and female humans acting in a particular capacity (forming and perpetuating community), then the destiny addressed to her alone in Genesis 3:15-16 should also be something directly related to that vocation and should be something both males and females can somehow experience, just as females can also experience the destiny of painful toil, return to dust, and loss of access to the tree of life (see further in excursus 4 below).

Answers to Frequently Asked Questions

1. What is the significance of naming the animals? Naming can sometimes be an exercise of authority, but naming at its heart reflects a larger concept of which authority is only one possible aspect. Naming, labeling, is intrinsically an order-bringing activity.[23] It distinguishes one (person or group) from others by recognizing distinguishable traits. It *recognizes* roles and functions, though it does not always

---

[23]Note how even today we order information by taxonomies and labels.

determine them. It confers identity. The one conferring the name may be exercising authority over that which is named, but the conferring can also be a reflection of insight, discernment, or even responsibility. When God names created features such as day and night, we are not inclined to think in terms of exercising authority over them. Naming, along with separating, is a key act of creation, since naming and separating establish order, and order bringing is a creative act.

In a similar way, Adam is exercising a role as delegated order-bringer when he names the animals. When a name is given, something is recognized about the identity, role, or function of that which is named. What is the significance of this task being taken up right after the observation that it is not good for man to be alone? The deficiency of aloneness is going to be resolved by the end of the chapter by providing man with a helper, and perhaps more to the point, the two become a family—a community (Gen 2:24). Since the naming of animals is placed in this context, presumably the point would be that the animals are not his proper community. This sort of thinking is also reflected in the Gilgamesh Epic, when the wild man, Enkidu, after being humanized through sex, is no longer accepted in his former community of animals. In Genesis, the recognition that animals are not the community for humans comes before the introduction of woman onto the scene rather than afterward, as in Gilgamesh. This stands as another example in which Genesis is charting its own course even as it offers perspectives on the values that informed concepts of order in the ancient world.

2. What is the significance of God "closing up the flesh" (Gen 2:21)?
I have claimed that Genesis 2:21 does not describe the surgical removal of part of Adam (whether rib or side) but that it details what Adam sees in a vision. Some have wondered, then, why the text specifically mentions the closing up of the flesh. It is easy to see how that would lead modern readers to think of a surgical procedure. Alternatively, it is not difficult to reason that, even in a vision, since Eve is being built

Genesis 2: Adam and Eve   163

as a whole person, it would be rather nonsensical for Adam to merely see himself as a partial being. One might logically compare the account of a similar scenario in Plato involving the slicing of humans in two and then closing up the flesh (done by Apollo and described at some length; see *Symposium* 189D-191E), an episode that, for those familiar with the Bible, is reminiscent of Genesis 2:21-22. Plato goes on to make the point that each half would long for the other and be grafted together again, as also indicated in Genesis 2:24. I am not suggesting that either Genesis or Plato knew of the other, but this demonstrates that even in nonsurgical scenarios, it would not be strange to refer to closing up the flesh.

3. What is the significance of their nakedness (Gen 2:25)? Gary Anderson notes, "Ephrem the Syrian believed, as did many other patristic writers, that Adam and Eve were *clothed* in glory prior to their sin."[24] Most early interpreters considered the statement in Genesis 2:25 to be about sex. Augustine's interpretation is notable and more extreme than most as it reflects his admitted struggles with lust and sexuality, yet his interpretation has had continuing influence on Christian thinking. He considers the "onset of uncontrollable lustful desires for sexual satisfaction" as the result of Adam's sin, therefore suggesting that Adam and Eve's pre-fall lack of shame about their nakedness reflects the absence of sexual desire.[25]

When we consider attitudes in the ancient world, however, we find that nakedness and the absence of shame about it are not connected to sexuality; rather, this is consistently a motif descriptive of those who

---

[24]Gary A. Anderson, *The Genesis of Perfection: Adam and Eve in Jewish and Christian Imagination* (Louisville, KY: Westminster John Knox, 2001), 104. This connection could easily have been reached through wordplay. The Hebrew word for "skin" in Gen 3:21 is *ʿôr* (beginning with the often-unarticulated consonant *ayin*), which sounds the same as the Hebrew word for "light," *ʾôr* (beginning with the often-unarticulated consonant *aleph*). One can imagine the suggestion being made that God clothed them in *ʿôr*, whereas they had been previously clothed in *ʾôr*; but the text never suggests the latter as their original situation.

[25]Anderson, *Genesis of Perfection*, 65, 67-68.

164   NEW EXPLORATIONS IN THE LOST WORLD OF GENESIS

are primitive/uncivilized.[26] It does not reflect an ideal situation, as in some Christian theology. In an ancient Near Eastern context, then, nakedness expresses the absence of the order that characterizes civilized life. We would capture this in modern language by stating that they were indecent and shameless.[27] This deficiency fits into the flow of Genesis 1–11, as it is considering various ways that order might be found. What is important here is not simply that they are without clothes but that, being without clothes, they are without shame. A deficiency (shamelessness as indicative of lack of civilization) is resolved (they are now ashamed), indicating that a higher level of civilization (order) has been achieved, but that gain remains insufficient—ultimately, order calls for more than higher levels of civilized behavior.[28] Note that even their animal-skin clothing is not a resolution since in the ancient Near East such clothing remained connected to the liminal world.[29] In answer to the question, then, the condition described in Genesis 2:25 is significant as an indication that the archetypal humans remain situated in a liminal world and are lacking civilization—a deficiency that will be resolved but whose resolution is not seen as being the basis for ultimate order.

4. You have said that Adam and Eve are functioning in the text as archetypes. Does that mean that they are allegorical? One of the major premises promoted in *The Lost World of Adam and Eve* was that the most important role of Adam and Eve was archetypal—that is, that they represent all of humanity. As such, they are being used by the narrator to address issues of human identity rather than to make statements about scientific human origins. I offered a caveat that the conclusion that

---

[26]This distinction can also be supported by analysis of the use of the Hebrew terms.

[27]J. Harvey Walton, personal communication.

[28]Walton, "Knowing Good and Evil."

[29]An example is in the Gilgamesh Epic, when the hero clothes himself with animal skins. Other examples of the need for proper clothing to be considered civilized are found in Adapa and the Gilgamesh Epic's Enkidu, and seen in reverse when Ishtar needs to dispense with clothing to enter the liminal realm of the netherworld. For details and elaboration, see Walton, "Knowing Good and Evil," 130-31, and especially 162.

Genesis 2: Adam and Eve 165

Adam and Eve were archetypal does not affect the question whether they were real people in a real past. Narrators can use real people in archetypal roles. In the Bible, Paul considers Abraham an archetype of faith. Outside the Bible, George Washington could serve as an archetypal president, while Joan of Arc could serve as an archetypal unlikely hero.

The point to be made is that archetypal characterizations are not rhetorical devices employed only in metaphor or allegory.[30] Those devices *could* create fictional characters to achieve their purposes (Tolkien's Sauron), but such purposes can also be achieved through real characters in a real past. The important discussion here is about the *literary* role of Adam and Eve—an issue that does not require resolving the question of their historicity (more on this in the next question).

The important distinction between allegory and archetype is that technically allegory refers to a type of literature.[31] A story (such as *Pilgrim's Progress, Lord of the Flies,* or *Brave New World*) can be defined as allegorical; the characters in the story should not be so described. Archetypes, in contrast, refer to characters, not the literature they are in. The literary category of allegory may at times use archetypal characters. But archetypal characters are used broadly in literature of all sorts. Even real people in a historical novel can be archetypes. An archetype is an exemplar of a category of person. In an allegory, characters personify concepts or abstractions.

Therefore, the real question is whether Genesis 2–3 has the hallmarks of allegory, and I would maintain that it does not, though others may differ. The point is that recognizing Adam and Eve as archetypes

---

[30]Abraham Lincoln is often invoked as an archetypal moral leader; Che Guevara as an archetypal revolutionary; Napoleon as an archetypal conqueror; Einstein as an archetypal genius; Galileo as an archetypal champion of knowledge; Martin Luther King Jr. as an archetypal champion of justice; etc.

[31]According to the *Cambridge Dictionary,* allegory pertains to a *work*: "a story, play, poem, picture, or other work in which the characters and events represent particular qualities or ideas that relate to morals, religion, or politics." Likewise, Britannica identifies allegory as a "symbolic fictional narrative." See "Allegory," Britannica, www.britannica.com/art/allegory-art-and-literature. Allegory has an intended double layer of meaning.

166 NEW EXPLORATIONS IN THE LOST WORLD OF GENESIS

does not automatically lead to identifying Genesis 2–3 as allegorical. In my view, Adam and Eve are serving as archetypes for the concepts tied up in human identity, especially with regard to seeking order.

5. How important is it that Adam and Eve are real people in a real past? This is perhaps one of the most difficult and controversial questions under discussion today. Conservative interpreters such as Tremper Longman have drawn criticism simply by suggesting that it may not be as important as we think.[32] Others who have been comfortable departing from traditional positions, such as Peter Enns, have abandoned any attempt to contend for a historical Adam.[33]

A first observation is that it is possible to retain the idea of Adam and Eve as real people in a real past while rejecting that they were the first and only of the species on earth at some point in time. To put it another way, it is possible to view their significance in terms other than biological. This would not be a problem even for those who wanted to trace sin back to them, since the pervasiveness of sin, its effect on all people, and the resulting need of salvation is not dependent on biological descent or genetic connections. When some insist on a biological model, they risk imposing a worldview on the text that is not the way that Israelites would have thought.

A second approach to the question is to inquire what would be lost if Adam and Eve were *not* viewed as real people in a real past. Some would see such a position as a threat to biblical inerrancy, but that would only be the case if it were determined that the text affirms or even demands that they be real people in a real past. Inerrancy cannot

---

[32]See Tremper Longman's contribution in Daryl Charles, ed., *Reading Genesis 1–2: An Evangelical Conversation* (Peabody, MA: Hendrickson, 2013), 122. See an attempt at nuancing the question in Dennis Venema and Scot McKnight, *Adam and the Genome* (Grand Rapids, MI: Brazos, 2017). See also van den Brink, *Reformed Theology and Evolutionary Theory*, 165-80, and Denis Alexander, *Creation or Evolution: Do We Have to Choose?*, 2nd ed. (Oxford: Monarch, 2014). For a comparison of various positions, see Matthew Barrett and Ardel Caneday, *Four Views on the Historical Adam* (Grand Rapids, MI: Zondervan, 2013), or Charles, *Reading Genesis 1–2*.

[33]Peter Enns, *The Evolution of Adam* (Grand Rapids, MI: Brazos, 2012), 119-27.

Genesis 2: Adam and Eve 167

be brought into play until the literary and exegetical issues are resolved, so making a case based on inerrancy is premature.

Even if one were to conclude that the genre of Genesis did not require them to be real people in a real past or even assume them to be so, it could be argued that Paul regarded them that way, and thus we would also be obliged to do so. This point, however, also remains debatable, as Scot McKnight demonstrates in his suggestion that a "literary Adam" or a "theological Adam" should be distinguished from a "historical Adam."[34]

If, in Genesis, Adam and Eve are archetypal, the focus is not anecdotal. That is, Genesis 2–3 is meant to be a story about *all of us* rather than a story about *them*. We are all dust; we all go our own way; we all want to be like God; we all are trying to find order in the liminal human realm as we battle ever-threatening chaos. We can therefore set aside the questions that prompted Augustine's formulation of original sin, and that have plagued all of us since then, concerning why everyone has to suffer for the error of one couple millennia ago. Furthermore, we do not have to have Adam as the biological parent of all in order to have sin spread to all. Sin does not have to spread to all; we all sin. Therefore, having Adam as the biological parent of all offers no theological payoff.

Paul is treating Adam and Eve differently. He uses them anecdotally as types rather than etiologically. That is, his comments are based on a traditional story found in his people's literature of the past (compare how we might talk about King Arthur), in that way reflecting on a literary Adam rather than commenting on the nature of all of us (etiology, such as making a claim that all women are by nature deceivable). Paul may well have considered Adam and Eve historical, but his opinion on that does not matter any more than his opinion about whether the earth is flat. Paul knows the story of Adam and Eve from the literature that represented the traditions of his people—which makes it real. A literary anecdote is not inherently less real or less meaningful than a historical

---

[34]Venema and McKnight, *Adam and the Genome*, 171-91.

one, especially if it is one deeply entrenched in the traditions that define the identity of a people group. Consider the following comparison:[35]

Table 6.1. Literary devices

DEVICE	DESCRIPTION	BIBLICAL EXAMPLE
History	"Person [X] did [Y], and [Z] happened because of that."	Nebuchadnezzar destroys Jerusalem; Paul gets approval for the mission to the Gentiles
Etiology	"Person [X] did [Y], and that is why [Z] is what it is."	Why Philistines will not step on the threshold in 2 Sam 5
Anecdote	"Person [X] is an example of someone who did [Y] and had [Z] happen as a result."	Pharaoh's magicians in 2 Tim 2; Eve in 2 Thessalonians; Michael and Satan in Jude
Allegory	"Person [X], who represents [A], did something to person [Y], who represents [B], and that tells us something about [A] and [B]."	Israel as an adulterous wife in Ezek 16
Typology	"Person [X] was or did [A], and person [Y] also is or does [A], so person [Y] is like person [X]."	Pharisees in Jn 8; Adam in Rom 5
Archetype	"Person [X] did or was [A], and people who are like them also do or are [A]."	Job; three friends in Dan 2; Daniel in Dan 6
Conceptual Story	"Person [X] did [Y], and [Z] happened, and that has implications for how we think about [A]."	Parables; search for meaning in Ecclesiastes; stories told to manipulate David's judgment
Fiction	"(Fabricated) person [X] said or did something amusing, tragic, poignant, or insightful."	N/A

Consequently, I would maintain that neither Genesis nor Paul is invested in the question of whether Adam and Eve were historical. It is irrelevant to these treatments whether they were. The archetypes of Genesis are meaningful, and what they declare is self-evidently true. The anecdotes of Paul make his theological points convincingly. Consequently, the authority of the Bible is not dependent on Adam's historicity. Just as the *Bible* does not have a position on the age of the earth, it does not have a position on the historicity of Adam, though people of the time may have had opinions on both. Just as the Bible does not offer an authoritative view on cosmic geography but only reflects what people of the time thought, it likewise does not offer an

---

[35]J. Harvey Walton, personal communication.

Genesis 2: Adam and Eve 169

authoritative view on the historicity of Adam but only reflects what people of the time thought. It is Scripture's affirmations that carry authority, and the affirmations of Genesis are defensibly archetypal.

As already indicated, one does not need a historical Adam to affirm that all humans are subject to sin and in need of salvation. These truths are assured based both on other parts of Scripture and on experience. Doctrines of sin and salvation are not jeopardized by decisions made about historical Adam. I propose, then, that the question is apologetic in nature, not theological (though, of course, others would differ).[36] In my view, exegetical, contextual issues are of first-level importance and theological ones close behind. I find concerns for apologetics much less pressing and resist any inclination to elevate them to too high a priority.

A final matter concerns what we can learn from how primordial individuals are treated in the ancient world. There we find that characters from the hoary past who take on archetypal significance generally are not fictional characters, though they obviously take on legendary status. In a discussion of the historicity of characters such as Gilgamesh, Enmerkar, and Lugalbanda, Assyriologist Bendt Alster strikes an admirable balance in drawing the relationship between history and texts.

> Let me state clearly that my purpose by raising this question is not to join the general line in much modern scholarship, one that sets itself as a task to deprive the ancient literary sources of actual reality whenever possible, instead of asking what the texts intend to say. My problem is of an entirely different nature, namely to try to find a way to read these texts which is in agreement with the message which they aim at communicating, being based on their own aesthetical norms. It may be

---

[36]By saying that the question is apologetic in nature, I mean that some are of the opinion that, to prove the Bible to be "true," one must contend for historical Adam.

considered an interesting historical problem whether or not rulers of the names of Lugalbanda, Enmerkar, and Gilgames have ever existed, but this would be completely insignificant with regard to the interpretation of these texts, if they are simply not in any way concerned with an aim at expressing historical data at all.[37]

This does not mean that Adam and Eve are not individuals. Judging from their role in genealogies, they are positioned at the headwaters of humanity, as the biblical authors thought about humanity. I do not regard them as the first and only of the species. These are complicated issues and require nuanced approaches. Several different sorts of conclusions can be found among those who treat the Bible as authoritative, and we need to keep working the problem as we continue to hope for new evidence or new insights. This topic will be treated in more detail in chapter seven below.

6. What is meant by Eve being the "mother of all living"? Based on the discussion earlier about naming, when Adam confers this name/epithet on Eve (Heb, *ḥawwāh* = "life"), I maintain that it is not essentially an act of authority but a recognition of identity. In Genesis 2:23, her name is related to her identity relative to man. Here the name given could reflect her role as progenitrix (mother), another important aspect of her identity. "Woman" is the source of "life." Perhaps also, recognizing that "Adam" (humanity) is archetypal of all people, Eve may be viewed as archetypal of the life of all people. She was provided to resolve aloneness, and the resolution is community. Life is found in community and perpetuated in each generation.[38] We

---

[37]Bendt Alster, "The Paradigmatic Character of Mesopotamian Heroes," *Revue d'Assyriologie et d'archéologie orientale* 68 (1974): 49-60, here 50.

[38]Ideas provided by Walton, "Knowing Good and Evil," 161, elaborated in personal communication. He suggests that her name indicates that she represents something comparable in some way to the tree in the garden. As in the Gilgamesh Epic, immortality is found not in a special plant but in family and community perpetuated generation to generation.

Genesis 2: Adam and Eve 171

will explore this more below (see excursus 5). An act of authority can use naming to try to alter someone's identity or impose a new identity on them, but that is not the case here. Adam does not determine Eve's identity; he acknowledges it.[39] This identity is true of all women, not just the archetype Eve.

Nevertheless, we can still ask whether it signifies something biological in nature. That is, does the text here claim that all humans (living beings) are biologically descended from Eve? The alternative that I would favor is that it indicates the archetypal role of woman as mother that is prominent in her identity, just as Adam's previous naming of Eve "woman" (Gen 2:23) indicated the archetypal role of woman as related to man, particularly as wife. Moreover, even though both of these pertain to the role of woman, they extend beyond her role to address abstractions such as family relationships rather than ones such as masculinity and femininity. As "mother of all the living," womankind is identified as the one from whom all future living descendants will come—they are mothers. This does not mean that all women are required to be mothers, but they have the potential ability to play that role, and all life comes from them. Having said that, it is obvious that both men and women together produce life, so this is the role of all humanity.[40]

7. Was humanity created immortal? I have already addressed this to some extent in the discussion about the translation of Genesis 2:7 (above under "New Explorations"). There humanity is identified as "dust," and dust is symbolic of mortality. Nevertheless, at this point more needs to be said. When we go back in the history of interpretation, there is no doubt that it was common to consider humanity to have been immortal before the fall. In one of the earliest known

---

[39]For discussion separating naming from authority, see Iain Provan, *Discovering Genesis: Content, Interpretation, Reception* (London: SPCK, 2015), 90-92.

[40]J. Harvey Walton points out that being the mother of all living is not gender related any more than Jubal being the "father" of all who play the harp and flute (Gen 4:21) is gender related.

172   NEW EXPLORATIONS IN THE LOST WORLD OF GENESIS

interpretations of the garden story, the Wisdom of Solomon (generally dated to the early first century AD), the sage writes, "God created us for incorruption (some translations read 'immortality') and made us in the image of his own eternity, but through the devil's envy death entered the world, and those who belong to his company experience it."[41]

This can be viewed as coinciding with Paul's contemporary statement that humans are subject to death because of sin (Rom 5:12), but at the same time we must note the ambiguity in both statements. The idea that humans were created *for* incorruption or immortality is not the same as saying that humans were created immortal. It could speak of the eventual achievement rather than the experienced reality. One could even question whether *incorruption* refers to physical immortality or to moral incorruptibility. In either case, being created *for* it (ultimate goal) is different from being created *with* it (inherent characteristic). Moreover, for Paul's part, it is unclear whether he is indicating that humans were originally immortal or that their loss of access to the tree of life doomed them to their natural mortality. In the latter view, they were subject to death because, having been driven from the garden, they were now without the antidote of the tree of life (a position I defended in *LWAE*).

Unarguably, Christian interpretation early on adopted the position that humans were created immortal.[42] Already, however, early Christians had adopted a theological paradigm in which this made sense in

---

[41]Wisdom 2:23-24, trans. Peter Enns, in *Outside the Bible: Ancient Jewish Writings Related to Scripture*, ed. Louis Feldman, James L. Kugel, and Lawrence H. Schiffman (Philadelphia: JPS, 2013), 2155-2207, here 2162. See discussion in Anderson, *Genesis of Perfection*, 24-27. Crowther surveys the views in Reformation writings (*Adam and Eve*, 88-98). The "devil's envy" is reflected in his refusal to bow to Adam. These ideas and even this wording are reflected in the work Life of Adam and Eve. The date of this work is uncertain but generally assigned somewhere in the first several centuries AD. It was used heavily by John Milton in *Paradise Lost*. For discussion and translation, see Gary A. Anderson, "Life of Adam and Eve," in *Outside the Bible*, 1331-58.

[42]For example, see discussion of Reformation positions in Crowther, *Adam and Eve*, 74-98.

Genesis 2: Adam and Eve 173

their larger framework. As always, we resist drawing a conclusion about how we should interpret Genesis by recruiting someone from the history of interpretation (Christian or Jewish)—they all have their reasons and their contexts.[43] A major contributing idea to this discussion was the assumption that Adam had been created perfect (see the following question below).

The question is whether the Israelite texts in the Old Testament in general, and Genesis in particular, imagined such a scenario. In the ancient Near Eastern literature, some texts consider humans to have initially not been subject to natural death (Atrahasis Epic), whereas other traditions view immortality as something that was unsuccessfully sought (as in the Gilgamesh Epic) or an opportunity lost (in the Epic of Adapa). This diversity of views shows that there was neither a monolithic view, nor even a consensus, but that it was a topic of great interest. In Genesis, the presence of a tree of life in the garden suggests that immortality was not already possessed but was in some way on offer and within their reach.[44] In this, it does not reflect any of the three scenarios in the ancient Near Eastern texts. Immortality is not the natural state, as in the Atrahasis Epic; it does not require a quest, as in the Gilgamesh Epic; and it is not specifically offered by a god, as in the Epic of Adapa. It is simply present in the Garden of Eden.

In the context of the order spectrum, when Genesis weighs in, it is addressing the question of whether immortality is a productive means to obtaining order. In such a case, Genesis 3 is not so much about something that Adam and Eve had and lost (whether that is immortality or the remedy for mortality). Instead, it concerns whether it should be sought and valued as a pathway to order or the

---

[43]For example, Irenaeus was arguing against Gnostics, Augustine was arguing against the Manichaeans and Pelagianism, and John Calvin and Martin Luther were arguing against Catholicism.

[44]Though the discussion remains open as to whether immortality is the point or just indefinite longevity.

foundation of order. Is immortality actually a good thing?[45] Death is classified in the ancient world as a liminal state, and is a component of nonorder. Note how it is described in Psalm 88. Nonorder, it will be recalled, is the default situation and precedes order. Arguably, immunity to death would have to be *established* in order bringing, and there is no indication in the text that it was. With regard to life (as order), the tree is what is provided in the ordered system. I would therefore consider both initial immortality and/or initial incorruptibility to be another case of later thinkers imposing their systems, preconceptions, and questions on a text that was not dealing with the same issues. We will discuss this further in chapter seven. The Israelites in general and Genesis in particular are not disinterested in immortality—it was a facet of order much in discussion in their cultural context, and it is natural for humans to be interested in such questions. But there is no reason to think that humankind was created immortal. The text suggests otherwise (dust), and neither Genesis nor Paul offers a different opinion. Most importantly, immortality is not set forth as the pursuit that will bring order.

8. Was Adam perfect? The immortality question is part of a larger discussion about initial perfection. Many early Christian writers believed that Adam and Eve were perfect in their pre-fallen state. Where did they get that idea, and what did they mean by "perfect"? Irenaeus illustrates some extreme thinking as he details the greater physical capabilities of the flawless human body before the fall:

---

[45]Lest this be considered a ridiculous question, given that people so often treat it as ideal (both in the desire to prolong life on earth endlessly and in the hope for eternal life), note that immortality is problematized in modern culture in the popular television series *Dr. Who* in the paired episodes "The Girl Who Died" (season 9, episode 5, October 17, 2015) and "The Woman Who Lived" (season 9, episode 6, October 24, 2015), reflecting on the experiences of Ashildr. Dr. Who himself struggles with his own immortality, and the pain of immortality is also articulated by Captain Jack Harkness, who cannot die but eventually longs to do so as the "Face of Boe."

Genesis 2: Adam and Eve   175

Before the Fall, the stomach digested food better, the liver produced purer blood, the heart was stronger and more resilient. All
of the senses were keener before the Fall. For example, "before
the Fall, man had bright, clear eyes, that gleamed and shone in
his head like carbuncles, with which he saw more sharply and
farther than even a lynx or an eagle."[46]

Eventually, therefore, interpreters were forced to posit comprehensive
physiological changes in the human body after the fall as they concluded that each human organ was affected by the fall. Nevertheless, a
moment's consideration would determine that Irenaeus could not have
gotten such details or reached such conclusions even from the New
Testament, let alone from Genesis. Moreover, despite Irenaeus's discussion of the physical state of Adam cited above, he describes Adam's
state as that of innocence (for him meaning "childlike, immature,
needing moral development") rather than perfection. In that regard,
Irenaeus is often contrasted to Augustine, who presents Adam as perfect.
As we can see, *perfection* can be defined in different ways, and the logic
to support such claims was often theological rather than textual.

Here we have to walk carefully, as always when we characterize the
early Christian writers. Augustine scholars indicate that he is more
nuanced than often represented in theological discussions.[47] His interest concerns whether Adam was capable of following the law (able
not to sin), not in the question of physical or even moral perfection,
though it was not unusual for interpreters to posit flawless bodies or
that Adam was spiritually and morally uncorrupted. Many modern
assumptions about Adam and Eve have been heavily influenced by

---

[46]Crowther, *Adam and Eve*, 75-76. For more detailed discussion of Irenaeus in his context,
see Thomas Holsinger-Friesen, *Irenaeus and Genesis: A Study of Competition in Early Christian Hermeneutics*, Journal of Theological Interpretation Supplements 1 (Winona Lake, IN:
Eisenbrauns, 2009).

[47]For carefully nuanced discussion of Augustine, see Gavin Ortlund, *Retrieving Augustine's
Doctrine of Creation: Ancient Wisdom for Current Controversy* (Downers Grove, IL:
InterVarsity Press, 2020).

176   New Explorations in the Lost World of Genesis

John Milton's *Paradise Lost*, where he reflects many of the theological conclusions current in his day. For example, in Milton's work, Raphael tells Adam that he was made perfect but not immutable. Gary Anderson believes that Milton was informed by a work from Second Temple Judaism titled Life of Adam and Eve (see 13:1–14:3, where Satan refuses to bow to the perfect creation, Adam) and also reflected Augustine's thinking. Anderson thus concludes that many ideas about the nature of Adam were driven by the need to reflect on Christ as the second and greater Adam.[48]

The point to be made is that much of what the church has come to believe about Adam is driven by Christian-theological discussions about Christ and Adam, and the role of Satan and the angels, rather than by what Genesis says. These discussions include the belief that protology (what happened at the beginning) and eschatology (what will happen at the end) are in balance, and in some cases these discussions work on the assumption that new creation is in some way a return to the garden, an idea not articulated in Scripture. I do not consider Adam to be perfect by any definition—moral, physical, psychological, or any other measure—because I find it unsupported in the text and theologically unnecessary.

J. Harvey Walton provides an important alternative to the moral paradigm for analyzing Adam that has been an essential building block for the idea that he be viewed as perfect. He calls for a shift from the dualistic moral perspective common in Christian circles, along with corresponding traditional interpretations regarding the fall, to a revised view based on the order spectrum that better describes the perspective of the ancient Israelites. I agree with his summary statement: "We propose that Genesis 2 depicts a chaotic state where order has not yet been established, and that the narrative of Genesis 2–4

---

[48]Anderson, *Genesis of Perfection*, 39. Added to that are the interests in the interrelationship of protology and eschatology, and the search for a theodicy. For them, to talk about Adam was to talk about sin and salvation.

Genesis 2: Adam and Eve 177

entails gradually replacing that chaotic state with various manifestations of order, while simultaneously devaluing those manifestations to
promote the Covenant by way of contrast."[49] In this view, Genesis does
not begin with humanity in an ideal state of any sort, let alone a perfect
state. Thus Genesis stands in contrast to the Greek myth of the golden
age, in which the beginning state was a state of perfection. This Greek
myth, undergirded by Platonism, is anachronistic to the ancient Near
East but foundational for aspects of Christian theology. So we cannot
assume that the narrator of Genesis had a state of perfection in mind
as he composed Genesis 2–3.[50] That would not have been part of
his worldview.

In contrast, when we apply the order spectrum to this question, we
find that we can no longer begin with the preconceptions that served
as the foundation for Christian-theological discussions, which were
more concerned with christological patterns and associations than
with anthropology or reading the text of Genesis in its cultural and
literary context. Reading the text for itself, can we really contend that
Genesis portrays perfection of any sort before the fall? In the ancient
Near Eastern context, nakedness is an undesirable state, in which case
Genesis 2:25 falls short of reflecting everything the way it should be.

In the cosmology of the ancient Near East and the Hebrew Bible, the
beginning state (cosmos or people) is not that of perfection or com-
pleteness. Rather, it is the default state of nonorder. Furthermore, there
is no moral assessment (positive or negative) of that original state.
Genesis 1:2 describes the initial nonorder—an undesirable state, yet the
default condition. Humanity is also initially in a state of nonorder in
several ways in Genesis 2, as expressed through the archetypal portrayals of humanity. They have not yet learned to work the ground,
Adam is alone (a situation specified as being not good), and they are

---

[49]Walton, "Knowing Good and Evil," 126.
[50]Recall that even Eden as the divine realm was a liminal realm for humans, not a perfect
one (see chap. 5 above).

indecent and shameless. In this description, the text of Genesis is not at all concerned with the later Christian questions, especially articulated by Augustine, about whether they were able to sin or, alternatively, able not to sin. Most of the discussion about Adam's perfection is based on an assumption that Genesis 2–3 is dealing with the issue of sin entering the world. Instead, I contend that sin is not the conversation that Genesis 2–3 is having (more about this in chapter seven below). If that is so, the question of perfection is anachronistic and moot.

7
Genesis 3
The Fall

Summary of Previous Material

Propositions 15-19 in *The Lost World of Adam and Eve* touch on issues in Genesis 3 in general and deal with the question of the fall in particular. I have been reluctant to pursue this in depth since I am neither a theologian nor a New Testament scholar. I was therefore happy to have N. T. Wright provide a chapter on Paul for *The Lost World of Adam and Eve*. In the interval since that book, others have contributed significant and productive analysis for both theology and New Testament.[1] The topic is complicated for many reasons, but among them is that neither the Old Testament nor the New Testament refers to Genesis 3 as recounting something called "the fall."[2] Moreover, the Old Testament never returns its attention to Genesis 3 at all. It shows no awareness of the chapter and what is recounted there. In particular, when it deals with the issue of sin, it is much more interested in Israelite violations of the covenant than it is in the question of where, when, and how sin had its origins.

The discussion must begin, as always, with the context of Genesis itself. In the analysis of that context and my interpretations of it, I

---

[1]Among the resources that I have found most helpful are Loren Haarsma, *When Did Sin Begin?* (Grand Rapids, MI: Baker, 2021); Gijsbert van den Brink, *Reformed Theology and Evolutionary Theory* (Grand Rapids, MI: Eerdmans, 2020); and Dennis R. Venema and Scot McKnight, *Adam and the Genome* (Grand Rapids, MI: Brazos, 2017).

[2]*LWAE*, 142-43.

focused most attention on the serpent and on seeking an understanding of the offense. The serpent was seen as a chaos creature in Israelite perception rather than as Satan. As I investigated the understanding of chaos creatures in the ancient world, I drew the conclusion that the serpent was not the embodiment or even the representation of either cosmic evil or moral evil but played a catalyst role, representing nonorder. Wherever disorder is present, people are responsible.

When I turned to consideration of the offense interpreted in the context of the order spectrum, I suggested, contrary to what has often been decided in the history of interpretation, that the prohibition of eating from the tree was not at all arbitrary. It was not, as often suggested, just a test of Adam and Eve's commitment to obedience that in and of itself had no intrinsic significance. In contrast, I maintained that the prohibition was all about the nature of the tree as providing a wisdom pathway to order.[3] The focus was not on what they *did* (traditionally construed as disobedience = sin) but on what they *seized* (wisdom for themselves to be like God). This concept set the course for humanity going its own way. I suggested that this was portrayed not so much as a fall from grace but as a choice that brought the loss of their access to God's presence in sacred space and loss of relationship with God as they sought to pursue order for their own benefits rather than on God's plans and purposes.

New Explorations

In *The Lost World of Adam and Eve* I discussed how there was nothing like the fall in ancient Near Eastern literature. Based on some of the insights of J. Harvey Walton's dissertation, I now maintain that, though there are no parallels to something like the fall, there *are* parallels to Genesis 3 in the ancient Near East. I had been looking for

---

[3]*LWAE*, 143-44.

Genesis 3: The Fall 181

parallels to the theological reading of Genesis 3 instead of parallels to the now-revised way of thinking about Genesis 3 with regard to the order spectrum.

If we are looking for a passage to talk about the origin of sin, or even the loss of relationship with God or access to the presence of God, it is true that we will find nothing quite like Genesis 3 in ancient Near Eastern literature. But Walton's dissertation suggests that regardless of whether Genesis 3 can be understood in those theological ways, something much more practical is going on. The primary thesis of his dissertation is that Genesis 2–4 (and even beyond) is not concerned with *events* or *actions* in the past but is interested in how people have tried to find order for themselves in ways that were conventional in ancient world thinking (strategies such as agriculture, community, civilization, city building). If Genesis 3 is talking about what constitutes order—that order was to be found neither by dwelling in the divine realm (with its benefit of immortality) nor by being like God—it can be seen to be in conversation with values that are the focus of some principal pieces of literature in the ancient world. The search for order is ubiquitous in the epic literature of the ancient world. Once we consider the potential of that as the literary objective of Genesis 3, as Walton proposes, we find easy parallels in the ancient Near East.

I had already proposed that Genesis 3 represented a shift in the whole question about humans' approach to order bringing—that people find order desirable, but rather than adopting God's plan, so we would bring his order working alongside him, we seize the wisdom to bring order so that we can try to bring order on our own, no longer dependent on God. This would still be seen as a violation of how things were supposed to be, as people set their own course, but it is not a corruption of an original pristine state; it is what we all always do. This direction of thinking, incidentally, runs in tandem with Augustine's definition of sin, *homo incurvatus in se*, which means "man turned inward on himself" ("incurvature").[4] In that sense, this interpretation is not a new idea.

J. Harvey Walton, however, has gone the next step. He suggests that in Genesis, the purpose of Genesis 3 is not to recount a deviation but yet another inadequacy concerning where order is to be found.

What the humans gain over the course of the narrative, of course, is that they "become like God, knowing good and evil." This is something the humans do not have at the beginning of the story, but they do have it by the end. . . . It is godlikeness, not chaos and/or death, that is the concept that forms the subject of the narrative. But the literary focus is still not on the actions and events that produced godlikeness at some point in the past; the focus is instead on the relative value and utility of godlikeness, specifically its inability to produce order in the human world.[5]

In this way, Genesis 3 fits into his proposal concerning the literary intent of the primordial history (Gen 1–11) as a whole, "to deconstruct and devalue various order-bringing institutions that other ancient Near Eastern cultures would have been inclined to assign the highest value," as it moves toward Genesis 12, where the covenant will be introduced as the desirable alternative. The conclusion, a rather uncomfortable one for readers holding traditional theology, is, "The loss of immortality is not a punishment; the action which incurs it is not a crime; and Yahweh's statement to abstain from the fruit of the knowledge of good and evil is a warning rather than a law or a threat."[6] The godlikeness Adam and Eve acquired (Gen 3:22) was not wrong for them to have; it was inadequate to achieve their desired outcome.

---

[4]See *City of God* 14.13, where Augustine describes sin as *inclinatus ad se*, "turning toward himself." For further discussion, see Matt Jenson, *Gravity of Sin: Augustine, Luther and Barth on 'Homo Incurvatus in Se'* (London: Bloomsbury Publishing, 2007).

[5]J. Harvey Walton, "Knowing Good and Evil: Values and Presentation in Genesis 2–4" (PhD diss., University of St Andrews, 2023), 168, http://hdl.handle.net/10023/27738.

[6]Walton, "Knowing Good and Evil," 177.

Genesis 3: The Fall 183

As mind-blowing on the one hand and perhaps disturbing on the other as this is for readers entrenched in traditional theology, it should only prompt us to dig deeper. Adopting this new proposal for the literary focus of Genesis 3—that it is on the order-bringing inadequacies of ideas such as dwelling immortally in the divine realm or achieving godlikeness—does not necessarily require rejection of the idea that humanity has deviated from its created purpose.[7]

In 1980, the Grammy award for the best country song was awarded to Johnny Lee for the song "Lookin' for Love." One of its memorable and repeated lines was "Lookin' for love in all the wrong places." The song was not reflecting a negative attitude toward love; in fact, it was pointing to how love was eventually found. Love was not the problem, but many of the singer's attempts to find it were flawed. In a similar manner, humans in general and Israelites in particular were lookin' for *order* in all the wrong places. There is nothing wrong with order, but attempts to find it may be misguided, especially when they are selfish. Nevertheless, the text does not identify a selfish, deviating intention. Even some pursuits that are not selfish remain inadequate. With this illustration in mind, we might be able to see that while Genesis 1–11 is most interested in the unsuccessful search, one element that makes those searches unsuccessful is that they lead people to pursue their own benefits rather than aligning with the plans and purposes of God. God wants order, but on his terms (eventually written into the covenant), not ours. What brings order for humanity may be contrary to what God's order would look like. Nevertheless, within the literary focus of Genesis, strategies for finding order in the human realm are at times simply recognized as inadequate rather than flawed.

The reasoning that can help us to accept Walton's proposal in the main without having to sacrifice the idea that Genesis 3 also reflects

---

[7]Humanity's created purpose is presumably found in carrying out the function given to it as image bearers. That called on humanity to be order bringers but did not necessarily fully equip it for that task.

deviation from God's plan was expressed well by Iain Provan well before these options were being weighed with each other.

In sum, the remainder of the OT does not view the events of Genesis 3 as *cataclysmic* events that somehow inevitably change everything about the world in which we live. Indeed, the rest of the OT does not ever again even refer *back* to the events of Genesis 3 as important for human beings in the present, when it comes to understanding the world in which we live, or how we should live in relation to God and the rest of creation. It does know that sin, chaos and darkness are threats to creation, and have been so ever since the beginning. It knows, further, that human beings can and do embrace sin, chaos and darkness and become implicated in it.[8]

My current position, beyond what I presented in *The Lost World of Adam and Eve*, is that Genesis 3 is intended to be a story neither about how sin came into the world nor about how the choices of two individuals have negatively affected all the rest of us. It is about how humanity is characteristically and constantly on a quest for order. Adam and Eve are all of us. Order is and has always been our quest. God created us with that intrinsic desire, yet we inevitably pursue that desire in ways that undermine his plans and purposes in favor of our own (corporately and individually). A focus on Adam and Eve's individuality or on the historicity of the narrative is misguided to the extent that these focuses represent the wrong questions. Questions about the origins of sin, as important as they may be to Paul (debatable) and to theologians throughout history (pervasively), are anachronistic when applied to Genesis. Genesis 3 is not about the *origin* of the human condition but about the *nature* of the human condition.

---

[8]Iain Provan, *Discovering Genesis: Content, Interpretation, Reception* (London: SPCK, 2015), 94. Provan, of course, was neither aware of nor commenting on Walton's proposals.

Genesis 3: The Fall

Now we need to circle back to ask whether this changes anything in regard to the metanarrative I have previously suggested, one focused on presence and relationship. I had previously maintained that God created us to be in relationship with us and to dwell among us.[9] I remain convinced that this reflects well a metanarrative that can be supported in the Old Testament and extends into the New Testament. The question is whether it can be found in these opening chapters of Genesis.

I also remain convinced that Genesis 2:1-4 points us to the idea that the climax of the seven-day account (understood in connection with Ex 20:8-11) is God's taking up his rule over the cosmos that he has ordered and that that rule finds its location on earth (eventually the tabernacle/temple) rather than just in heaven. This concept would remain intact even if Eden were more about people dwelling in the divine realm than God dwelling in the human realm.

Likewise, the concept of the image of God in Genesis 1 already assumes a working relationship focused on how God intends to carry out his plans and purposes. In these ways, the metanarrative remains intact even if Genesis 2–3 is not as supportive of it as previously proposed. Even in the new model, the aftermath of Genesis 3 shows people having less access to the presence of God (which is granted in the covenant). The covenant reforges a relationship.

ANSWERS TO FREQUENTLY ASKED QUESTIONS

1. If the serpent is not identified with Satan in the Old Testament, how should we understand the serpent and its role? In *The Lost World of Adam and Eve* I adopted the position that the serpent would have been viewed by the original audience as a chaos creature.[10] This

---

[9]For the most recent articulation of this metanarrative, see John H. Walton, *Wisdom for Faithful Reading: Principles and Practices for Old Testament Interpretation* (Downers Grove, IL: InterVarsity Press, 2023), 199-200; see also John H. Walton, *Old Testament Theology for Christians* (Downers Grove, IL: InterVarsity Press, 2017), 27-28.

[10]*LWAE*, 128-39. For discussion of the varieties of chaos creatures, see Joan Goodnick Westenholz, *Dragons, Monsters and Fabulous Beasts* (Jerusalem: Bible Lands Museum, 2004);

186   NEW EXPLORATIONS IN THE LOST WORLD OF GENESIS

differs greatly from the traditional Christian view that the serpent was Satan. In that traditional view, theological questions such as these often were raised:

- How did Satan get access to the Garden of Eden?
- Does this mean that evil already existed before the fall?
- How were Adam and Eve expected to resist temptation if they were forbidden to partake of the tree of the knowledge of good and evil?

The entire conversation is redirected if we recognize that in Genesis (and in the Old Testament in general), the serpent is not associated with Satan—it has a different role altogether.[11]

We therefore cannot begin by asking how Satan gets access to the garden, since the Old Testament does not view the serpent as Satan. Still, we might raise the alternative question concerning what a chaos creature is doing in the Garden of Eden. In previous chapters I have considered positively the position that Eden is in the divine realm. If that position is adopted, it might seem that it is even less likely that people would encounter a chaos creature there.[12] Nevertheless, such a scenario is not uncommon in the ancient Near Eastern literary world. In Enuma Elish, the Babylonian creation epic, for example, Tiamat is a chaos creature, and her army of monsters inhabits the divine realm, as Tiamat herself likely does. In the Tale of Anzu, Anzu is a chaos creature that lives in the divine realm as a quasi-domesticated servant of Enlil. In fact, the emblem animals of numerous gods are chaos creatures and would be present in the divine realm.[13]

Gina Konstantopoulos, *The Divine/Demonic Seven and the Place of Demons in Mesopotamia*, Ancient Magic and Divination 20 (Leiden: Brill, 2023). Notice also that in Revelation, the serpent is a dragon.

[11]Note that the serpent is not presented in the text as evil. The description of it uses a wisdom term (ʿārûm) rather than a term designating badness (whether moral or in terms of order).

[12]This paragraph and the next developed in personal conversation with J. Harvey Walton.

[13]Most notably, Marduk's emblem animal, *Mušḫuššu* (Westenholz, *Dragons, Monsters and Fabulous Beasts*, 25-26). A boundary marker (*kudurru*) from the Kassite period portrays

Genesis 3: The Fall

Figure 7.1. A boundary marker (*kudurru*) from the Kassite period portrays the various realms, and in the uppermost realm (top register) some of the gods are represented by their emblem animals. Photo credit: Kim Walton.

Furthermore, though the serpent can be seen as a chaos creature, the text is also clear in identifying it as an animal, and there are explicitly animals aplenty in Eden. Moreover, in the monumental parks kept by ancient kings, wildlife of all sorts was abundant. This included lions, whose presence constituted a declaration of the king's ability to bring order into the midst of nonorder. Some chaos creatures are hybrid monsters, but others are simply creatures in the known world. The author of Genesis apparently feels no need to explain how the serpent could be in the garden, suggesting that he assumed his audience would not stumble over it.[14]

We need to note further that temptation per se is not in the purview of a chaos creature. The questions posed and statements made by the serpent are intentionally provocative in that they prompt some rethinking.[15] The serpent never suggests that they should eat the fruit, though by questioning what reasons they might have for not doing so, it leads them in that direction. In the Genesis account, the serpent is not a central character but a bit player who serves in the role of catalyst. It should not be identified as a tempter, nor should it be considered inherently evil (chaos creatures are amoral). Certainly, it should not

---

the various realms, and in the uppermost realm (top register) some of the gods are represented by their emblem animals.
[14]Note also that chaos creatures in the literature of the ANE regularly engage in dialogue.
[15]For discussion of the adjective describing the serpent, ʿārûm, see *LWAE*, 132.

be seen as representing an evil force already in the world. We therefore do not have to try to explain how evil existed in the world before the fall. It is order that is being addressed, not sin or metaphysical evil. I agree with Gijsbert van den Brink when he states, "At the end of the day, we can blame neither God nor the devil for our moral evil, but only ourselves."[16]

2. Was there death before the fall? In chapter six above I addressed the question of whether humanity was created immortal and concluded that was not the case. In this question we must turn attention to the larger issue of whether there was death of any sort prior to the fall.[17] Given that I have already defended the view that humans were created mortal and that there would therefore have been human death before the fall, there remains little reason to think that death at other levels would not have been taking place.

The traditional idea that there would have been no death before the fall was based on the premise that the goodness of creation was indicative of a paradise setting where nothing negative existed (see chapter five above, FAQ 1). I have contended that that is neither the picture given in Genesis nor the implication of the word *good*. The term *good* refers to order, not perfection.[18] Creation brought order into the midst of nonorder, but it did not dispel all nonorder. Death is one of the characteristics of nonorder and, according to the New Testament, was overcome in the resurrection of Jesus and will be fully eliminated in new creation, but the Old Testament never anticipates or endorses a state of human existence where death is absent.[19]

If these textual points are insufficient to establish the idea that there was death before the fall, some practical observations can be

---

[16]Van den Brink, *Reformed Theology and Evolutionary Theory*, 183.
[17]Initially discussed briefly in *LWAE*, 159-60.
[18]*LWAE*, 53-57.
[19]Interestingly enough, even the description of new creation in Is 65 features long life rather than the absence of death (Is 65:20).

Genesis 3: The Fall 189

garnered for further support. Plants grow through a process of cellular death; fall colors that impress us with their beauty reflect death; animals and humans alike would have been eating plants. If there was death at the cellular level and at the biological level, then what logic would draw the line at sentient life?[20] There is no reason to believe that predation was absent from the world prior to Genesis 3 (see the next question). Of course, people in the ancient Near East would not have thought about death in such terms (e.g., cellular). Nevertheless, given the significance of death, if it did not exist, we might well expect that a statement about its absence would have been made.

The idea that cells, plants, animals, and even humans would have experienced death prior to the fall has nothing in Scripture to contradict it, only the misguided presuppositions of theologians who assume that *good* must imply a paradise of perfection. Romans 5, for example, speaks only of humans being subject to death because of sin. This is not a claim of original immortality but of the destiny that was inevitable without access to the tree of life.

More provocatively, however, I have suggested that the text is not trying to convey something that we call the fall. Therefore, there can be no consideration of "before." If, as I contend, the text is less interested in an event than in an evaluation of strategies for finding order, comparison of a before and after is irrelevant. Even the idea that Genesis 3:15 conveys the idea that God has turned the struggle against chaos over to humanity does not invite us to consider a "before" scenario. Its focus is describing our current plight more than providing an etiological explanation of how it got that way (see further below in FAQ 4).

3. *Was there pain and suffering before the fall?* This question is simply a corollary to the previous one, and the answer goes roughly

---

[20]Note that human skin, epidermis, is dead cells.

in the same direction (based on the implications of the word *good* and the hazard of before/after thinking).[21] People and animals have always had nervous systems, so there could have been pain. Survival is threatened if we cannot feel pain on the physical level.[22] Moreover, suffering is not limited to the physical level. Psychological suffering can occur in the context of loss. If there is love, for example, there can be unrequited love and therefore psychological suffering. These reflections, however, come from our modern ways of thinking. We find that the only scriptural defense for the absence of suffering is the assumption that new creation will constitute a return to an Edenic state (eschatology recapitulates protology), a view already refuted above (see chap. 6, FAQ 8). The final state is defined by the absence of tears and suffering (Rev 21). But that is only possible in resurrection bodies. The suggestion that predation will be absent (the lion lying down with the lamb) likewise derives from portrayals of new creation (Is 11:6-9). Once we draw a line of differentiation between the beginning and the end, we no longer have the option of characterizing Eden by descriptions offered of new creation.

I have already pointed out that to defend a prelapsarian state of such assumed perfection, the early Christian writers had to go to great extremes that resulted in a human body entirely different from what we know.[23] But this would be true of animal bodies too, since the anatomy and physiology of predators is designed for the diet and lifestyle we observe. Yet, the concept of predation before what has been called the fall is one of the most persistent sticking points in

---

[21]*LWAE*, 57.

[22]A ready example is when those who have type 2 diabetes gradually lose feeling in their feet, sometimes resulting in injuries that become infected and require amputation. Also consider the much more serious condition of Hansen's disease.

[23]See chap. 6 above, FAQ 8, and Kathleen Crowther, *Adam and Eve in the Protestant Reformation* (Cambridge: Cambridge University Press, 2010), 74-81, discussing the views of Irenaeus.

Genesis 3: The Fall

this whole conversation and overlaps with the questions surrounding evolutionary models.[24]

For those who consider predation the result of the fall, it (and all of its required teeth, claws, and digestive systems) is viewed as being imposed on the animal world through the curse of a creator. We search in vain, however, for any inkling of such a curse referred to in Scripture. Furthermore, such a solution would not spare God the responsibility for predation. Rather than inferring some curse that the Bible never mentions and that suffers from illogic (animals being punished for human offense), we find a better solution in the pathway we have been following in this book. Creation is not yet complete; nonorder remains. Predation could perhaps be viewed as nonorder but not disorder; predation does not reflect moral deficiencies in animals. We should also recall the lesson taught to Job in the Yahweh speeches, where the discussions of all sorts of animals is meant to press the point that there is more order than we know lingering behind what we often perceive as nonorder (Job 39, which includes predation in Job 39:30; see also Ps 104:21).

How, then, should we interpret the "groaning of all creation" (Rom 8:22)? J. Richard Middleton suggests that Paul is adopting the picture of Israel groaning under the weight of their slavery (Ex 2:23-24).[25] Whether that is the case or not, the question posed is a question about Romans and Paul's intention, not a question about the intentions of the author of Genesis. Nevertheless, we could suggest

---

[24]It prompted Darwin, was lamented by Friedrich Nietzsche, was pondered by C. S. Lewis, is a central accusation of Richard Dawkins, and is the primary concern of Ken Ham, just to mention a few voices who have taken up the topic. For extensive treatment, see Michael Murray, *Nature Red in Tooth and Claw: Theism and the Problem of Animal Suffering* (Oxford: Oxford University Press, 2008); Ronald Osborn, *Death Before the Fall: Biblical Literalism and the Problem of Animal Suffering* (Downers Grove, IL: InterVarsity Press, 2014); Christopher Southgate, *The Groaning of Creation: God, Evolution, and the Problem of Evil* (Louisville, KY: Westminster John Knox, 2008).

[25]J. Richard Middleton, *A New Heaven and a New Earth: Reclaiming Biblical Eschatology* (Grand Rapids, MI: Baker, 2014), 159-60.

192   NEW EXPLORATIONS IN THE LOST WORLD OF GENESIS

that we still might understand such a concept in the context of the order spectrum. People were supposed to be working alongside God to bring order. Having strayed from this commission, we sought order that would serve our own agendas and desires.[26] "We have subjected creation to futility or frustration, much as the Egyptian king oppressed the Israelites."[27] As Romans 8:23 indicates, all creation is awaiting redemption—freedom from the nonorder and disorder that continues to characterize our present life. We, not God, are the reason for this continuing condition (see Gen 6:11).[28] Creation could be said to groan under the weight of our selfish deviations and deficiencies as God's order is neglected. We could therefore conclude that no evidence in the text suggests that pain and suffering were absent at some pristine time in the past, but a case could be made that these have been accelerated due to human actions.

4. Is the origin of sin the focus of Genesis 3? When Paul wants to discuss sin and salvation, he looks to Genesis 3 to illustrate the need for salvation. In this he was not prompted by any preserved teaching of Jesus. Some think he is reflecting a view represented in the extant literature of Second Temple Judaism.[29] Yet, at the same time, a close reading of Genesis 3 without Pauline lenses would raise the question

---

[26]As we have experienced in our modern times, this often comes at the expense of the natural world around us (killing elephants for their tusks, devastation of rainforests), though Paul would not have anticipated these activities.

[27]Middleton, *New Heaven and a New Earth*, 160.

[28]N. T. Wright, *The Day the Revolution Began: Reconsidering the Meaning of Jesus's Crucifixion* (New York: HarperOne, 2016), 370-71.

[29]Admittedly, this issue has been long debated. Ben Sira (second century BC) offers the clearest connection of the origin of sin to Gen 3: "From a woman sin had its beginning, and because of her we all die." Wisdom of Ben Sira 24:25, trans. Benjamin Wright III, in *Outside the Bible: Ancient Jewish Writings Related to Scripture*, ed. Louis Feldman, James L. Kugel, and Lawrence H. Schiffman (Philadelphia: JPS, 2013), 3:2277. Suggested parallels occur in Life of Adam and Eve, but that work is generally dated to the first century AD at the earliest. Adam as a character is addressed by numerous Second Temple Jewish sources, but not as the one through whom sin entered the world. For analysis of the pertinent texts, though with controversial results, see John R. Levison, *Portraits of Adam in Early Judaism: From Sirach to 2 Baruch*, Library of Second Temple Studies (London: Bloomsbury, 2015).

Genesis 3: The Fall 193

whether the narrator of *Genesis* is addressing sin at all (despite Ben Sira). We need to be reminded that what Paul does with Genesis can be different from what the narrator of Genesis is doing. Many readers note that the word *sin* is not used in the passage. The reality of sin is first noted in Genesis 4:7 and is universalized in Genesis 6:5; 8:21. Augustine's infamous misinterpretation of Romans 5:12 is also complicit in the development of ideas relating to how sin is perceived in Christian theology.[30] Whatever interpretation of Paul one might choose, in Genesis, I would contend that Genesis 3 read in context is not the story of how sin began. By way of corollary, that also means that in Genesis (again, despite Ben Sira), woman is not carrying the blame for bringing sin into the world, if, in Genesis, this is not a story of how sin came into the world.

When we ask questions about the beginning of sin, they overlap with the doctrine of original sin, a concept popularized in Christian doctrine by Augustine. For many today, original sin is often not clearly understood, rarely explored, but generally assumed as a pillar of Christian doctrine.[31] Somewhat in contrast, New Testament scholar Joel Green observes that the particulars of the doctrine "have been

---

[30]Based on Jerome's Latin translation, Augustine referred to all people sinning *in* Adam rather than *because of* Adam ("in whom all have sinned" rather than "because all have sinned"). See Willemien Otten, "The Long Shadow of Human Sin: Augustine on Adam, Eve and the Fall," in *Out of Paradise: Eve and Adam and Their Interpreters*, ed. Bob Becking and Susanne Hennecke (Sheffield: Sheffield Phoenix, 2011), 29-49, here 30-31; Joel B. Green, "'Adam, What Have You Done?' New Testament Voices on the Origins of Sin," in *Evolution and the Fall*, ed. William T. Cavanaugh and James K. A. Smith (Grand Rapids, MI: Eerdmans, 2017), 98-116, here 108-9. As Sanlon shows, though Augustine may be the most prominent voice as we look at the history of the doctrine, he was certainly not the first to articulate it or the only one in his time. See Peter Sanlon, "Original Sin in Patristic Theology," in *Adam, the Fall, and Original Sin: Theological, Biblical, and Scientific Perspectives*, ed. Hans Madueme and Michael Reeves (Grand Rapids, MI: Baker, 2014), 85-107, here 86-88. See also Robert Kolb, "The Lutheran Doctrine of Original Sin," in Madueme and Reeves, *Adam, the Fall*, 109-27.

[31]Primarily in Roman Catholic and Protestant contexts. For a helpful discussion of its development as a Christian doctrine, see Sanlon, "Original Sin in Patristic Theology"; Kolb, "Lutheran Doctrine of Original Sin"; and Donald Macleod, "Original Sin in Reformed Theology," in Madueme and Reeves, *Adam, the Fall*, 129-46.

194   New Explorations in the Lost World of Genesis

and are the subject of ongoing negotiation." As evidence, he points out, "Original sin may belong to our Christian heritage, particularly though not exclusively among Protestants, but, absent from the church's ecumenical creeds, it lacks magisterial definition for the whole church."[32]

No hesitation can be entertained concerning the pervasiveness of sin. I have already referred to Old Testament passages such as Genesis 6:5; 8:21 that attest to this concept in the earliest periods, and those ideas are only strengthened as we move through Scripture.[33] Nevertheless, the pervasiveness of sin and its logical corollary, the need for salvation, are not the same as the doctrine of original sin, though they are incorporated into it. The doctrine pertains not only to the etiology of sin but to its transmission to all (imputation).[34] On the latter point, Scripture has little to offer. As Green concludes at the end of his careful analysis, "Both Paul and James thus emphasize sin's corporate dimension and assume sin's heritability—not in the sense of passing sin down through procreation, but in the sense of pattern and influence."[35] This coincides with the archetypal understanding I have presented. Adam and Eve are not to be blamed for our sin and its resulting condition—we each individually and universally carry that load quite adequately on our own.

Note finally that the doctrine of original sin is dependent on seeing Adam acting in his individuality, a view that Romans 5 could be seen to endorse. Without deciding on the question of whether Adam was indeed an individual, a real person in a real past, the point I have been making is that the focus of Genesis 2–3 is not on his individuality—his actions as a person—but rather on his archetypal role, through which humanity is seen as acting. Though I

---

[32]Green, "'Adam, What Have You Done?,'" 99.

[33]Note, however, that though the pervasiveness of sin is evident in the OT, there is no corresponding need for salvation. The OT understands that sin needs to be addressed but does not have any concept of being saved from sin.

[34]Macleod, "Original Sin in Reformed Theology," 139-44.

[35]Green, "'Adam, What Have You Done?,'" 115.

Genesis 3: The Fall

contend that Genesis is not discussing sin, if we want to talk about sin using Genesis (as Paul does), sin need not be transmitted to us—we were there. This is not the same as Augustine's mistranslation of Romans 5:12 that we all have sinned "*in* Adam"—to the contrary, we *are* Adam. At the same time, Paul, his predecessors in Second Temple Judaism, and his successors in the church who formulated doctrine and commented on Scripture did indeed think of Adam as an individual (note, as an example, Paul's "one man" language in Rom 5:12-19). This issue warrants further explanation, which J. Harvey Walton offers in this excursus.

EXCURSUS 4: WHAT IS PAUL'S INTEREST IN ADAM IN ROMANS 5?

J. HARVEY WALTON

When Augustine proposed the doctrine of original sin, his objective was to remove any involvement of human will from the process of salvation, so that the receipt of grace could be attributed to God alone with no human participation. For Augustine, Adam's transgression eliminated the ability of subsequent humans to exercise their will toward godliness. Modern Christians, on the other hand, are more inclined to view original sin as a *theodicy*, an etiology of evil that preserves the justice of God. For these theologians, all the evil of the world is a just punishment for Adam's original crime, for which all subsequent humans are (one way or another) equally culpable. Both interpretations rely heavily on Romans 5, which is simultaneously read as a kind of director's cut of Genesis 3, offering new scenes and details that change the theme and plot of the story entirely.

Romans 5 in context, however, is not interested in the subject of either divine supremacy or divine justice, and also is not a commentary on Genesis. Instead, it is part of a lengthy discussion about the law of Moses and whether obedience to the law is sufficient to save a person from death. In the Judaism of Paul's day, the law of Moses was understood to represent the kind of civic *rule of law* that governs a democratic society (Greek *nomos*), similar in concept to the collection of legislation, executive orders, international treaties, and judicial decisions that govern our democracy today. Yahweh, as the author of the law, was therefore understood to essentially represent the government, and accordingly, sin—breaking the law—was essentially a crime that demanded a judicial response. Legal integrity upheld the order of Roman society, so order demanded that justice *always* had to be served. A Roman judge could be lenient, but he could not forgive. Yahweh, on the other hand, as a deity and therefore author of the world order, *could* forgive without undermining the integrity of the legal order that upheld society. Yahweh's decision to show mercy was thought to be based on the defendant's *repentance*, which in turn was demonstrated by their earnest efforts to live as a law-abiding citizen—in other words, their efforts to obey the law and commit no further crimes. When Paul and the other New Testament writers are interacting with the idea of salvation through (the works of) the law, this is what they are talking about: scrupulous obedience to the legal decrees of a divine government in order to demonstrate the proper penitence that will earn them a reprieve from a judicial sentence for a crime.

The pervasive discussion throughout the New Testament, including Romans, is whether the observance of the law is sufficient and/or required to earn the mercy of the divine judge, and the consistent answer to both (for a variety of reasons) is no. That in turn creates a different problem. In early Judaism, the economy of guilt and punishment was individualistic; the one who sinned was the one who died, and the one who was righteous was the one who lived (e.g., Ezek 18:20). If keeping the law—the only recourse a guilty person has available—cannot earn divine mercy, there must somehow be a *different* way for people who cannot earn mercy for themselves to nonetheless gain life. If life can be provided vicariously to people who are not personally righteous,

that means the economy of guilt and punishment works differently, and *that* is what Romans 5 is talking about.

Paul finds a precedent for the new economy in an anecdote about Adam as the character and his story were commonly understood at the time. Guilt for crime was not possible before the law (by definition, Rom 5:13), but nonetheless Adam's personal transgression of divine command was sufficient to vicariously bestow death on people who lived before Moses and who therefore had no law to break (Rom 5:14). If one person's guilt can earn punishment for a whole group of people who are meaningfully associated with them (in some unspecified way; Rom 5:12, 19), then the reverse is also true; one person's righteousness can earn mercy for a whole group of associated people as well (Rom 5:18-19). Adam in Romans 5 is not an archetype of humanity, and the interpretation of his story is not an etiology of human crime; he is a *pattern* (*typos*) of *Jesus* (Rom 5:14) in that his actions in an anecdotal story are establishing a meaningful precedent for something similar (though not identical, Rom 5:15-16) that Jesus will do.

My argument does not concern this interpretive and theological direction but is only trying to address what issues are being discussed in the context of Genesis.[36] If Genesis is not discussing sin and its

---

[36]I continue to emphasize the point that all interpreters are in conversation with the people and issues in their world. In this case, for example, Augustine's interpretations and doctrinal deliberations reflect his controversy with Pelagius and his followers.

Genesis 3: The Fall 197

origin, what is it discussing? Some commentators have contended that Genesis 3 portrays a movement to a higher plane (coming of age), while others have perceived a descent to a lower plane (transition to a state of sin and death). Alternatively, I interpret it as a discussion of what is capable of bringing order and the lack of ultimate success of the various options. Genesis 3 is unquestionably presented as a narrative. Nevertheless, I maintain that it is less about recounting an event and more about describing a reality—becoming like God does not provide the answer to establishing order in the human realm. The transitions from the divine realm to the human realm and to godlikeness simply illustrate how such possibilities fail to bring further clarity to achieving ultimate order. If this is the case, the theological significance of the passage does not address how sin began. The Genesis account is not seeking to establish blame in a discussion of the etiology of sin, and it certainly does not offer suggestions for how sin spreads. If we want to have those discussions, we will have to find them elsewhere. Genesis is talking about us (all humans), not them (Adam and Eve), and its focus is on the now, not in contrasting a before and an after.

5. Are Adam and Eve being punished for sin? To make a convincing case for this, we would want to identify specific terms in Genesis that make this point. Many Hebrew terms occupy the semantic domains of sin and punishment, but Genesis 3 uses none of them. Rather, the language reflects shame (Gen 3:10) and recognition of failure to heed the warning concerning the tree and its fruit. Genesis 3:11 implies accusation in the question as to whether they have eaten from the forbidden tree. Furthermore, Genesis 3:13, "What is this that you have done?" is language that recognizes the fact of the violation. Then the narrative proceeds by seeing their actions as the cause for the statements in Genesis 3:14-19. We need to analyze these nuances carefully in evaluating the question of sin and punishment.

First of all, according to the interpretation I have offered, Adam and Eve are already mortal. The reality of death is not a punishment, then, but the inevitable result of being separated from the tree of life in the divine realm, the consequence of their choice. Being doomed to death was what would result if they ate from the tree (Gen 2:17), but here in Genesis 3, God does not include a pronouncement of physical death. Death is not presented as a punishment but an inevitable reality as God prevents access to the tree of life. As Genesis 2:17 indicated, death is the consequence of their act rather than punishment for it. Note also that the text does not emphasize that they will now experience death. The consequence cited is that now they are like one of us.

Second, interpreters have traditionally seen Genesis 3:14-19, the so-called curse, as a punishment. Nevertheless, as we will see in chapter eight, it is a pronouncement, which I will suggest is descriptive, not prescriptive. As such, it also pertains to consequences, not punishment.[37] If neither death nor the pronouncement reflects punishment, but rather these are the outcomes of being relocated from the divine realm, then the only other factor we have to consider is whether "driving them out" is the punishment that itself then brings about the consequences of death and the challenging reality delineated in the pronouncement.

Genesis 3 indicates that they are "sent" (*piel* stem of *šlḥ*) from the divine realm (Gen 3:23, NIV: "banished") and that God "drives them out" (*piel* stem of *grš*, Gen 3:24).[38] Hebrew usage shows that these are not verbs of punishment. With regard to the former, consider when parents make their adult children leave the home. In most cases it is not punitive and generally does not involve banishment. They are sending them out to enter the world to which they belong, to a new phase of life. Even when parents do this forcibly, it is done for the sake

---

[37]I have often used the analogy of a teenager who gets in a car accident and totals the family car. "Punishment" might be something like being grounded; "consequence" would be the considerable increase in insurance costs.

[38]The root also occurs in the *qal* stem seven times characteristically to refer to a divorced ("driven out") woman (e.g., Lev 21:7, 14; 22:13).

Genesis 3: The Fall

of the one being sent out, not as punishment on them. The *piel* stem of *šlḥ* can refer to sending out on a mission (the birds in Gen 8:7-12; messengers in Gen 19:13); sending out to remove one from an area (Gen 12:20) or dismissing one from someone's presence (Job 22:9 and many passages about divorce); sending out as an act of deliverance (Gen 19:29; often in Exodus, and of freeing slaves in Jer 34:9-16); and sending out to the next phase (Gen 24:54-59; 25:6; 30:25). God does not send Israel into exile (punishment), but he does send them home from exile (Is 45:13).[39] God can send armies, fire, locusts, or plagues as punishment, but that is not the same as sending someone away as punishment.[40]

Turning now to the second verb, in the over thirty-five occurrences of the *piel* or *pual* stems of *grš*, about one-third of them relate to either Yahweh or Israel driving out the peoples of the land at the time of Joshua. I have argued elsewhere that there is no indication that this is punishment being visited on the peoples of the land.[41] The other uses of this verb indicate that the person or group is being driven out not as punishment for something they did but to protect, defend, or maybe even seize something of value.[42] This usage profile would suggest that driving Adam and Eve out is not punishment but either protection for

---

[39]Jer 24:5 does speak of God sending Israel into exile (*piel* stem of *šlḥ*), but there it is referred to as being good, not as a punishment (see Jer 29:20).

[40]In over 250 occurrences, the only possible exception is Jer 28:16, and there it is used in a collocation for death ("send away" + "from the earth").

[41]*LWIC*, 38-47.

[42]For examples using the *piel* stem of *grš*, see Gen 21:10 (protecting covenant inheritance); Ex 2:17 (protecting water rights); Ex 6:1; 11:1 (Pharaoh protecting his country from further harm); Num 22:6, 11 (king of Moab protecting his land); Judg 9:41 (protecting his authority); Judg 11:7 (protecting inheritance); Mic 2:9 (seizing property of widows); Zeph 2:4 (seizing cities). Seen in this light, driving out the peoples of the land is to protect the Israelites from being corrupted, to defend the sanctity of Yahweh's land, or even to seize their cities—not as punishment. The one occurrence that looks like it could be punishment is in God's treatment of Cain in Gen 4:14. But here Cain is being banished from the ground not as punishment for his sin but as the destiny of calamity (*ʿāwôn*) that has come upon him for defiling the ground with Abel's blood. For this understanding of *ʿāwôn*, see *LWIC*, 54-57.

200   NEW EXPLORATIONS IN THE LOST WORLD OF GENESIS

the tree of life (something for only the divine realm) or even protection of humans from the tree of life (Gen 3:22). Humans have discovered that the divine realm is not a suitable place for them. Immortality is possible only in the divine realm, and being like God equips them to live in the human realm, where they belong.

As a side note, consider that if driving out is not punishment, and if Eden is the divine realm, then the parallels often drawn between Genesis 3 and the exile become less defensible and less plausible. The *piel* stem of *grš* is never used of sending Israel into exile, which *was* judgment. That means that the interpretation of Genesis 3 as an allegory concerning Israel's exile from the land cannot be defended from the Old Testament.

I am not questioning that Adam and Eve disregarded God's warning; failing to heed a divine warning could be labeled a form of sin.[43] But the consequences of disregarding the warning do not come because they have offended God; the consequences come because the warning was for their own good. Their neglect and its consequences are drawn out in their confrontation with God ("What is this you have done?").[44]

The question still remains, Is this an account of the first sin and its punishment that extends to all humankind? The data presented here leave that case unsettled in that the text contains nothing that makes these aspects explicit. I conclude that in Genesis the author is not telling the story of the first sin and its punishment. Moreover, it is what the Genesis author intends to do that carries the authority of the

---

[43]For other examples, we may well reflect on Abraham's mating with Hagar or Rahab's misdirection of the king's soldiers as sins. But the text does not so identify them and is not interested in whether they are.

[44]Consider the example of a parent who warns a child not to touch the hot stove. The child's curiosity leads them to neglect the warning, and as a result they suffer a burn. This is not punishment but consequence. Since the child knows that they disregarded the warning and is now suffering as a result, they try to hide the burn from their parent. But the parent recognizes that the clumsily wrapped hand is being hidden and confronts the child, "What have you done? Did you touch the stove that I warned you not to touch?"

Genesis 3: The Fall 201

text. While it is clear that the text *could be* redeployed with those questions in mind if the interpreter had those questions on the table, that does not allow us to disregard what the text was doing.[45] Nor should it be taken as permission to redeploy the text in any way we choose. Even if those *are* the questions on the table for Second Temple Judaism, for Paul, and for Christian writers throughout history, that does not mean that those are the questions that the ancient Israelites were raising or the answers they were offering. Our hermeneutics bind us to the authors' literary intentions. Even if *Paul's* intentions are to discuss sin and punishment, that does not mean that the narrator of Genesis has the same concerns, and our first obligation is to read that text in context.

6. Is Genesis 3 a theodicy? I have already expressed the reasons I believe that Genesis 2–3 does not offer an etiology of sin. Another part of traditional Christian doctrine is that Genesis 2–3 offers a theodicy— an explanation for why there is suffering and evil in the world, particularly an explanation that puts the blame somewhere other than on God. So now we must address the question of whether Genesis 2–3 actually plays that role in the context of Genesis.

To begin with, we should ask the question, What makes people believe that Genesis 3 is a theodicy? Why do they find such an interpretation necessary? Even in the ancient Near East, people were interested in trying to explain evil in the world, and it remains one of the biggest questions in philosophy today.[46] It is therefore no surprise that people who value the Bible have wanted to find an answer to the problem of evil, and likewise no surprise that they should turn to the opening chapters of Genesis in search of such an answer. People wonder whether there was evil in the world before the garden. If they understand the serpent as Satan, then they look earlier than the garden

---

[45]Again, compare Rahab's lie.

[46]For examples, see the numerous articles from various ancient cultures in Antti Laato and Johannes C. de Moor, eds., *Theodicy in the World of the Bible* (Leiden: Brill, 2003).

to explain that evil and devise stories of the fall of Satan (not offered in the Bible).[47] Others look to the act of disobedience as the beginning of sin and see that event as offering an explanation of how evil came into the world as the result of human action. Even in those two scenarios (sometimes blended), questions are asked about why God created beings who were able to sin (fall) and whether that makes him complicit.

These options and variations of them all find supporters in the history of interpretation of Genesis, but we have to ask whether they are the questions Genesis is asking. The interpretations of passages in Genesis I have offered thus far maintain that these are not the issues important to the author and ancient audience of Genesis. The issue in the book is the pursuit of order. The evidence of the book itself cannot sustain the idea that it is asking about the origin of evil or proposing how it came into the world. It is not attempting to blame or exonerate God, Satan, or humanity. If we want answers to those questions and seek a theodicy, we should look elsewhere.[48] The text does not begin by depicting a world devoid of evil. The nonordered world is not a desirable world, so Genesis is not starting with a pristine environment and therefore does not document when it become nonpristine—that is, it is not trying to pinpoint when evil began.

---

[47]For full discussion, see John H. Walton and J. Harvey Walton, *Demons and Spirits in Biblical Theology* (Eugene, OR: Cascade, 2019), 212-28.

[48]For extended discussion of theodicy and Gen 3, see Walton, "Knowing Good and Evil," 101-7.

8

Genesis 3

The Pronouncement

SUMMARY OF PREVIOUS MATERIAL

I gave little attention to what is often referred to as "the curse" in the Lost World books, though I treated it at some length in my Genesis commentary.[1] There I observed that the term *curse* is not applied to humans but to the serpent and the ground. I also noted that the translation "curse" even in Genesis 3:14, 19 is misleading, but regardless, it is not applied to people. We will dig deeper into the terminology in the next section, but I proposed that if we have mislabeled this "the curse" (on people), we have to reconsider what the nature of this section is. The position I adopted is that it should be viewed as *descriptive* (of a situation) rather than *prescriptive* (imposing a punishment on people). I compared it to a parental discussion with a wayward teen whose behavior resulted in negative consequences. In such a case, the existing scenario is laid out even if the parent is not punishing the son or daughter. The conversation is meant to offer a reality check.

Likewise, I discussed Genesis 3:15 specifically only in passing in *The Lost World of Adam and Eve* but extensively in the earlier commentary.[2] The two main points I made pertained to the singular pronouns and the verbs used to describe the conflict. I analyzed the singular verbs as

---

[1]John H. Walton, *Genesis*, NIV Application Commentary (Grand Rapids, MI: Zondervan, 2001), 224-29, 236-39.
[2]*LWAE*, 135.

204   NEW EXPLORATIONS IN THE LOST WORLD OF GENESIS

grammatically appropriate in connection with a collective noun ("seed") rather than as indicative of a future singular descendant. Since the verbs expressing the conflict between the parties were the same, I contended that they should be considered as having equivalent potential impact. That is, the serpent's bite and the human's trample are equally potentially mortal blows. I therefore concluded that the verse does not indicate a victory and therefore should be considered neither a proclamation of the eventual defeat of the devil (also remember that the serpent would not have been seen as Satan) nor a messianic promise of hope.

I gave Genesis 3:16 considerable attention in the commentary but did not mention it in *The Lost World of Adam and Eve*. I argued strenuously against the traditional interpretations that suggest that the woman's desire was to control her husband (traditionally based on nuances derived from Gen 4:7), was a sexual desire (based on Song 7:10), or was reflecting a psychological weakness.[3] All of these read too much into the word *desire*. Instead, I contended that based on usage (infrequent and diverse as it is), the word must reflect a larger sense of instinct or inclination applicable across a broad spectrum that could be defined in many different ways by contextual factors.

Other main points that I made were that the word *pain* is better understood as *anxiety*, which makes much more sense in that it is related to conception rather than to childbearing, the latter chosen by most translations despite the indisputable fact that the Hebrew term refers to conception. Once we recognize anxiety as the issue rather than just physical pain, the connection to conception makes much better sense since conception for women in the ancient world was fraught with anxiety. Women were not considered to have a stable place in the family until they had conceived and given birth to a child.

---

[3]Such an interpretation of Gen 3:16 is interpretively made explicit in several translations. "Your desire shall be contrary to your husband, but he shall rule over you" (ESV); "you will desire to control your husband, but he will rule over you" (NLT); "You will want to control your husband, but he will dominate you" (NET).

Genesis 3: The Pronouncement

Furthermore, maternal mortality was high in the ancient world, so though pregnancy was considered a gift from God, it also brought the realization that the soon-to-be mother may have had only eight months to live. This high anxiety for the mother was intensified greatly when taking account of all the things that could go wrong with the baby.

I then suggested that, given all the hazards surrounding the process that led to being fruitful and multiplying, one might imagine that women would be hesitant to put their lives at risk. Nevertheless, that a woman's status depended on bearing children meant that she would continue to have a desire (natural inclination as well as social mandate) to do so. Obviously, however, she could not do so alone. Since she needed her husband's cooperation to fulfill this essential role, she was dependent on him, and he could therefore lord it over her by withholding his seed (a scenario occasionally found in biblical narrative; see Gen 38:8-10).

The man would likewise experience anxiety when the unproductive ground made survival difficult. This finds support in the linguistic data showing that the reference to sweat in the ancient world is typically related to anguish or anxiety, not to hard labor.[4] Thus God indicates to the humans that they will face challenges in the most basic aspects of life: reproduction (though the blessing remains intact) and food (still made available but accompanied by great anxiety). On both counts, people experience anxiety because failure threatens and death is always looming.

New Explorations

Cursed. The Hebrew verb ʾārûr is one of several words translated "curse" in the Old Testament. This particular verb can refer to a hex (like its Akkadian cognate), but when used in combination with the m- preposition (only in Gen 3:14; 4:11), it refers to banishment or disenfranchisement.[5]

---

[4]Daniel E. Fleming, "By the Sweat of Your Brow: Adam, Anat, Athirat and Ashurbanipal," in *Ugarit and the Bible*, ed. George J. Brooke, Adrian H. W. Curtis, and John F. Healey, Ugaritisch-Biblische Literatur 11 (Münster: Ugarit-Verlag, 1994), 93-100.

[5]Josef Scharbert, "ʾārûr," in *Theological Dictionary of the Old Testament*, ed. G. Johannes Botterweck and Helmer Ringgren, trans. John T. Willis et al. (Grand Rapids, MI:

It reflects an interruption of order, as it implies the object is relegated in some way to a liminal state. For example, Cain's reaction indicates that he is removed from the protection of family and society, the foundation of order, as he is driven out into the liminal world, where his life is in jeopardy, leading him to seek ways to bring order (such as city building). Specifically, however, the judgment removes him from the support of the produce of the ground, which is what necessitates his wandering.

When we consider the curse on the ground (Gen 3:17), we have another unusual contextual factor to consider—that the object of the verb is impersonal. All but three of the forty occurrences of the curse formula in the Hebrew Bible refer to beings (mostly people but also the serpent). The inanimate exceptions are Genesis 3:17 (ground); Deuteronomy 28:17 (basket and kneading trough); and Jeremiah 20:14 (day of his birth).[6] Both the ground in Genesis 3:17 and the vessels for food production reflect their cursed nature by being unproductive or uncooperative—again, relegation to unproductive liminality.

Genesis 3:15. As developed in my Genesis commentary, the idea that the serpent and its seed will be mutually exchanging potentially mortal blows with the woman and her seed (that is, generation to generation) argues against interpreting this verse as an announcement of victory. How then shall we interpret the passage? Once we identify the serpent as a chaos creature, we can consider how that identity would offer an interpretation of this verse.

Eerdmans, 1974–2006), 1:408-9; Anne Marie Kitz, *Cursed Are You: The Phenomenology of Cursing in Cuneiform and Hebrew Texts* (Winona Lake, IN: Eisenbrauns, 2014), 138-39, 238-39. For extensive semantic analysis, see Scharbert, "ʾārûr," 405-18; Kitz, *Cursed Are You*. Ziony Zevit encapsulates the English word as containing the "notion of malevolent power triggered by some supernatural authority that wreaks destruction or vengeance." See Zevit, *What Really Happened in the Garden of Eden?* (New Haven, CT: Yale University Press, 2013), 193-94.

[6]Days are considered "cursed" because of a devastating event that took place on the day, such as how we talk about 9/11 as the day of the terrorist attack in 2001. Similarly, March 11 is now remembered as "Covid day." Because of the terrifying role that Jeremiah had to play, he considered the day of his birth such a cursed day.

Genesis 3: The Pronouncement

J. Harvey Walton observes that this verse can be interpreted in light of ancient Near Eastern contexts, in which the gods did battle with chaos creatures in the order-bringing activities of creation.[7] This well-known motif in ancient Near Eastern literature, referred to as *Chaoskampf* (battle against chaos), is most prominent in the Babylonian creation epic, Enuma Elish.[8] Evident in Genesis is that instead of the god doing battle with the chaos creature (here the serpent), a concept that Genesis 1 ignores, *people* are given the ongoing task of combat with chaos. Here all of humanity is given the task of battling against chaos, a role that was often considered the task of the king in the ancient Near East.[9] From generation to generation, humans, having the delegated responsibility to bring order, will have to sustain a battle against the

---

[7]J. Harvey Walton, personal communication.

[8]For major discussions on the *Chaoskampf* motif, see Bernhard W. Anderson, *Creation Versus Chaos* (New York: Association, 1967); Debra S. Ballentine, *The Conflict Myth and the Biblical Tradition* (New York: Oxford University Press, 2015); Bernard F. Batto, *Slaying the Dragon: Mythmaking in the Biblical Tradition* (Louisville, KY: Westminster John Knox, 1992); Paul K.-K. Cho, *Myth, History, and Metaphor in the Hebrew Bible* (Cambridge: Cambridge University Press, 2019); John Day, *God's Conflict with the Dragon and the Sea: Echoes of a Canaanite Myth in the Old Testament* (Cambridge: Cambridge University Press, 1985); Carola Kloos, *Yhwh's Combat with the Sea* (Leiden: Brill, 1986); Susan Niditch, *Chaos to Cosmos: Studies in Biblical Patterns of Creation* (Atlanta: Scholars Press, 1985); JoAnn Scurlock and Richard H. Beal, *Creation and Chaos* (Winona Lake, IN: Eisenbrauns, 2013); J. Toyraänvourl, *Sea and the Combat Myth: North West Semitic Political Mythology in the Hebrew Bible*, AOAT 457 (Münster: Ugarit-Verlag, 2018); David Tsumura, *Creation and Destruction: A Reappraisal of the Chaoskampf Theory in the Old Testament* (Winona Lake, IN: Eisenbrauns, 2005); Mary K. Wakeman, *God's Battle with the Monster* (Leiden: Brill, 1973); John H. Walton, "Creation in Gen 1:1–2:3 and the Ancient Near East: Order Out of Disorder After *Chaoskampf*," *Calvin Theological Journal* 43 (2008); Rebecca S. Watson, *Chaos Uncreated: A Reassessment of the Theme of "Chaos" in the Hebrew Bible* (Berlin: de Gruyter, 2005).

[9]Portrayed most prominently in the Assyrian king's lion hunts. See Chikako E. Watanabe, *Animal Symbolism in Mesopotamia: A Contextual Approach* (Vienna: Institut für Orientalistik der Universität Wien, 2002), 42-56; Brent D. Strawn, *What Is Stronger Than a Lion? Leonine Image and Metaphor in the Hebrew Bible and the Ancient Near East*, Orbis Biblicus et Orientalis 212 (Göttingen: Vandenhoeck & Ruprecht, 2005); Benjamin R. Foster, "Animals in Mesopotamian Literature," in *A History of the Animal World in the Ancient Near East*, ed. Billie Jean Collins (Leiden: Brill, 2002), 271-88; Margaret Cool Root, "Animals in the Art of Ancient Iran," in Collins, *History of the Animal World*, 169-209; Tallay Ornan, "The Defeat of the Lion: A Visual Trope Promoting Ancient Near Eastern Kings," in *Picturing Royal Charisma: Kings and Rulers in the Near East from 3000 BCE to 1700 CE*, ed. Arlette David, Rachel Milstein, and Tallay Ornan (Oxford: Archaeopress Archaeology, 2023), 23-50.

208　New Explorations in the Lost World of Genesis

constant tension that the ordered world will revert to nonorder, thus undermining attempts to bring and sustain order. Contrary to the traditional interpretation that this pertains to the ultimate victory of God, in this interpretation God removes himself from the conflict.

Genesis 3:16. The position I had proposed was that the desire (natural inclination) toward the husband reflected procreation dependence (the woman could not have children on her own), leading to possible male domination (withholding seed).[10] Though this remains a possible interpretation, several problems can be identified with this view. First, if conception were the focus of the narrator, it would have been clearer to say that the woman's desire was to conceive rather than her desire being for her husband. Second, while the scenario of a husband exercising power by withholding seed or refusing responsibility is attested (besides Gen 38, possibly David and Michal, 2 Sam 6:23), husbands were generally highly motivated to have children as well, so withholding may not have been a common enough occurrence to be featured so prominently here. Third, the Hebrew term used to express the rule exercised by the husband is not typically a negative term, as would be required by this interpretation.

A second option also interprets the verse in the context of sexual domination but goes the opposite direction. Instead of withholding seed, male domination is viewed as taking the form of the husband demanding that his wife produce more and more children in order to strengthen the family line and to provide workers for their challenging agrarian lives. This is supported by translating, "I will greatly increase your hard labor and your pregnancies" and "your turning will be to your husband."[11]

A third option has been proposed by J. Harvey Walton, summarized in his excursus.

---

[10]Reflected in my Genesis commentary but not addressed in the Lost World Series (see Walton, *Genesis*).

[11]Interpretation adopted by Carol L. Meyers, *Rediscovering Eve: Ancient Israelite Women in Context* (Oxford: Oxford University Press, 2013), 95-121. Her discussion of turning is on 94 and could be supported by the LXX variant (*apostrophē* < *təšûbâ*).

EXCURSUS 5: WHAT IS GOING ON IN GENESIS 3:16?

J. HARVEY WALTON

The destiny in Genesis 3:17-19, decreed for Adam alone, does not reflect a life experience unique to human males. As discussed in excursus 4, Adam is not an archetype of human males; he is an archetype of humans who work the ground—established in Genesis 2:5-7 by the negative condition he is created to correct—and his destiny reflects the struggles of both male and female humans as they attempt to fill that void and work the ground. Eve's character was likewise created to correct a negation (Gen 2:18), and her destiny should similarly reflect the struggles of both male and female humans as they attempt to fill the void of isolation and alterity.

The struggle that Adam—representing agrarian humanity—will face is brought about by a curse not on him but on the ground. The struggle that Eve—representing communal humanity—will face is likewise brought about by a curse not on her but on the serpent. Eve is addressed alone (without Adam) in Genesis 3:15, as an object of the serpent's enmity together with her offspring. The reciprocating mortal injuries of the head crush and heel strike represent God delegating the task of subduing chaos to humanity, a condition that will persist down through future generations. Just as thorns and thistles will impede the human effort to work the ground, so will the animosity of personified chaos impede the human effort to perpetuate their community into the future through procreation.

Genesis 3:16 does not begin with a new "Because you [did] . . . cursed" statement.

Instead, it continues the thought of the previous verse, providing more detail about what effect the animosity of personified chaos will entail. Specifically, the process of conceiving and bearing children will now occur in a state of anxiety and fear. "Conceiving and bearing children" does not refer to the biomechanical processes of gestation and birth (an experience unique to females, which uses different words; see Gen 35:17-18; Is 13:8; 26:17-18; Jer 4:31; Mic 4:9-10) but instead refers to the social and communal implications of the next generation, something both male and female humans are deeply invested in (see especially Gen 5, where the word translated "became the father of" is the same word translated "give birth" in Gen 3:16).

If the destinies of Genesis 3:17-19 and also Genesis 3:15-16a apply equally to both male and female humans, Genesis 3:16b probably does as well. The juxtaposition of the wife's desire and the husband's rule could potentially represent something that will make the attempt to overcome solitude through community more difficult, as also seen in the serpent's enmity and heel strike. Alternatively, it could represent a reassurance of (partial) success, as also seen in the destiny of crushing the serpent's head. Because a positive and a negative destiny (for the humans) are juxtaposed in Genesis 3:15—the defeat and victory of the serpent, respectively—and because Genesis 3:16 is an extrapolation of that destiny and its implications, a hopeful or reassuring statement seems more likely. Nonetheless, the final reading should be based on whether the *reading audience of Genesis* would have imagined the condition of a wife's desire and a husband's rule as a desirable or an undesirable state of affairs, and whether it would be a good or bad thing for the successful propagation of community.

In all likelihood, the authors and audience of the Old Testament were all male and would have not been interested in how a woman might experience her own desire or her husband's rule. The relevant question for modern readers is whether these male authors and audience—based on their experience as males—would have understood the picture of a woman desiring and a husband ruling to represent a harmonious relationship or a dysfunctional relationship. If the dynamic described in Genesis 3:16b would have been seen as dysfunctional, the dysfunction (whatever it specifically looks like) represents a further obstacle to overcoming solitude that both males and females will have to endure. If, alternatively, the dynamic would have been seen as harmonious—which is quite possible, given the positive connotation of a spouse's desire in Song of Songs 7:10 and the overall culture's inclinations toward patrimonial and hierarchical social structuring—then it represents a reassurance that, despite the aforementioned obstacles, both males and females will still be able to find security and stability (whatever that specifically looks like) and successfully sustain their community despite the animosity of personified chaos. The destiny of Genesis 3:16b does not decree gender roles; it decrees either social harmony or social dysfunction. Both harmony and dysfunction can manifest in a variety of different ways in a variety of different social relationships. Whatever connotation the destiny specifically has, harmony or dysfunction can both be experienced by both males and females, and both are relevant to both male and female humans attempting to overcome the undesirable state of "being alone," which is who Eve's character archetypally represents.

The main difference between these interpretations is that both my previous interpretation and the one proposed by Carol Meyers represent a negative reading of *mšl* ("rule"). This also characterizes the traditional interpretations that view the husband's rule as punishment on the woman, with the assumption that this section was imposing subjugation as a curse on womankind as the one who first ate the fruit and then gave it to her husband. This view presumed that a power struggle was inherent in the role the woman played in taking the fruit. Walton's option, which I have now adopted, treats the husband's rule

Genesis 3: The Pronouncement

as indicative of a structured society. There is no question that those in a position of rule (whether husbands, employers, or kings) can be abusive, tyrannical, or despotic, but this verb is consistently used in connection with a positive view of authority structures. This should be differentiated from the traditional interpretation that reads this verse as establishing a universal biblical mandate for male authority (which, since it is viewed as biblical, is considered positive), which likewise considers the imposed structure to be a punishment on women. As I had previously proposed and continue to maintain, this section is descriptive, not prescriptive. What it describes is not something we should take as a biblically mandated scenario. It is also not a biblical assessment of the institution of patrimonial hierarchy as a household structure (as opposed to egalitarian equality) any more than the lack of a king in Israel in Judges is a biblical assessment of the institution of monarchy as a political structure (as opposed to democracy).[12]

In contrast, then, I now hold that the text describes an ancient Israelite mode of thinking. Ruling in this sense is an order-bringing role rather than an exercise of power. Genesis 3:16, then, should be seen as elaborating one of the main implications of Genesis 3:15, specifically dealing with women producing offspring, an activity that will be fraught with anxiety.

Community is the sought-after solution—a positive destiny for humans, who find it to be order bringing. The patrimonial form of community is alluded to neither as a negative nor as a positive—it just is. The alternative is not some other form of rule but isolation from community. As such, it is not about gender roles but about the order that community offers, just as Genesis 3:17-19 is not about gender roles but about the order that tilling the ground offers. The order found in both community and tilling the ground, however, brings anxiety, since people are staving off the threat of chaos as they face the potential of death and extinction.

---

[12]J. Harvey Walton, personal communication.

Answers to Frequently Asked Questions

1. Should we consider Genesis 3:15 messianic? On the basis of both my previous analysis and the new interpretive information offered here, I find no reason to think that Genesis 3:15 is a declaration of the gospel (referred to as the protoevangelium) or a messianic prophecy. Both of these perspectives are ruled out specifically by the recognition that no victory is envisioned by the narrator of Genesis. If we are tracking with the narrator as a hermeneutical necessity of submitting to the authority of the text, we cannot allow this deviation from the meaning of the text-in-context.

Furthermore, we cannot adopt a messianic reading on the basis of some assumed affirmation in the New Testament; it never suggests the work of Jesus as a fulfillment of Genesis 3:15. At this point, we can pick up the argument that I made in *Wisdom for Faithful Reading*, where I pointed out that the only possible reference to Genesis 3:15 in the New Testament is Romans 16:20.[13] Paul includes in his final greeting to the church at Rome, "The God of peace will soon crush Satan under your feet." Three pieces of evidence suggest that this does not support a messianic interpretation of Genesis 3:15.

1. If it were a reference to Genesis 3:15, it would undermine a messianic interpretation. In Romans 16:20, the foot that is expected to crush Satan is the church at Rome (empowered by "the God of peace"), not Jesus.

2. The Greek word Paul uses for the verb "crush" in Romans 16:20 is not the same one that his likely Greek translation of the Old Testament used in Genesis 3:15. If Paul wanted to make the connection, it would have been logical to use the Greek verb familiar from that passage.

---

[13]John H. Walton, *Wisdom for Faithful Reading: Principles and Practices for Old Testament Interpretation* (Downers Grove, IL: InterVarsity Press, 2023), 24-25. Rev 12 makes an explicit allusion to Gen 3:15 but does not offer an interpretation or a fulfillment.

Genesis 3: The Pronouncement

3. Paul does not speak of crushing under the *heel*, as Genesis 3:15 does, but under the *foot*. That distinction is significant because the idea of placing enemies under one's feet is a widespread idiom throughout the ancient and classical worlds communicating conquest or subjugation (see Ps 110:1).

Consequently, Paul is likely not referring to Genesis 3:15, but even if he were, he would not be interpreting it in a messianic way.

2. Does Genesis 3 have anything to contribute to questions concerning the roles of women? Whether Genesis 3:16 refers to procreation dependence (as in my former view), male demands for more offspring (Meyers's view), or the stability of community, this verse does not suggest that God is *imposing* an authoritarian structure on the family as consequence for Eve's role in the preceding events. If, as I maintain, it is not a curse, not punishment, and not imposing a hierarchy, then it can have nothing to say about any mandated role of women in the home or in the church today. The text refers to how Israelite family structures worked and how those structures could bring order in the threatening context of childbearing. Nothing in the text of Genesis 2–3 could be used to defend a lesser position for women.

3. What is the significance of the guardian with the sword? This is not a topic I addressed in *The Lost World of Adam and Eve*, and I did not even give it much attention in my Genesis commentary.[14] A student paper recently prompted me to consider the ancient Near Eastern background of this verse and its significance.[15] The cherubim are well-known in the Old Testament as the composite

---

[14]Walton, *Genesis*, 230.

[15]Adrien Hayward, "Your Storybook Bible Needs New Pictures!: A Re-picturing of Genesis 3:24 in Its Ancient Near Eastern Context" (unpublished, cited with permission). See Ronald S. Hendel, "The Flame of the Whirling Sword: A Note on Genesis 3:24," *Journal for Biblical Literature* 104 (1985): 671-74; Abraham Winitzer, "Etana in Eden: New Light on Mesopotamian and Biblical Tales in Their Semitic Context," *Journal of the American Oriental Society* 133 (2013): 441-65.

214 NEW EXPLORATIONS IN THE LOST WORLD OF GENESIS

creatures that guard both sacred space (prominent in the sanctuary decor, even flanking the ark of the covenant) and royal space (flanking the throne).[16] They are also ubiquitous in ancient Near Eastern iconography, serving the same functions. They are not gods but in Assyrian and Babylonian contexts are specified as part of the divine realm.[17]

In Genesis 3:24 no grammatical analysis would suggest that the two or more guardians (plural, cherubim) are wielding a weapon. In fact, such guardians are not portrayed in either the literature or iconography as having weapons. The Hebrew indicates that God stationed the guardians (direct object 1) and Lahaṭ ("flame"? direct object 2), the whirling sword (descriptor of Lahaṭ), to guard the way to the tree of life.[18] Note that it is not the entrance to the garden that is guarded but the path to the tree of life.

Of particular interest is the common idea in the ancient Near East that deities had weapons that could at times take on a deified nature themselves and were given names.[19] Typically, special weapons were wielded by deities in battles against chaos (Baal against Yamm, the Sea, and Marduk against Tiamat, the Sea; Ninurta fighting the chaos creature Anzu).[20]) Given that possibility, *Lahaṭ* may be the name of

---

[16]Raanan Eichler, *The Ark and the Cherubim*, Forschungen zum Alten Testament 146 (Tübingen: Mohr Siebeck, 2021).

[17]Akkadian *kuribu*. Note that here again we have chaos creatures, here hybrids, in the divine realm.

[18]The word translated "whirling" is a rarely used Hebrew term referring to circular movement, whether rolling, wheeling, or whirling.

[19]Michael B. Hundley, *Yahweh Among the Gods: The Divine in Genesis, Exodus, and the Ancient Near East* (Cambridge: Cambridge University Press, 2021), 266-68; Hundley, "Here a God, There a God: An Examination of the Divine in Ancient Mesopotamia," *Altorientalische Forschungen* 40 (2013): 68-107; Barbara Nevling Porter, "Blessings from a Crown, Offerings to a Drum: Were There Non-anthropomorphic Deities in Ancient Mesopotamia?," in *What Is a God? Anthropomorphic and Non-anthropomorphic Aspects of Deity in Ancient Mesopotamia*, ed. Barbara Nevling Porter (Winona Lake, IN: Eisenbrauns, 2009), 153-94 (see 180-81 for examples of such named weapons).

[20]Baal's weapons, Yagarrish and Ayyamarri, in the Baal Epic; Enuma Elish 4.91-104; in the Epic of Anzu, Ninurta's weapon is Šarur (2.86), also known from the epic Lugale. On

Genesis 3: The Pronouncement   215

the deified whirling sword. Alternatively, *Flame* may be considered the name of a being who wields a whirling sword.[21] The difference is in whether the whirling sword is an animate object or wielded by a being. Either of these options could be supported by Psalm 104:4, "He makes winds his messengers, flames of fire his servants."[22] From our cultural context, we might just think of this psalm as indicative of natural elements being controlled by God, but in the ancient context, the (four) winds and "flame" would be beings.

Regardless of whether we understand Lahaṭ as an animate object or as a being, it is clear that this verse, like so many others, reflects an ancient Near Eastern cultural context. The gods in the ancient world had weapons as well as attendants who served them. The gods also guarded their prerogatives, in this case, the life that characterized the divine realm, represented in the tree of life. In the ancient Near East, the gods generally were viewed as withholding immortality from humanity, though in the case of Adapa, it appears that it was on offer, but Adapa refused it, as counseled by his god Ea (who perhaps wanted to withhold it from him). In Genesis, God does not withhold immortality, but its properties are made inaccessible with fearsome guardians as sentries.

4. Why does Genesis 3:22 use the plural form ("like one of us")?

Plural pronouns pertaining to deity occur a number of other times in the Old Testament (Gen 1:26; 11:7; Is 6:8). It is easy to see why Christian interpreters generally agreed that this was a reference to

---

Yagarrish and Ayyamarri, see Manfried Dietrich, Oswald Loretz, and Joaquín Sanmartín, eds., *Die keilalphabetischen Texte aus Ugarit* (Münster: Ugarit-Verlag, 2013), 1.2: IV, 24.

[21]Hendel, "Flame of the Whirling Sword," 673. Wilfred G. E. Watson lists lesser deities with similar names, e.g., Nablum. See Watson, "Flame," *Dictionary of Deities and Demons in the Bible*, 2nd ed., ed. Karel van der Toorn, Bob Becking, and Pieter W. van der Horst (Grand Rapids, MI: Eerdmans, 1999), 335; see also Hundley, *Yahweh Among the Gods*, 268; Douglas R. Frayne and Johanna H. Stuckey, *A Handbook of Gods and Goddesses of the Ancient Near East: Three Thousand Deities of Anatolia, Syria, Israel, Babylonia, Assyria, and Elam* (University Park, PA: Eisenbrauns, 2021), 220.

[22]This also uses Lahaṭ, and in the singular, not a plural, as implied by this NIV translation.

216   NEW EXPLORATIONS IN THE LOST WORLD OF GENESIS

the Trinity, but it should also be acknowledged that the Israelite author and audience would not have come to that same conclusion.[23] If we value tracking with the author's intentions, then we must look for another explanation. Other interpretations, documented at length in almost every academic commentary, have included grammatical ones (plural pronouns to correspond to the plural noun for God, Elohim) as well as rhetorical ones (plural of majesty). Though maintained by some, the drawbacks to these options have to do with how difficult it is to substantiate them in light of Hebrew usage.

The more common interpretation, and the one I have also adopted, is that it is a reference to the divine council. The divine council (sometimes referred to as the heavenly court) is well attested both in the Hebrew Bible and in the ancient world.[24] Even so, I disagree with those, such as Michael Heiser, who propose that the Bible's reference to the divine council must be taken as affirmation of its existence and so mandate that we must also adopt such a view of how God works.[25] Rather, I am inclined to think of Old Testament references to the divine council as similar to its references to cosmic geography (solid sky, etc.). That is, they simply accommodate how people thought in the ancient world for communication purposes rather than offering scriptural truth about how things really are.

---

[23]Note further that the NT offers no trinitarian interpretation of the plural pronouns either, so that cannot be used as support for interpreting them that way.

[24]OT references include Job 1; 1 Kings 22; Is 6; Dan 7; and several psalms (e.g, Ps 82; 89). For further discussion, see Ellen White, *Yahweh's Council* (Tübingen: Mohr Siebeck, 2014); Theodore Mullen, *Assembly of the Gods* (Missoula, MT: Scholars Press, 1980). For discussion of the question, including in early Judaism, see Archie Wright, *Origin of Evil Spirits* (Tübingen: Mohr Siebeck, 2005), 61-75.

[25]Michael Heiser, *The Unseen Realm* (Bellingham, WA: Lexham, 2015).

9

Genesis and Science

SUMMARY OF PREVIOUS MATERIAL

In *The Lost World of Genesis One*, several propositions addressed scientific issues:

- the metaphysical differences between science and Scripture, particularly contrasting the teleology (having a purpose and a goal) of theology, Scripture, and Genesis, to the dysteleology of science;
- the question of intelligent design;
- the ultimate compatibility between the Bible and models that posit evolutionary mechanisms as descriptive of God's creative work;
- and the question of public education.

I also addressed the (ultimately scientific) question of the age of the earth. Since I had proposed that the seven-day creation account was focused on ordering the cosmos with a purpose rather than on scientific origins of matter, it became clear that Genesis did not offer a view of the age of the earth (a material question).[1] Instead, the seven days reflected the seven-day inauguration of sacred space. If the Bible does not offer information on the age of the earth, then people are free to follow the science. Even young-earth creationists admit that the earth

---

[1] J. Harvey Walton (personal communication) makes the interesting comparison that the age of the temple as a structure has nothing to do with the age of the rocks it is made out of.

looks old; that is why they have to offer explanations for the "apparent age" of the earth.

My attention turned to the questions of human origins in *The Lost World of Adam and Eve*. Proposition 20 addressed the question of whether it was essential for all humans to be descended from Adam and Eve, and proposition 21 dealt with the issue of human distinctiveness. On the latter, I maintained that even if material continuity were established (as evolutionary models indicate), human distinctiveness was still identifiable in spiritual and functional terms. As discussed there and also in chapter five above, I do not believe that the Bible requires material discontinuity, in which case it would not be incompatible with evolutionary models on that point.

NEW EXPLORATIONS

One development since the publication of the Lost World books can be seen in the position of computational biologist S. Joshua Swamidass regarding what he terms "genealogical Adam."[2] His is a scientific study, not a theological one. His research maintains that population genetics, which suggests that humanity evolved as a population, can demonstrate that single-couple origins are genetically possible. He explains that there were various points in history at which there was a single couple from whom all modern humans were descended. That does not suggest that any of these couples were the first and only of the species but that all humans happened to share descent from them. This is an admittedly complicated and technical discussion, and I am in no position to critique the validity of the science. My only comment is that, while such a demonstration may be vital for those who believe that the Bible teaches that all humans descend from Adam and Eve, I am not

---

[2]S. Joshua Swamidass, *The Genealogical Adam and Eve: The Surprising Science of Universal Ancestry* (Downers Grove, IL: InterVarsity Press, 2019). Swamidass's research into genealogical Adam is summarized, discussed, and for the most part accepted by William Lane Craig, *In Quest of the Historical Adam: A Biblical and Scientific Exploration* (Grand Rapids, MI: Eerdmans, 2021), 338-55.

Genesis and Science   219

convinced the Bible requires that. Consequently, I view Swamidass's position as intriguing but not essential.

I remain convinced that material de novo creation is not the question in the biblical text, nor is it a point the Bible affirms (see discussion of Gen 2:7 in chapter five above). The biblical text is more interested in human identity, and therefore it is not material discontinuity that must be established or maintained but a human particularity. Human particularity can be maintained on the basis of the image of God and the functions associated with it even in the context of material continuity (descent from a common ancestor). To say it another way, God's "creation" of people in Genesis entailed making humanity his image, a characteristic that does not describe any other living creature. It is a fundamentally ontological description regardless of biological details.

This conviction was strengthened by insights gained in conversation with my son, J. Harvey Walton. The important observation he made was, "God made us more than what he made us from." This is what God did to Israel when he chose them as a covenant people. He took a people group from nondescript ethnic stock (Deut 26:5; Ezek 16:3) and *created* them as his people. Their creation was in their change of status. They were an ethnic mix; he gave them an identity that made them theologically central. In the same way, he has created us, the church, as his people. Paul observes that though many were immoral in a variety of ways, we were "washed, sanctified, and justified" in Jesus' name and by the Spirit (1 Cor 6:9-11; see also Eph 2:12-13). We have been crucified with Christ, yet live through him—reborn (Gal 2:20), created anew as new creation (2 Cor 5:17; 1 Pet 2:10). These passages offer patterns that reflect how God works—he makes things new, more than what they have been made from.

We could theoretically view this same pattern at work within an evolutionary model. It does not matter whether our human species evolved from a pool of amino acids or through a line of primates or hominids—or, for that matter, sprung from dust in the hands of a crouching creator. The point is that however God did it, he made us more than what we were made from. Teleology (our destiny) is more significant than ontology (what we came from). Though biologically we may be similar to various primates, in the end, it is only the work of God that made us more than animals. But for the grace of God, we would have been what we were—just another mammalian creature. I do not say all of this to promote an evolutionary model but to explain why such a model would not pose a problem.

A second area in which I have gained greater clarity in presenting these important ideas comes in how we can distinguish between what Scripture and science are and what they are doing. In *The Lost World of Genesis One* I frequently discussed how the Bible had little to say about physical mechanisms. The spoken word of God stands as the effective mechanism but is not offered as a physical mechanism. That is, what God speaks into existence may actually come into existence in any number of physical ways. Some may come into existence immediately; others may do so through processes. Presumably, no physical mechanism would always be detectable or even have existed. But the mechanism of his spoken word does not offer any clarification of such things.

Listening to a 2016 TEDx talk by April Cordero Maskiewicz, however, added the other side of the equation, clarifying an important distinction.[3] She helpfully contrasted mechanisms with agency.[4] That provided a convenient way to present the sort of thinking I have been espousing. The Bible is most concerned with agency, that is, God is the active agent in creation of everything at every level. This is the truth claim of the Bible. It has little to offer on the question of physical, material mechanisms. As is often said, the

---

[3]April Maskiewicz Cordero, "The E Word," TEDx talk, April 6, 2016, 17:34, www.youtube.com/watch?v=ttt0p-dO8XQ.

[4]In personal communication, Cordero informed me that she in turn had gotten those terms from a book: Robert J. Asher, *Evolution and Belief: Confessions of a Religious Paleontologist* (Cambridge: Cambridge University Press, 2012).

Genesis and Science 221

Bible is interested in the *who* and *why* questions of creation, not the *how* and *when* questions.[5]

In contrast, scientists are engaged in learning all they can about mechanisms but cannot say anything about agency.[6] That is, science cannot address *who* and *why* questions. Consequently, the Bible and science cannot be in disagreement about agency because most scientists without a metaphysical axe to grind admit that science cannot contribute to that discussion. Science can neither assume nor detect the existence of some agent, nor can it prove that there was none. On the other hand, the Bible and science cannot be in disagreement about mechanisms if the Bible maintains no position concerning material mechanisms. If the claims of science pertain to mechanisms and not agency, science is not in conflict with the Bible, which makes no such claims. One may not agree with science's proposed mechanisms, but that is a matter of scientific debate and has nothing to do with the Bible. Likewise, if the claims of the Bible pertain to agency, not mechanisms, it is not in conflict with science, which makes no such claims. One may not agree with the Bible's proposed agency, but that is a matter of theological or metaphysical debate and has nothing to do with science.

ANSWERS TO FREQUENTLY ASKED QUESTIONS

1. How can you claim that the Bible is compatible with evolutionary models, given that those models are by nature godless? This question is based on a false assumption—that evolutionary models are by definition godless. It is true that some people who have adopted an

---

[5]I have furthermore claimed that even the *what* question is different. The scientist (and much of modern culture) who asks the *what* question gives the answer as the material universe. The Bible (and the ancient world in general) asking the *what* question would give the answer as order in the cosmos and in society.

[6]Many proclaim that a self-sufficient mechanism (such as they believe evolution to be) obviates the need for an agent, which in their mind proves there is no agent. That may be the belief of some scientists, but it is not something that science can demonstrate.

evolutionary model see it as an alternative to theism or as an expression of their commitment to atheism. Nevertheless, that simply reflects their personal beliefs or metaphysics. Evolution does not and cannot claim that no God is behind the process, speaking the world into existence through change over time. Consequently, someone could theoretically be committed both to Christianity and a divine Creator and still adopt an evolutionary model of creation. One example, the BioLogos organization, adheres to what it calls "evolutionary creation." "Evolutionary creation (EC) is the belief that God is the Creator, and science gives an accurate (though not complete) description of how God's creation has changed over time. Evolutionary creationists accept the scientific consensus when it comes to ideas like the Big Bang model of cosmology, the tectonic plate model of geology, and the evolutionary model of biology."[7] Evolutionary creation is not an oxymoron. In fact, an increasing number of people are committed to that combination (see more below).

2. If one believes that the Bible is inerrant and should be read literally, can one also accept an evolutionary model? This represents the next step from the previous question. Since evolutionary models do not intrinsically rule out the agency of a creator, the two positions can be held simultaneously with no cognitive dissonance. As noted, a position called "evolutionary creation" maintains that God is the Creator actively engaged not only at one launching point in the distant past but throughout evolutionary history and continues to be involved today as evolution continues at its measured pace. Such a view could be maintained by someone who claimed to read the Bible literally if

---

[7]BioLogos Integrate curriculum glossary. BioLogos president Deborah Haarsma offers further theological clarification: "Evolutionary Creation is the belief that God creates all living things through Christ, including humans in his image, making use of intentionally designed, actively-sustained, natural processes that scientists today study as evolution." See Haarsma, "A Flawed Mirror: A Response to the Book 'Theistic Evolution,'" BioLogos, April 18, 2018, https://biologos.org/articles/a-flawed-mirror-a-response-to-the-book-theistic-evolution.

Genesis and Science   223

they understood literal reading to represent a commitment to reading the Bible as its human authors intended it to be read. If they determined that the authors of Scripture did not intend to offer scientific information, a literal reading would find no claims regarding the processes or mechanisms of creation, and therefore their thinking would be able to accommodate an evolutionary model to describe God's creating. In like manner, someone who adopted the view of biblical inerrancy would not struggle with evolutionary models if they believed that the Bible was not making any affirmations that would eliminate the possibility of evolutionary models.

   3. Where can I learn more about committed Christian scientists who also adopt an evolutionary model of creation? Books addressing such issues and offering testimonies of believing scientists have proliferated in the twenty-first century.[8] Even more information can be found on the websites of those organizations that support believing scientists who are committed to evolutionary models, most notably BioLogos, founded by geneticist Francis Collins, and the Faraday Institute in Cambridge, founded by biochemist Denis

---

[8]Denis Alexander, *Creation or Evolution: Do We Have to Choose?*, 2nd ed. (Oxford: Monarch, 2014); Kathryn Applegate and J. B. Stump, *How I Changed My Mind About Evolution: Evangelicals Reflect on Faith and Science* (Downers Grove, IL: InterVarsity Press, 2016); Robert C. Bishop, Larry L. Funck, Raymond J. Lewis, Stephen O. Moshier, and John H. Walton, *Understanding Scientific Theories of Origins: Cosmology, Geology, and Biology in Christian Perspective* (Downers Grove, IL: InterVarsity Press, 2018); Greg Cootsona, *Mere Science and Christian Faith: Bridging the Divide with Emerging Adults* (Downers Grove, IL: InterVarsity Press, 2018); Darrel R. Falk, *Coming to Peace with Science: Bridging the Worlds Between Faith and Biology* (Downers Grove, IL: InterVarsity Press, 2004); Mark Harris, *The Nature of Creation: Examining the Bible and Science* (Durham, UK: Acumen, 2013); Matthew Nelson Hill, *Embracing Evolution: How Understanding Science Can Strengthen Your Christian Life* (Downers Grove, IL: InterVarsity Press, 2020); Dru Johnson, *What Hath Darwin to Do with Scripture? Comparing Conceptual Worlds of the Bible and Evolution* (Downers Grove, IL: InterVarsity Press, 2023); Kenneth Keathley, J. B. Stump, and Joe Aguirre, *Old-Earth or Evolutionary Creation? Discussing Origins with Reasons to Believe and BioLogos* (Downers Grove, IL: InterVarsity Press, 2017); Denis Lamoureux, *Evolutionary Creation* (Eugene, OR: Wipf & Stock, 2008); Lamoureux, *Evolution: Scripture and Nature Say Yes* (Grand Rapids, MI: Zondervan: 2016); James Stump, *The Sacred Chain: How Understanding Evolution Leads to Deeper Faith* (San Francisco: HarperOne, 2024).

Alexander and geophysicist Bob White.[9] These sites feature articles by scientists who are committed Christians on almost every imaginable aspect of science as well as contributions by theologians, biblical scholars, and philosophers. In addition, numerous blogs and podcasts address such issues.[10]

4. Why would God use an instrument of creation that entailed endless millions of years of animal suffering through predation? This question voices a common problem for people who cannot accept evolution, and it is not hard to understand the urgency and gravity that fuel it. Could God not have found a better way? Yet, we must realize the position that we put ourselves in by posing this question or any like it that begins with "Why would God . . . ?" By posing such questions, we are presuming that we could be wiser, better, be more compassionate. The problem is that we cannot penetrate the mind or motives of God. He does not need our defense (theodicy), and he is not in the dock to answer our accusations (a lesson learned by Job, with whom we do well to sit and learn). His response would be the same to us as it was to Job: Would you discredit my justice? Would you condemn me to justify yourself? (Job 40:8). Isaiah 55:8-9 is fairly clear on this point: "'For my thoughts are not your thoughts, neither are your ways my ways,' declares the Lord. 'As the heavens are higher than the earth, so are my ways higher than your ways and my thoughts than your thoughts.'" We cannot out-God God. Yes, it baffles us; yes, we are incredulous. Our response should be to trust, not to deconstruct; to admit that we do not have the wisdom and insight of God. To some this sounds like evasion, but when we are trying to understand the Creator God of the universe, a little humility is in order.

---

[9]Collins led the group that mapped the human genome and served for twelve years as the director of the National Institutes of Health under three presidents. For BioLogos, see http://biologos.org; for the Faraday Institute, see www.faraday.cam.ac.uk.

[10]Many podcasts occasionally feature an episode or two on the Bible and science, but of those that focus exclusively on issues of science and faith, perhaps one of the best known is the Language of God podcast, https://biologos.org/podcast/language-of-god.

Genesis and Science 225

5. Don't the biblical genealogies make an old earth, and therefore evolution, impossible? This question has already assumed that Adam and Eve are the first and only of the species, a view I have argued against. It also assumes that genealogies in ancient Israel work the same as the genealogies that we use in our culture. Genealogy is a genre, and we must confess that overlapping genres may work differently in one culture than in another. We cannot assume that the values and conventions reflected in ancient genealogies are the same as those that characterize our own use of genealogies. Caution and reserve are the essential attitudes to bring to genre research. For example, from what we can tell of genealogies in the ancient world (admittedly with less information than would be desirable), they were subject to fluidity in names and sequence, and characterized by rhetorical use of numbers in the details. To the extent that this is so, we must refrain from thinking that we can simply do the math and thereby calculate the time span or reconstruct the history. If genealogies were not designed to work that way in the ancient world, and evidence suggests that is so, then we cannot use them in that way.[11]

6. What about all the arguments that people use to refute or at least undermine evolutionary models? Evolutionary theory has been constantly under scrutiny since the inception of its fundamental ideas. Critics, religiously motivated or otherwise, well informed or not, have found fault with it in innumerable ways. At the same time, scientists who have accepted its premises are also continually engaged in

---

[11]An older seminal work still of value is Robert R. Wilson, *Genealogy and History in the Biblical World* (New Haven, CT: Yale University Press, 1977). For a specialized study on the Sumerian King List, see Piotr Steinkeller, "An Ur III Manuscript of the Sumerian King List," in *Literatur, Politik und Recht in Mesopotamien: Festschrift für Claus Wilcke*, ed. Walther Sallaberger, Konrad Volk, and Annette Zgoll (Wiesbaden: Harrassowitz, 2003), 267-92. In an interesting example, when Esarhaddon presents his claim of descent in the Zincirli stele, he names his father and his grandfather, then jumps back a thousand years to name two of those whom tradition held were the founders of the line. See Esarhaddon 098, in The Open Richly Annotated Cuneiform Corpus, http://oracc.museum.upenn.edu/rinap/corpus, reverse side, lines 15-18. See other examples of Ashurbanipal and Nebuchadnezzar given above in chap. 6 under "Adam and Adapa."

modifying it. Variations and new ideas have been proposed, including the punctuated equilibrium model of Stephen Jay Gould (Harvard), the evolutionary convergence model of Simon Conway Morris (Cambridge), and the natural genetic engineering model of James Shapiro (University of Chicago), who is an advocate of non-Darwinian evolution and critiques the modern synthesis.[12] Meta-Darwinian models in general have turned their attention to mechanisms beyond natural selection and mutation.

Evolution is variously defined. For some it is (too generally) simply a theory of biological change over time. To others it is a metaphysical explanation of origins without God. The definition adopted by BioLogos in its Integrate curriculum is, "Evolution is the process by which a population of organisms changes over time. Given enough time and gradual changes, the process of evolution results in new life forms that have descended with modification from pre-existing life forms. The evolutionary model of common descent explains the great diversity of life observable on earth today and in the fossil record."[13]

Given the breadth and range of the topic, it has also become increasingly necessary to separate different levels of evolution from one another. Arnold De Loof from the Functional Genomics and Proteomics Group at Leuven delineates three general categories:

> Micro-evolution is the change in allele frequencies that occur over time within a population. It is relevant to the emergence

---

[12]On the punctuated equilibrium model, see Stephen Jay Gould, *Punctuated Equilibrium* (Cambridge, MA, Belknap, 2007). This refers to long periods of species stability interspersed with moments of greater change. Consequently, the rate of evolution is not constant but variable. On the evolutionary convergence model, see Simon Conway Morris, *Runes of Evolution* (New Brunswick, NJ: Templeton Press, 2015). Evolutionary convergence describes the process whereby organisms not closely related (not monophyletic) evolve independently yet develop similar traits as they adapt to similar environments. On the natural genetic engineering model, see James A. Shapiro, *Evolution: A View from the 21st Century* (Chicago: Cognition, 2022).

[13]BioLogos Integrate glossary. For further discussion of definitions, see Bishop et al., *Understanding Scientific Theories of Origins*, 456-57.

Genesis and Science 227

of new species. Macro-evolution acts on a scale of separated gene pools. It occurs at or above the level of species. Mega-evolution is a more recent approach. It does not specifically focus on genetic changes but it attempts to describe the evolution of Life in its totality, irrespective of the way Life manifests itself in the wealth of prokaryotic and eukaryotic species and their communities.[14]

All of this demonstrates that evolutionary theory has not remained static over decades. Many of the critiques found in popular Christian apologetics are still addressing evolution in its Darwinian form, which most evolutionary biologists no longer accept, despite the fact that that is what is often taught in the educational system. It would take considerable expertise and advanced degrees to be able to launch a scientific critique of evolution, but legitimate critiques do exist. Nevertheless, identifiable cracks in the theory are continually being addressed by scientists, and it is still considered the model with the most explanatory power.

Other critics focus more on theological issues, and, as I have indicated, I am not convinced that such criticism takes account of the Israelite author's intentions, the realities of the ancient world's cultural context, or the nature of the literature. Our understanding of both Scripture and science results from interpretation of the data, and given that new evidence for interpretations of both Scripture and science is always emerging, we must always recognize that our interpretations in both categories are to some extent provisional.

7. How is your view the same or different from Stephen Jay Gould's proposal that science and religion are nonoverlapping magisteria? Gould's explanation of his terminology indicates that science is

---

[14]Arnold De Loof, "The Evolution of 'Life': A Metadarwinian Integrative Approach," *Communicative and Integrative Biology* 10, no. 3 (2017), www.ncbi.nlm.nih.gov/pmc/articles/PMC5501214/.

empirical by nature and pertains to the constitution of the universe, whereas religion is exclusively ethical and spiritual in nature.[15] Be that as it may, that distinction is far broader than that which I am making. The high level of interpenetration between these two warn us against claiming that the two conversations are saying different things about different things.[16]

I have adopted the two-books metaphor, which refers to the two primary ways that revelation takes place.[17] The two books are described as the book of the world (revelation mediated through nature) and the book of the word (revelation mediated through humans). In the two-books model, the book of the world shows God's glory, while the book of the Word tells God's story.

Gould's model can be evaluated in light of the two-books metaphor. If we adopt a metaphor of a jigsaw puzzle, his nonoverlapping magisteria model would suggest that religion and science are two different jigsaw puzzles, each with their own pieces—mutually exclusive realms of thought. This would be distinguished from concordance models such as young-earth creationism, which would envision only one puzzle, with both religion and science contributing pieces.[18]

In contrast to both of these, a partial-views model is more defensible. Here we abandon the jigsaw puzzle metaphor as inadequate. Rather than mutually exclusive, we can view science and religion as mutually informing. An example might be the comparison between a soil-moisture map of the United States and a geothermal energy map.[19] They are both of the same geographical territory, yet they give different sorts of information, though not entirely unrelated. Both would

---

[15]Stephen Jay Gould, "Nonoverlapping Magisteria," *Natural History* 106 (March 1997): 16-22.

[16]For description and critique, see Bishop et al., *Understanding Scientific Theories of Origins*, 89-90.

[17]This metaphor was used as early as Origen and Augustine and as well by Galileo. For full discussion see Bishop et al., *Understanding Scientific Theories of Origins*, 63-96.

[18]For the puzzle metaphor, see Bishop et al., *Understanding Scientific Theories of Origins*, 87-92.

[19]For this analogy, see Bishop et al., *Understanding Scientific Theories of Origins*, 90-91.

Genesis and Science 229

be correct, yet they are not the same. They are answering different questions, but they are intertwined with each other in complex ways.

8. Some have claimed that all of your conclusions in Genesis are proposed only to accommodate an evolutionary model. Is this true? Evolutionary theory is the reigning paradigm, so it makes sense to ask whether it is compatible with the Bible. If it is compatible with the Bible, as I contend, then it makes sense to give it careful consideration. A few scientists consider it deeply flawed. A high percentage of scientists consider it to have more explanatory power than any other idea yet, as addressed above, recognize that it needs to continue to adapt as new research is done. Many will admit that the mechanisms that have traditionally been invoked as the primary drivers of evolution (mutation and natural selection) are insufficient in and of themselves, and therefore they continue to seek additional mechanisms. All of this to say, evolutionary theory is still a work in progress.

Any critique of it as a science needs to be carried out by those who are competent scientists, and, preferably, who are well versed in the nuances. Consequently, since I am not qualified to critique it scientifically, I can only evaluate whether it is compatible with Genesis. Just as I am not able to offer valid critique, I am in no position to endorse it; that too would imply more expertise than I have. My willingness to consider the plausibility of an evolutionary model, then, is based on my trust of friends and acquaintances who are both good scientists and also Christians who heartily embrace the faith.

To answer the question, then, my work in Genesis is not driven by an already-decided scientific view. I was raised in a young-earth context and remained in that camp well into my professional career. What changed was not that I was convinced that evolution was true but that I gained insights into the text of Genesis that led me to believe that it was not making scientific claims regarding cosmic or human origins from a scientific standpoint. If the reigning paradigm changed to something else, it would make no difference to my

230   New Explorations in the Lost World of Genesis

position—Genesis is what Genesis is, regardless of the scientific theories that dominate the discussions.

My methodological approach agrees with the succinct statement by Annette Yoshiko Reed, "I am more interested in analyzing ancient theories and categories of knowledge than in judging them against modern criteria of scienticity."[20] In part, this is due to my conviction that the Bible is not presenting authoritative scientific perspectives, but, just as importantly, accountability to the authority of Scripture and the integrity of our hermeneutics are preserved when we track with the authors and read the text as they intended it to be read in their insider-to-insider communication. That I find the Bible and evolutionary theory to be compatible is premised on my interpretation of the biblical text, not on my assessment of the scientific credibility of evolutionary theory.

9. Is there a war between science and the Bible? The short answer is that no, there is not, and on the larger scale there never was. At least there never was a major conflict inherent in the magisteria of science and religion.[21] Nevertheless, both scientists and theologians have at times tried to portray a scenario of deep-seated conflict and have told their constituencies that one must make a choice—science or the Bible, you cannot have them both. I categorically reject this premise as a false dichotomy.

The best book I have encountered tracing the details of the supposed conflict is Derrick Peterson's *Flat Earths and Fake Footnotes: The Strange Tale of How the Conflict of Science and Christianity Was Written into History.*[22] Peterson capably wears the hat of historian and

---

[20]Annette Yoshiko Reed, *Demons, Angels, and Writing in Ancient Judaism* (Cambridge: Cambridge University Press, 2020), 141.

[21]Unquestionably, philosophically localized skirmishes have taken place between entrenched, sometimes misguided adherents on both sides. See Timothy Larsen, "'War Is Over, If You Want It': Beyond the Conflict Between Faith and Science," *Perspectives on Science and Christian Faith* 60 (2008): 147-55.

[22]Derrick Peterson, *Flat Earths and Fake Footnotes: The Strange Tale of How the Conflict of Science and Christianity Was Written into History* (Eugene, OR: Cascade, 2021). Peterson's

Genesis and Science

to some extent philosopher, so he is not discussing science or theology. Instead, he focuses his detailed attention on key moments in history as he evaluates the collective social memory that has developed over the centuries regarding the likes of Christopher Columbus, Copernicus and Galileo, Darwin, Thomas Huxley and Samuel Wilberforce, Andrew Dickson White, John William Draper, and the Scopes trial. He guides readers through movements such as positivism, scientific naturalism, and the rise of modern creationism and the new atheism. In this penetrating and heavily documented investigation, Peterson lays bare the ways in which reconstructions of history and minority agendas have forged the fiction of conflict between science and religion/theology/Bible. In Peterson's conclusion, he laments,

> In the world of religion and science we are still living amidst a world torn by the warfare thesis. While deconstructing many of the historical misunderstands [*sic*] that have gone into the thesis and continue to linger in our consciousness does not solve all our problems, or prove Christianity true, or that God is real, it does help us precisely by clearing the decks.[23]

---

thirty-page bibliography will give readers many other resources to consider. For a more accessible volume, see Jeff Hardin, Ronald L. Numbers, and Ronald A. Binzley, eds., *The Warfare Between Science and Religion: The Idea That Wouldn't Die* (Baltimore, MD: Johns Hopkins University Press, 2018). Other important studies include Peter Harrison, *The Territories of Religion and Science* (Chicago: University of Chicago Press, 2015); Peter Harrison and Jon H. Roberts, eds., *Science Without God? Rethinking the History of Scientific Naturalism*, Ian Ramsey Centre Studies in Science and Religion (Oxford: Oxford University Press, 2018); Kenneth W. Kemp, *The War That Never Was: Evolution and Christian Theology* (Eugene, OR: Cascade, 2020); Bernard Lightman, ed., *Rethinking History, Science, and Religion: An Exploration of Conflict and the Complexity Principle* (Pittsburgh: University of Pittsburgh Press, 2019); David N. Livingstone, D. G. Hart, and Mark A. Noll, eds., *Evangelicals and Science in Historical Perspective* (Oxford: Oxford University Press, 1999); Ronald L. Numbers, ed., *Galileo Goes to Jail and Other Myths About Science and Religion* (Cambridge, MA: Harvard University Press, 2009); James C. Ungureanu, *Science, Religion, and the Protestant Tradition: Retracing the Origins of Conflict* (Pittsburgh: University of Pittsburgh Press, 2019).

[23]Peterson, *Flat Earths and Fake Footnotes*, 316.

Peterson agrees that the vestiges of the concept of warfare remain ubiquitous as the staple in popular works of polemical history, characteristic of what Ronald Numbers calls the "cliché-bound mind." He also quotes with approval the assessment of David Bentley Hart, that such warfare ideas are fueled by little more than "attitudes masquerading as ideas, emotional commitments disguised as intellectual honesty . . . ballasted by a formidable collection of conceptual and historical errors."[24]

---

[24]Peterson, *Flat Earths and Fake Footnotes*, 4-5, citing Ronald Numbers, "Science and Religion," *Osiris* 1 (1985): 59-80, here 65, and David Bentley Hart, *Atheist Delusions: The Christian Revolution and Its Fashionable Enemies* (New Haven, CT: Yale University Press, 2009), 19.

10

Conclusion

The purpose of this book, as the title indicates, has been to advance the conversation that began more than two decades ago. Consequently, the book has addressed ways in which my thinking has been refined and has deepened in a variety of ways by addressing new terminology, new resources, new insights, and new strategies for communication of the ideas, while also addressing many of the questions that have arisen over the years. At the same time, astute readers who are familiar with my work will note that there have also been a few issues on which I have changed my mind. These have been discussed throughout the book but can be summarized here as follows:

EDEN AS TEMPLE

The shift in this issue began with the slight change in terminology regarding the purpose of the seven-day account. It was a relatively minor adjustment when I revised my terminology from "cosmic temple" to the cosmos as "sacred space." That shift led to a reevaluation of the concept of Eden as a temple. Based on a variety of nuanced insights offered by Daniel Block and J. Harvey Walton, I would now be inclined to think that even though the tabernacle and temple in Israel were designed to portray the divine realm (thus the furniture and decor as revealed to Moses), Eden itself was in the divine realm rather than the human realm. Having said that, in some ways this may be a difference without a distinction, since the holy of holies in the tabernacle/temple was probably believed to be in both realms concurrently. Nevertheless, such nuances may have ripple effects in other factors, such as the next one.

Priestly Roles

If both the holy of holies and the Garden of Eden are seen to be in the divine realm, reason exists to revisit the priestly roles. Neither location requires priests. Consequently, it seems now less likely to me that Adam and Eve were seen to be priests, and, as discussed in chapter six, are more likely portrayed as wardens, a role that is associated with royal imagery rather than temple/priestly imagery.

The Individuality of Adam and Eve

This is the next domino to fall. In my previous work, it was the priestly role of Adam (and Eve) that was the main element distinguishing them from the rest of humanity (since everything else in the chapter focused on their archetypal role). The question I had raised was that if Genesis has no interest in the idea that Adam and Eve were the first and only of their species, and therefore they are not biologically significant, then why are they being singled out for attention in Genesis 2–3? The provisional answer I previously offered was that they had a theological significance bound up in their priestly role. If their priestly role is now open to doubt, we return to the prior question, Why are they singled out for attention? The position I have now taken is that the intent of the narrator is not to single them out as individuals. Their role in the garden remains an archetypal one, and they have no significance in Genesis as individuals—they are all of us. Even if their individuality is irretrievably submerged in their role as archetypes for humanity, that is not to say that they were not individuals, only that the message of Genesis is not invested in their individuality (see excursus 3).

Conclusion 235

PUNISHMENT IN GENESIS 3

This is probably the revision that has the most significant impact. In the Lost World material, I did not give too much attention to this issue, but my broad acceptance that Genesis 3 featured punishment was evident. Based on revisiting the question of the rhetorical strategy of the author of Genesis, I have now adopted the view developed by J. Harvey Walton that not only is Genesis 3 not about sin, but it also does not feature punishment (see chapter seven). This challenges whether the very familiar Christian metanarrative of creation–fall–redemption–consummation represents well what the author of Genesis was doing. I now maintain that Genesis is engaged in consideration of order and how it is to be found. Though Adam and Eve fail to heed God's warning against eating the fruit from the tree of the knowledge of good and evil and suffer the consequences, it is only later that New Testament authors recast this for the context of sin and punishment (see below).

LOSS OF RELATIONSHIP

My understanding of the metanarrative launched in the Old Testament and continued in the New Testament is that God created us to be in relationship with us and to live with us, what I call an Immanuel theology. The Old Testament, though not a documentary by any means, is revealing (among other things) how God, through history, has worked out his plans and purposes to achieve those goals. This topic is not treated systematically, but these ideas are pervasive. I have not changed my mind about this, but in light of ongoing research, some adjustments are necessary. I continue to maintain that Genesis 3 conveys how people pursued a path of their own, and thereby their relationship with God as those intended to be coworkers was disrupted. Yet at the same time, I now recognize that that is not the central focus of that chapter. Nevertheless, since the covenant relationship represents the book's view of order as God has formulated it, we can see that relationship remains an important focus.

GENESIS 3:16

I continue to maintain that Genesis 3:14-19 is not a curse on humanity and not punishment of the woman and man; rather, it deals with the destinies that they face in their existence in a more liminal environment. Now, however, I have a revised understanding of Genesis 3:16 based on the interpretation offered by J. Harvey Walton, who contends that the desire of the woman is for a stable, functioning community provided in Israel by a spouse within a patrimonial structure (represented in her husband's rule) that was considered as providing it. As such, Genesis 3:16 is addressing human community, itself an order structure, as a positive solution to humans not being alone. Both males and females will require order (through community) against anxiety (for the continuation of the community). Community, not femaleness, is the aspect of human existence that is placed under chaotic threat. In my current view, it is not about power, as many have assumed, and not about sexual dependence, as I previously suggested.

OUR PERSPECTIVES SHOULD BE SUBJECTED TO
CONSTANT RECONSIDERATION

In the last two decades I have continued to become more informed and nuanced in my understanding of the relationship between Genesis, the New Testament, and the history of Christian interpretation. Specifically, how much should our interpretation of Genesis be driven by how New Testament authors are using Genesis to generate their messages? How should we assess how the early Christian writers were using Genesis in their sermons, commentaries, theological formulations, and council decisions? I discussed these issues in detail in chapter two.

I am now convinced that we should not feel compelled to think that Jesus and Paul are doing the same things as Genesis. For example, if the New Testament can be shown to be interested in Adam and Eve as

Conclusion 237

individuals, that would not mean that Genesis had that same interest. Some might claim that the concept of the unity of Scripture could be invoked to claim that Genesis and the New Testament ideas about Adam should be conflated, but that cannot be maintained. As mentioned in chapter two, we do not have to see Scripture's voice being in unison, but we do expect harmony and coherence. As expressed eloquently by Michael Graves,

> Belief in the unity of Scripture does not require that all biblical texts say the same thing; rather, the expectation is that the various things Scripture says can be put together in a meaningful whole. One should not think of the Bible as "unified," in the sense of a canvas covered with solid green or solid red. Instead, the Bible is like a painting made up of many colors: blues, greens, red, browns, and so forth—all of which come together to make a coherent and meaningful picture.[1]

Others might invoke the principle that Scripture interprets Scripture, but again we have to consider carefully what that principle claims. At the first level, it involves inner-biblical interpretation. This expresses what biblical authors are sometimes doing as, for example, Daniel 9 interprets Jeremiah, or Hebrews 7 interprets Psalm 110. Paul is arguably engaging in this exercise when he makes use of Genesis 3. Having said that, the principle of Scripture interpreting Scripture is often invoked today as an interpretive tool for people as they seek to understand Scripture, especially in the formulation of theology. Following this methodology, interpreters are told that they ought to use clear passages to aid in understanding more obscure passages on the same topic.

As helpful as this may seem to its adherents for sorting out theological issues, it does not rule out diversity of perspectives on complex

---

[1]Michael Graves, *How Scripture Interprets Scripture: What the Biblical Writers Can Teach Us About Reading the Bible* (Grand Rapids, MI: Baker, 2021), 17. It is worth noting that *meaningful* does not imply linear or systematic or simple and straightforward.

238   *Conclusion*

issues, though it does assume that coherence can be reached.[2] We have to exercise caution in imposing clear texts on obscure ones when doing exegesis because texts can be redeployed.[3] Again, Graves provides helpful explanation: "In principle there is no reason why a later biblical writer cannot apply an earlier biblical tradition in a way that fails to adhere to a specific trajectory—if, for example, the needs of the later writer require an application that does not exhibit development."[4] So, for example, the identity of the serpent in Genesis 3 could certainly be considered an obscurity, but the reference to the dragon in Revelation might better be considered a redeployment rather than merging the texts to claim that the serpent in Genesis is Satan. Some may use Revelation to draw a theological conclusion that the serpent in the garden should be identified with Satan, but that does not change the fact that there is no evidence to think that an Old Testament audience would have come to that conclusion. The same cautions should be in place when we discuss whether the divine use of plural pronouns in Genesis 1:26; 3:22; 11:7 refers to the Trinity. In like manner, the autonomy of Genesis regarding Adam and Eve must be retained. What Paul says has to do with the points Paul is making as he redeploys Genesis for his audience in the theological discourse in which he is engaged; that neither dictates nor changes how we understand the message in the context of Genesis.

A second aspect of the principle of "Scripture interprets Scripture" is that, given the premise of progressive revelation, interpreters are advised to allow later revelation to inform and deepen what had come earlier. This is also often invoked when formulating theology but again is less useful when doing exegesis. Even when further revelation about a topic occurs, such as how to understand the resurrection, the

---

[2]For balanced, wise, and nuanced discussion, see Iain Provan, *The Reformation and the Right Reading of Scripture* (Waco, TX: Baylor University Press, 2017), 283-312, and Graves, *How Scripture Interprets Scripture.*

[3]Graves, *How Scripture Interprets Scripture*, 21.

[4]Graves, *How Scripture Interprets Scripture*, 23.

Conclusion   239

afterlife, or the doctrine of the Trinity, that later revelation may help us formulate our theology, but it does not change what was going on in the minds of the earlier authors and audiences. Consequently, the principle of Scripture interpreting Scripture does not give us permission to allow New Testament voices and perspectives to dictate the exegetical conclusions of the Old Testament.

We should also be very intentional as we consider how the history of Christian interpretation should factor into our own processes. Again, we may find it useful to distinguish between doing exegesis and formulating theology. In chapter two, I indicated that many who preceded us were not doing what we refer to as exegesis in a technical sense and, even when they were, were not employing the same hermeneutical controls we feel constrained to use today. Most did not have the basic tools of exegesis that we consider most essential today.

More specifically, we often have a misguided perception of the history of interpretation. We often do not realize how messy it is. Unanimity is a rarity. Conclusions are not monolithic. On almost any theological topic, one can find a variety of opinions. More problematically, we rarely take the time to understand the context of what a particular theologian of the past was actually saying. Early interpretations were consistently flavored by christological, millennarian, pastoral, moral, apologetic (whether against Jews or Gnostics), or philosophical concerns that drove the methodology and offered the backdrop for the understanding of the biblical text. "We must have the historical honesty to allow past figures to be 'foreign' and conditioned by their immediate intellectual circumstances. The false alternative is to 'plunder only those extracts that serve [our] present-minded purposes.' Ancient heroes are often not interested in answering the questions we would like to ask them."[5] I have made this point with regard to the biblical authors, but here Andrew Brown makes it with

---

[5] Andrew Brown, *Recruiting the Ancients for the Creation Debate* (Grand Rapids, MI: Eerdmans, 2023), 18 (his quotations from Stefan Collini).

240   *Conclusion*

regard to the likes of Augustine, John Calvin, and Martin Luther, in which case it is no less true but equally neglected. To say it another way, it is no more acceptable to cherry-pick the early Christian writers than it is to cherry-pick the text itself. It remains true that context is everything.[6]

Consequently, we recognize that the doctrine of original sin was formulated early in the history of Christian doctrine (in the West at least), but we also must realize that it has always been controversial among Christian theologians. That being said, and considering all the factors we have been discussing, we should resist any inclination to read that concept back into Genesis as if that were what it is talking about.

A FINAL WORD

For decades I have had a plaque in my office perched near the shelf that holds copies of the books that I have written and edited. The plaque says, "Lord, give me this day my daily opinion and forgive me the one I had yesterday." Of course, it can apply to all sorts of areas in life, from political positions to impressions of people. It recognizes that we learn and grow. But as might be expected, I think of it in terms of my opinions about the meanings of texts. My exegetical conclusions are always provisional, and, if they are truly based on evidence, they must be held lightly, because there is always the possibility of new evidence. Perhaps it might be reflected in archaeological finds or new texts. Perhaps it might take the shape of new insights or research. Perhaps it might come as we recognize that our interpretation was driven by a presupposition we were hardly aware of and that, placed under scrutiny, must be discarded. As I have taught this material over

---

[6]Brown uses the term *prolepsis* to describe the practice of using a work "to address a contemporary problem, without first, considering the original intentions of the author, and producing the work" (*Recruiting the Ancients*, 282-84). He gives a number of guidelines for using material from the ancient Christian writers, and they are very much like the ones that I use when I talk about engaging the cultural river of the ancient world.

Conclusion 241

the decades, I have found my views at times reshaped when prompted by someone asking a question I had never thought to ask.

Given all the possible contingencies, we should expect to occasionally change our minds about the interpretation of one text or another. It is not dangerous to change our minds; it is dangerous to be determined not to do so even in the face of new evidence, ideas, or insights we might encounter. Such a determination would stand at odds with most Christian writers throughout the centuries. The patent approach of Jesus was precisely to challenge some of the traditions of those who would have been considered the most godly and educated people of his time. If we are inclined to look to Jesus for models, that is certainly one we should take seriously.

Despite the changes and shifts I have outlined, some with significant ramifications, the basic thrust of my position remains largely unaltered. The basic elements of my methodology remain: tracking with the authors as those vested with the authority of God, careful semantic analysis of Hebrew terminology, close attention to literary features, and deep investigation of the cultural context based on the windows provided by ancient literature. Furthermore, the order spectrum continues to provide a trove of implications as we continue to understand its centrality and its significance for interpretation of these Old Testament texts, which have come to us from the ancient Israelite world.[7] These fundamentals continue to challenge any conviction we might have that Genesis should guide our science. They also raise questions about some of the textual interpretations that have shaped our theological convictions.

---

[7] I introduce the order spectrum in *LWAE*, 149.

For Further Reading

Allert, Craig D. *Early Christian Readings of Genesis One.* Downers Grove, IL: InterVarsity Press, 2018.

Anderson, Gary A. *The Genesis of Perfection: Adam and Eve in Jewish and Christian Imagination.* Louisville, KY: Westminster John Knox, 2001.

Arnold, Bill T., ed. *The Cambridge Companion to Genesis.* Cambridge: Cambridge University Press, 2022.

Brink, Gijsbert van den. *Reformed Theology and Evolutionary Theory.* Grand Rapids, MI: Eerdmans, 2020.

Brown, Andrew. *Recruiting the Ancients for the Creation Debate.* Grand Rapids, MI: Eerdmans, 2023.

Evans, Craig A., Joel N. Lohr, and David L. Peterson, eds. *Book of Genesis: Composition, Interpretation and Reception.* Leiden: Brill, 2012.

Graves, Michael. *How Scripture Interprets Scripture: What the Biblical Writers Can Teach Us About Reading the Bible.* Grand Rapids, MI: Baker, 2021.

———. *The Inspiration and Interpretation of Scripture: What the Early Church Can Teach Us.* Grand Rapids, MI: Eerdmans, 2014.

Greenwood, Kyle R. *Since the Beginning: Interpreting Genesis 1 and 2 Through the Ages.* Grand Rapids, MI: Baker, 2018.

Haarsma, Loren. *When Did Sin Begin?* Grand Rapids, MI: Baker, 2021.

Hall, Christopher A. *Reading Scripture with the Church Fathers.* Downers Grove, IL: InterVarsity Press, 1998.

Heine, Ronald E. *Reading the Old Testament with the Ancient Church.* Grand Rapids, MI: Baker, 2007.

Hilber, John W. *Old Testament Cosmology and Divine Accommodation: A Relevance Theory Approach.* Eugene, OR: Cascade, 2020.

For Further Reading   243

Holsinger-Friesen, Thomas. *Irenaeus and Genesis: A Study of Competition in Early Christian Hermeneutics.* Winona Lake, IN: Eisenbrauns, 2009.

Levenson, Jon D. *Israel's Day of Light and Joy.* University Park, PA: Eisenbrauns, 2024.

Lyon, Jeremy D. *The Creation Account in the Dead Sea Scrolls.* Eugene, OR: Pickwick, 2019.

Meyers, Carol. *Rediscovering Eve: Ancient Israelite Women in Context.* Oxford: Oxford University Press, 2013.

Ortlund, Gavin. *Retrieving Augustine's Doctrine of Creation: Ancient Wisdom for Current Controversy.* Downers Grove, IL: InterVarsity Press, 2020.

Peterson, Derrick. *Flat Earths and Fake Footnotes: The Strange Tale of How the Conflict of Science and Christianity Was Written into History.* Eugene, OR: Cascade, 2021.

Provan, Iain. *The Reformation and the Right Reading of Scripture.* Waco, TX: Baylor University Press, 2017.

Simonetti, Manlio. *Biblical Interpretation in the Early Church: An Historical Introduction to Patristic Exegesis.* Edinburgh: T&T Clark, 1994.

Venema, Dennis R., and Scot McKnight. *Adam and the Genome.* Grand Rapids, MI: Brazos, 2017.

Zevit, Ziony. *What Really Happened in the Garden of Eden?* New Haven, CT: Yale University Press, 2013.

FURTHER ARTICLES AND CHAPTERS BY JOHN H. WALTON ADDRESSING THE LOST WORLD OF GENESIS

"Adam and Eve as Archetypal Humans." In *Four Views of Adam*, edited by Ardel Canaday and Matthew Barrett, 89-118. Grand Rapids, MI: Zondervan, 2013.

"Babel's Invitation." *Christianity Today* (March 2023): 73-77.

"Biblical Interpretation: What Is the Nature of Biblical Authority?" In *Old Earth or Evolutionary Creation? Discussing Origins with Reasons to Believe and BioLogos*, edited by Kenneth Keathley, J. B. Stump, and Joe Aguirre, 27-48. Downers Grove, IL: InterVarsity Press, 2017.

"Cosmic Origins." In *Understanding Scientific Theories of Origins*, by Robert C. Bishop, Larry L. Funck, Raymond J. Lewis, Stephen O. Moshier, and John H. Walton, 99-116. Downers Grove, IL: InterVarsity Press, 2018.

"Creation, New Creation, and the So-Called Mission of God." In *Creation and Doxology*, edited by Gerald Hiestand and Todd Wilson, 133-44. Downers Grove, IL: InterVarsity Press, 2018.

"Flood." In *Understanding Scientific Theories of Origins*, by Robert C. Bishop, Larry L. Funck, Raymond J. Lewis, Stephen O. Moshier, and John H. Walton, 237-44. Downers Grove, IL: InterVarsity Press, 2018.

"Genesis and the Conceptual World of the Ancient Near East." In *The Cambridge Companion to Genesis*, edited by Bill T. Arnold, 148-67. Cambridge: Cambridge University Press, 2022.

"Hermeneutical Humility and Origins in Genesis." *Cultural Encounters* 12, no. 2 (2017): 34-43.

"Hermeneutics." In *Understanding Scientific Theories of Origins*, by Robert C. Bishop, Larry L. Funck, Raymond J. Lewis, Stephen O. Moshier, and John H. Walton, 9-13. Downers Grove, IL: InterVarsity Press, 2018.

"Human Origins." In *Understanding Scientific Theories of Origins*, by Robert C. Bishop, Larry L. Funck, Raymond J. Lewis, Stephen O. Moshier, and John H. Walton, 547-57. Downers Grove, IL: InterVarsity Press, 2018.

"Human Origins and the Bible." *Zygon* 47 (2012): 875-89.

"Interactions in the Ancient Cognitive Environment." In *Behind the Scenes of the Old Testament*, edited by Jonathan S. Greer, John W. Hilber, and John H. Walton, 333-39. Grand Rapids, MI: Baker, 2018.

"Origins in Genesis: Claims of an Ancient Text in a Modern Scientific World." In *Knowing Creation*, edited by Andrew Torrance, 107-21. Grand Rapids, MI: Zondervan, 2018.

"Reading Genesis 1 as Ancient Cosmology." In *Reading Genesis 1–2: An Evangelical Conversation*, edited by Daryl Charles, 141-69. Peabody, MA: Hendrickson, 2013.

"Response to Richard Averbeck ('The Lost World of Adam and Eve: A Review Essay')." *Themelios* 40 (2015): 240-42.

"The Temple in Context." In *Behind the Scenes of the Old Testament*, edited by Jonathan S. Greer, John W. Hilber, and John H. Walton, 349-54. Grand Rapids, MI: Baker, 2018.

Scripture Index

APOCRYPHA

4 Ezra
6:1-6, 79
6:6, 79
6:38, 79
6:38-54, 79
8:52, 147

OLD TESTAMENT

Genesis
1, 1, 3, 8, 34, 41, 64, 70, 71, 73,
74, 75, 77, 78, 79, 81, 83, 85,
87, 89, 91, 92, 93, 94, 95, 97,
99, 101, 102, 103, 104, 105,
106, 107, 108, 109, 111, 112,
113, 114, 115, 117, 119, 121,
123, 125, 127, 129, 131, 133,
134, 142, 150, 153, 154, 157,
158, 185, 207
1–2, 86, 116, 133, 166
1–2:4, 127
1–3, 7, 9, 16, 48, 117
1–11, 11, 12, 15, 49, 50, 51, 52,
53, 70, 104, 105, 155, 160,
164, 182, 183
1:1, 10, 70, 71, 101, 102
1:1–2:3, 112, 207
1:1–2:4, 112
1:2, 3, 10, 71, 97, 104, 107, 153,
177
1:6-8, 41
1:26, 215, 238
1:26-28, 158
1:28, 94
1:29, 94, 95
2, 8, 133, 135, 137, 139, 141,
142, 143, 144, 145, 147, 149,
150, 151, 153, 154, 155, 157,
159, 161, 163, 165, 167, 169,
171, 173, 175, 176, 177
2–3, 26, 52, 140, 141, 143, 145,
147, 154, 159, 160, 165, 166,
167, 177, 178, 185, 194, 201,
213, 234
2–4, 7, 12, 13, 136, 154, 176,
181, 182
2–11, 13, 14
2:1-3, 28, 127, 128
2:1-4, 185
2:2, 71
2:2-3, 112, 117, 125
2:4, 150
2:5, 161
2:5-6, 153, 154
2:5-7, 209
2:5–3.24, 90
2:6, 119
2:7, 155, 156, 157, 158, 161,
171, 219
2:8-14, 144
2:15, 134, 140, 141, 151
2:17, 198
2:18, 154, 161, 209
2:19-20, 144
2:21, 162
2:21-22, 163
2:23, 170, 171
2:23-25, 161
2:24, 161, 162, 163
2:25, 154, 163, 164, 177
3, 8, 13, 14, 143, 145, 173, 179,
180, 181, 182, 183, 184, 185,
187, 189, 191, 192, 193, 195,
197, 198, 199, 200, 201, 202,
203, 205, 207, 209, 211, 213,
215, 235, 237, 238

3:5, 154
3:10, 197
3:11, 197
3:13, 197
3:14, 203, 205
3:14-19, 197, 198, 236
3:15, 189, 203, 206, 209, 211,
212, 213
3:15-16, 161, 209
3:16, 204, 208, 209, 210, 211,
213, 236
3:17, 206
3:17-19, 160, 209, 211
3:18, 94
3:19, 152, 203
3:21, 163
3:22, 146, 154, 182, 200, 215,
238
3:22-24, 160
3:23, 198
3:24, 198, 213, 214
4–5, 143
4:1, 142
4:7, 193, 204
4:11, 205
4:14, 199
4:17, 155
4:20-21, 155
4:21, 171
5, 209
5:24, 15
6, 159
6:1-4, 28, 45
6:5, 193, 194
6:11, 192
8:7-12, 199
8:21, 193, 194
8:22, 128, 129
9, 158

Scripture Index

10, 13
11:1-9, 28, 155
11:7, 215, 238
12, 11, 46, 182
12–37, 29
12–50, 47, 50, 52, 53
12:20, 199
15, 46
15:6, 54
18–19, 29
19:13, 199
19:29, 199
20, 46
21:10, 199
24:54-59, 199
25:6, 199
26, 46
30:25, 199
30:37-42, 23
35:17-18, 209
38, 208
38:8-10, 205
42:25, 157

Exodus
2:17, 199
2:23-24, 191
6:1, 199
11:1, 199
19, 138
20:8-11, 28, 117, 127, 185
23:10, 129
24:9-11, 137, 138
24:10, 39
25–30, 118
25–31, 117
25:1–30:10, 118
30:11-16, 118
30:17-21, 118
30:22-33, 118
30:34-37, 118
31:1-11, 118
31:12-17, 118
31:13-17, 126
31:17, 118
32, 29
39–40, 117
40, 11

Leviticus
11, 23
21:7, 198
21:14, 198

22:13, 198
25:1-7, 129
26:11-12, 15

Numbers
22:6, 199
22:11, 199

Deuteronomy
1:39, 144
3:20, 129
5, 130
26:5, 219
28:17, 206
28:28, 43
32:11, 97

Joshua
1:13, 129
10:12-15, 28
21:44, 129

Judges
9:41, 199
11:7, 199

1 Samuel
28, 24

2 Samuel
5, 168
6:23, 208
7:1, 129
19:35, 144

1 Kings
3:9, 144
5:4, 129
6:4, 137
8:57, 15
19, 138
21:2, 140
22, 24, 216

2 Kings
17:16, 41, 44
19:37, 50
21:3-5, 41, 44
21:18, 140
21:26, 140
23:5, 41, 44
23:11, 128
24:8-17, 50

25:4, 140
25:27-30, 50

1 Chronicles
22:18, 94

2 Chronicles
36:21, 129

Nehemiah
2:8, 140, 141, 147
3:15, 140

Esther
2:5, 50
3:1, 50
7:8, 94

Job
1, 216
22:9, 199
26:11, 39
38:4, 107
39, 191
39:30, 191
40:8, 224

Psalms
8, 157
17, 67
27:4, 137
82, 216
84:4, 137
88, 174
89, 216
97:2, 137
103:14, 152, 157
104:2, 107
104:4, 215
104:5, 107
104:21, 191
110, 237
110:1, 213
132:13-14, 117, 124
132:14, 127, 128
139:13-15, 107

Proverbs
8, 67, 68

Ecclesiastes
1:1, 12
1:12, 12

Scripture Index

2:4-9, 12
2:5, 147
4:7-8, 12
9:13-16, 12

Song of Solomon
4:13, 147
7:10, 204

Isaiah
6, 216
6:1-4, 138
6:8, 215
7:15-16, 144
11:6-9, 96, 190
13:8, 209
13:11, 128
17:3, 128
26:17-18, 209
42–48, 74
45:13, 199
51:3, 149
55:8-9, 224
58, 126, 130
58:13-14, 122
65, 188
65:20, 188

Jeremiah
4:31, 209
8:2, 41, 44
11:20, 43
17:10, 43
19:13, 41, 44
20:12, 43
20:14, 206
24:5, 199
28:16, 199
29:20, 199
34:9-16, 199
39:4, 140
52:7, 140

Ezekiel
16, 168
16:3, 219
18:20, 196
34:30, 15
37:26-28, 15
47, 136

Daniel
2, 168

6, 168
7, 216
9, 237

Hosea
6:7, 151

Amos
4:13, 107

Jonah
1:9, 107

Micah
2:9, 199
4:9-10, 209
7:19, 94

Zephaniah
1:5, 41, 44
2:4, 199

Zechariah
12:2, 157

New Testament

Matthew
11:28, 130
12:9-14, 130
28:20, 15

Mark
2:27, 122
3:1-6, 130

Luke
6:5, 123
6:6-11, 130
13:10-17, 130
14:1-5, 130

John
1:14, 15
5:1-18, 130
8, 168

Acts
7, 23

Romans
5, 168, 189, 194, 195, 196
5:12, 152, 172, 193, 195, 196

5:12-19, 195
5:13, 196
5:14, 196
5:15-16, 196
5:18-19, 196
5:19, 196
8:22, 191
8:23, 192
16:20, 212

1 Corinthians
6:9-11, 219

2 Corinthians
3:6, 66
5:17, 93, 219
6:16, 16

Galatians
2:20, 219

Ephesians
2, 92, 93
2:8-9, 92
2:8-10, 92
2:12-13, 219

Colossians
1, 130
1:15, 93
1:17, 74

2 Timothy
2, 168
3:16, 62

Hebrews
3–4, 130
7, 237

1 Peter
2:10, 219

Revelation
2:7, 148
12, 212
21, 116, 190
21–22, 149
21:3, 16

The Lost World Series

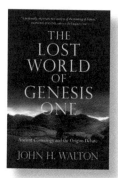

The Lost World of Genesis One
978-0-8308-3704-5

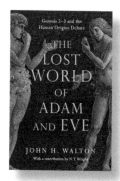

The Lost World of Adam and Eve
978-0-8308-2461-8

**The Lost World of the
Israelite Conquest**
978-0-8308-5184-3

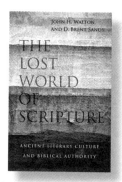

The Lost World of Scripture
978-0-8308-4032-8

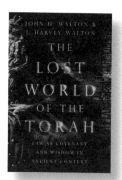

The Lost World of the Torah
978-0-8308-5241-3

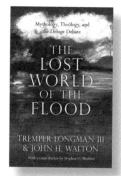

The Lost World of the Flood
978-0-8308-5200-0

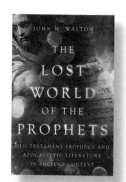

The Lost World of the Prophets
978-1-5140-0489-0